SPIRIT OF THE RAINFOREST

Dedicated to the memory of Renee and Kinza with love.

O, when I am safe in my sylvan home,
I tread on the pride of Greece and Rome;
And when I am stretched beneath the pines,
Where the evening star so holy shines,
I laugh at the lore and the pride of man,
At the sophist schools, and the learned clan;
For what are they all, in their high conceit,
When man in the bush with God may meet?

Ralph Waldo Emerson

SPIRIT OF THE RAINFOREST

A YANOMAMÖ SHAMAN'S STORY

Second Edition

MARK ANDREW RITCHIE

ISLAND LAKE PRESS
CHICAGO

Also by Mark Andrew Ritchie
God in the Pits (Macmillan, 1989)

For books and tour information contact the publisher: 1-800-245-1022
Island Lake Press, P.O. Box 710, Island Lake IL 60042

Publisher's Cataloging-in-Publication
(Provided by Quality Books, Inc.)

Ritchie, Mark A.
     Spirit of the rainforest : a Yanomamo shaman's
story / Mark Andrew Ritchie. —2nd ed.
     p. cm.
     Includes index.
     LCCN: 99-73686
     ISBN: 0-9646952-3-5

     1. Yanomamo Indians—Social conditions.
2. Yanomamo Indians—Religion. 3. Yanomamo
mythology. 4. Shamanism—Orinoco River Valley
(Venezuela and Colombia) 5. Orinoco River Valley
(Venezuela and Colombia)—Social life and customs.
I. Title:

F2520.1.Y3R57 2000   987'.6400498
                    QBI99-1181

CONTENTS

Map 6
Introduction 7

Prologue:
A Long Story Goes Before Every Fight 13

The Beginning: Split Truth 19
1 It's Never Beautiful Where You Aren't Wanted 21
2 You Are So Brave 33
3 Not Every Spirit Is What He Appears 51
4 Our Pain Is Not Our Spirits' Fault 63
5 We Want You So Much 79

The Middle: Doesn't-Grab-Women 91
6 The Father Eagle Never Found His Eaglet 93
7 Blinded By Lies 113
8 A Very Nice Word 125
9 Pulling His Eye Down 139
10 We Can Have Both Ways 155

The End: Nobody's That Stupid 173
11 They Think We're Animals 175
12 Why Don't You Leave? 185
13 Vengeance Is Mine 205
14 Killers Like Me 225
15 Epilogue: Be Good To Her 233
16 Author's Addendum: So Many Of Them Are Dead 239

Appendix 253
"Yanomamö: Noble Savages or Hobbesian Brutes?" 253
"Missionaries 1, Anthropologists, 0" 254
"Yanomamology, Missiology, and Anthropology" 256
Glossary 260
Family Relations 262
Legend of Characters and Locations 264
Documentation 268
Index 276

Photographs may be found following page 128.

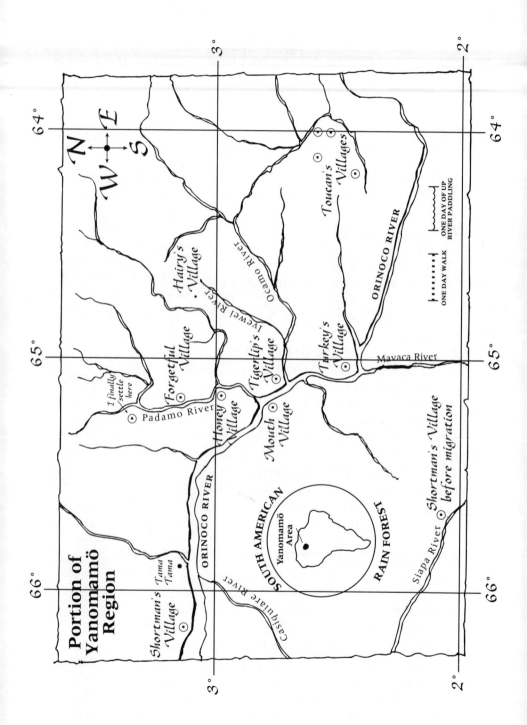

Portion of Yanomamö Region

Shortman's Village

Tama Tama

ORINOCO RIVER

Casiquiare River

SOUTH AMERICAN

Yanomamö Area

RAIN FOREST

Siapa River

Shortman's Village before migration

I finally settle here

⊙ Padamo River

Forgetful Village

Honey Village

Mouth Village

Tigerlip's Village

Iyewei River

Ocamo River

Hairy's Village

Turkey's Village

Mavaca River

Toucan's Villages

ORINOCO RIVER

N
W   E
S

┊┈┈┈┊ ONE DAY WALK

├────┤ ONE DAY OF UP RIVER PADDLING

6

INTRODUCTION TO THE 2ND EDITION

I first met Keleewa and his Yanomamö friend, Shoefoot, seventeen years ago in the jungles of southern Venezuela. Skepticism has always come easy to me, but they introduced me to the concept that truth is stranger than fiction. Not only that, it's harder to believe, funnier, and far more adventuresome. I'm a nonfiction writer because fiction has to be "real," but nonfiction only has to have happened. So when I hear someone say, "That's unreal. It couldn't have happened," I know it is a story that must be told.

The Yanomamö are one of the world's most mysterious peoples. Small, rarely over five feet tall, they have the speed, strength, and agility of a jungle cat. Their women can tote their own weight up and down a jungle trail that would challenge me even if I were empty handed. Their men can call, track, and shoot anything that breathes in a jungle that is hostile enough to kill anyone but a trained survivalist.

After that first visit, I consulted with Venezuelan anthropologist and medical doctor Pablo Anduce, who had worked with and studied the Yanomamö people for much of his life. Dr. Anduce told me that his source of information on the Yanomamö culture, language, and Amazon plant life was a jungle-raised U.S. citizen named Gary Dawson. I had already met him—Shoefoot's friend, the one the Indians called Keleewa. "He knows Yanomamö language and culture better than anyone else alive," Anduce told me. Dawson has since translated for a nationally televised *National Geographic* special on the Yanomamö.

In the decade following my meeting with Dr. Anduce, I

returned to Amazonas many times. His commendation of Keleewa proved invaluable. Over countless moonlit nights on sandbars with fish lines in the water, or floating quietly down broad rivers in dugout canoes, or just relaxing around camp-fires, I listened with ever mounting curiosity to the stories that make up the trauma of jungle life. They presented me with a picture of Yanomamö culture which is amazingly unknown—amazing in light of the widespread attention they have received.

All of the stories you are about to read were told to me personally over a period of thirteen years during my six visits to Amazonas. *Nothing herein is fiction, not even slightly exaggerated.* Having seen the Indians repeatedly exploited, Keleewa agreed to serve gratis as translator and researcher for the project under the condition that all royalties would be owned by the Indians.

Researching a culture known for its violence is an almost impossible task when that same culture has a powerful taboo against speaking of its dead. I should have kept track of the number of times that I heard the line, "I just don't like talking about it because it brings back so much pain," or the number of times Keleewa said, "Well, I can't mention *her* name; she's dead."

Indeed, the crowning achievement of this story lies in the quantity of intimate secrets that Jungleman and his people were willing to reveal. The credit for this belongs to Keleewa. His life has been so characterized by care for the Yanomamö people that they will trust him with stories which would otherwise be heard only by the closest and most trusted friend in the most quiet of whispers in the remotest corners of the darkest *shabonos*. Apart from Keleewa's special relationship with the Yanomamö people, the most powerful of these stories would never see the light of day.

To represent their story authentically, I have told it through the eyes of Jungleman, one of their most charismatic leaders. Readers may be troubled, possibly even disconcerted, by this shaman's ability to get inside everyone's head, in some cases making it appear that another person has taken over as narrator. I found myself repeatedly asking Jungleman, "How did you know that, if you weren't there and he didn't tell you?"

He always answered the same: "I just knew," an answer

that presents no confusion to rainforest peoples. My western mind, of course, required verification, so I checked everything he said with other sources. But I never found Jungleman to be mistaken about anything that he "just knew."

It has often been said that we in the "civilized" world can learn as much from primitive peoples as they can learn from us. I had always thought this to be the politically correct misunderstanding of the naïve. After traveling the U.S. with Keleewa and Shoefoot, my view is quite different. Shoefoot and Keleewa shatter stereotypes—even some of their own. The reception they have received has varied widely. Some refuse to hear them at all. Some say they live in Eden. Shoefoot knows otherwise.

My goal is to turn you over to a colorful storyteller, Jungleman, and allow you to judge for yourself.

Mark Andrew Ritchie

SPIRIT OF THE RAINFOREST

Way up in the top of a tree a howashi monkey jumped, grabbed the soft bark of a branch, and scampered for those berries at the very top. He was so far up into the bright sunlight that he couldn't see the humid jungle floor below. A toucan whistled. The monkey turned his head, chattered back, grabbed the berries, settled in the crook of a branch, and began filling his cheeks. He looked out through the leaves. The treetops went on forever, with every color of green reflected in the warm morning sunlight. In his world of peace and beauty, he couldn't see the open spot that was two bends down the crawling Padamo River. In this clearing sat a village called Honey.

Smoke from morning cooking fires rose from the village. Palm-leaf roofs held large circles of white yucca drying in the hot morning sun. But a Yanomamö village is never as peaceful as it looks.

A LONG STORY GOES BEFORE EVERY FIGHT

The warriors of Honey Village stood in a line that curved to form a half moon. The damp morning grass under their feet was drying from the morning sun, but not fast enough for what they needed. Warriors from Mouth Village faced them, also in a half-moon shape. Some of them wore clothes they had gotten from the *nabas*, white people who talk like babies. The rest wore loincloths. Each man in the circle held a club he had carefully crafted from the hardwood palm. In the bright sunlight you could see deep lines in every face.

Hairy could beat a man to death with a club, but it might take a lot of time and effort. He stood outside the circle, off to the side. This wasn't really his fight. If he were to become involved, he wouldn't use a club. He would use the weapon in his hands, the one that had made him so famous and feared.

He looked relaxed holding his bow and arrows. It was a look he had perfected over many seasons, arms crossed over the weapon, the fingers of one hand over his mouth. The hand was everything. It hid the big wad of tobacco that hung in his lower lip and kept anyone from seeing his mouth move. The enemy never saw fear. But I know what Hairy felt inside his body; he felt that great excitement begin to build, a feeling he knew well. In a flash this fight could turn from clubs to arrows. And his stomach screamed to the rest of his body to get ready for action. His long arrows extended from the ground at his feet up through his folded arms. The sharpened points rested perfectly still in front of his eyes. He heard the sounds of a battle about to begin. Between two of the points, painted dark red with poison, he saw Legbone, maybe the best warrior on the enemy side. *He'll be the target for one of these points if I have to use them*, Hairy thought.

Hairy's eyes watered a little from the smoke of the morning cooking fires. He wanted to rub them, but he wouldn't move that hand off his mouth. It showed he had no fear. And this wasn't the time to make any unnecessary motion.

Beside Hairy stood the Honey leader, Shoefoot. This leader didn't look like the others; his hands were empty. No club. No bow. No arrows. Not even a wad of tobacco in his lower lip. In the land of Yanomamö Indians, Shoefoot always has been and still is a mystery. His friendship with the whites did something strange to him. He used to be a brave warrior and was a great hunter still. Even I, his relative and teacher, did not understand him. Now he tried to *stop* fights. He had done everything he could to stop this one, but Mouth Village wouldn't leave. Still he knew right where his bow and arrows were, a lot closer than anyone thought.

Slothtail also stood outside the curved line of warriors. Like Hairy, he held bow and arrows, and watched. Unlike Hairy, he had never killed a man. No Yanomamö would brag that he had never killed a man. Beside Slothtail stood his lifelong friend, Keleewa, who had persuaded him to avoid these fights—and he had. Keleewa talked just like a Yanomamö, but he was a naba; white just like the rest of them.

A few others were in important places outside and behind the two facing lines of warriors. No clubs, just bows and arrows. They would only watch until arrows were needed. But nobody could watch like Hairy. He saw every warrior on the other side, especially the ones behind the line—the ones standing and watching. They stood just like Hairy, arms folded over the chest, bow and arrows under the arms, one hand over the mouth, as still as trees when there's no wind. Some had even removed their big wad of tobacco and handed it to their woman. So Hairy watched. If one of those men moved, Hairy's bow would be drawn.

All the Honey Village women were there too of course. They wouldn't miss this. Women were always close to fights. They moved in freely to help the wounded, carry out the dead, and hold their men's weapons. Sometimes they were quiet, but not very often. When it was time to throw insults, every warrior wanted the help of a woman who often knew the most private and humiliating information about the enemy.

One woman, Deemeoma, knew all the men in this fight. She's old enough now that her children have children. She knew the long story that went before this fight. She knew it from the very beginning—and every man in it, on both sides. She'd known them longer than anyone, and better too.

All the rest of the warriors were part of the curved lines that faced each other. Everyone wondered who would be the first to step to the center of the circle and fight. The men of Honey wouldn't step out first. Even though they had more warriors, they still didn't want to fight. Mouth Village had come to beat the men of Honey and steal some of their women.

Mouth sent one of their best fighters into the center, carrying a huge, long club. Won't-Grow, Crossedeye, Toughfoot, Bighead, Trip, Funnyman, and the other Honey warriors all looked at each other. Who would be first to defend Honey Village? A little wind came through, but no one noticed.

Won't-Grow stepped out. All the time he was a child, he had been so sick that everyone said he'd never get big. Even now Won't-Grow wasn't an experienced fighter. What chance would he have against a real fighter? Mouth Village roared with laughter when they saw that his club was hardly any longer than his arm. "Look at that tiny little stick!" Mouth Village mocked, while Won't-Grow walked toward the center. The Mouth warrior's club was as long as two or three of Won't-Grow's little club.

But Won't-Grow was quick with his club. As the Mouth warrior drew his long club back for a vicious swing, Won't-Grow struck him five quick blows on the head. Blood gushed. The Mouth warrior ran back into his half-moon formation to let someone else try.

Hairy watched Spear and his son, Fruitman, who were among the warriors on the Mouth side. They were the cause of this fight. *They're our friends,* he thought, *but because we wouldn't let their family take the girl that they wanted, now their whole village wants to fight us.* Spear stood behind the Mouth line with his friend, Smallmouth—and Smallmouth just stood and watched, like Hairy.

Another Mouth warrior stepped to the center and was met by Funnyman from the Honey side. Funnyman also held a small club and Mouth Village laughed again, but not as loudly. Funnyman made everything funny. He looked at the little club in his hand and laughed too. He was good with a canoe and motor on the river and did most of Honey's river travel, but he had never fought. Joining in his enemy's laughter, he wondered if this would finally be the day that he would take his first big beating to the head.

Everything turned quiet. Funnyman blinked his eyes to clear them from the sting of the smoke, felt the grain of the palm wood as he firmed his grip, and watched the eyes of his approaching enemy. He squatted to avoid that first big blow, used his little club the same as Won't-Grow, and turned the Mouth warrior's head bloody.

The Honey men never approached the center first. They only defended their positions each time an attacker came out from the other half moon. Their short clubs were effective up close; they sent each attacker back to his village's line with a bloody head.

Finally Legbone's turn came. Everyone knew about Legbone, Mouth's best warrior. He walked to the center and waited.

Trip, the youngest warrior, stepped forward, slowly. There was a girl in Honey who Trip held in his heart. She was the real reason behind this fight.

Now Hairy really watched because he's related to Trip, and Trip was only a beginning warrior. Hairy taught Trip how to fight, and Hairy really wanted Trip to get that girl. Both Trip and Hairy were from a village that was friendly with Honey, and Hairy knew how much they needed more girls to help their village grow. Trip had already taken a club blow to the head a few days ago from the boy in Mouth Village who wanted her.

You see, there are always many little quarrels that lead up to a big fight like this one. A long story goes before every fight.

Mouth villagers laughed. "He's just a boy!" they yelled. They were right. He'd never fought.

Behind the Mouth line, Legbone's father, Smallmouth, watched his son stand and wait for Trip to get closer. He knew that his son was a great warrior.

Hairy watched Smallmouth.

Hairy unfolded his arms. His thumb plucked the bow string so softly that only he could hear the sound. It was tight. With his fingertips he felt the smooth shaft of the arrow. He was ready. *If Legbone does anything unfair: Vooom!* he thought. "Vooom" is the sound of Hairy's poisoned arrow leaving his bow to kill Legbone.

Trip felt the damp grass under his toes as he approached the center to face Legbone. He would have to move fast to avoid that big club. If the grass were drier, it would be easier to avoid falling. And if he fell, he might never get rid of his name.

Trip didn't hear the howashi chatter in the distance, or the toucan whistle, or the slow-moving river touch its bank. He heard nothing. He saw only his target, Legbone's eyes, and the club he swung. *If they knew that the hit I took a few days ago was my first,* Trip thought, *they would really be laughing. But that hit came from a boy like me.* Everyone knew that Legbone used his club for killing. *If that club hits me even once,* Trip thought, *I'll be through.*

Legbone's club was so big that Trip easily dodged it. Before Legbone could draw it back for another swing, Trip jumped close and whopped him a bunch of quick blows to the head. Blood squirted and ran down Legbone's face.

Mouth Village watched Legbone go back to their line. He wasn't just driven back, he was beaten badly. Their best warrior had just been humiliated by a boy with no fighting reputation.

Mouth Village had come to beat the heads of these cowardly enemies until they had to run away, but they showed no signs of having been in a fight, while Mouth's warriors stood injured and bloody. The disgrace was more than anyone could stand. Legbone walked back to the women. *If I can't draw blood from a warrior,* he told himself, *at least I'll get something from someone.* His wife handed him a small club. He walked over to an old woman who sat on the ground watching, drew the club back and struck her a cruel blow to the side of the head. The club laid her scalp open to the bone.

That was it; that's when everything happened, and it all happened in the snap of a bowstring.

Legbone had just clubbed Slothtail's mother. In Yanomamö

land, the protection of the weak is a family obligation. Like his Honey leader, Slothtail had been taught strange new ways of peace. But when the blow cut into his mother's scalp and laid it open to the skull, everything Slothtail had been taught, all the influence of the naba, was forgotten. In the next moment he would react like a son.

No one was quick enough to stop him, not even his white friend standing next to him. Before Slothtail knew what he was doing, his arrow flew straight at Legbone's shoulder blades. No one strikes an old woman without starting a war.

Hairy drew his bow on Legbone. But the mysterious Honey leader was already at the center of the group screaming, "No arrows! No arrows!" And now his hands were no longer empty, his bow and arrows having somehow instantly appeared. He couldn't stand in the center of a group of killers without a weapon. Suddenly every club was gone, replaced by bows and arrows.

But a peace-loving leader screaming for no arrows will never stop a war after a death. Slothtail's bow had been drawn and his arrow released in one action—an action that would take him back to his roots. An experienced hunter knows when the arrow leaves his bow if it has found its mark. And Slothtail knew that this shot was perfect.

In the warm sunlight that morning, Slothtail saw that his life of peace was over. His village, led by the mysterious peace-loving chief, would finally return to a killing war. But remember, I said that a long story goes before every fight. And this story started back before Slothtail was born. In Yanomamö land there are very few secrets. None are kept from me. That's because my spirits saw everything and told me anything I need to know.

I'm a man of the spirit world, "shamans" we are called. The shaman is almost always the leader of his village. If he is a good shaman—I mean that if he can avoid the bad spirits and get the good ones—he can lead his village to good hunting, tell them when and where to plant, who to make war with— all the things that will make them into a great village.

The long story that goes before the fight on the grass at Honey is a story I know better than anyone—I was a part of what started it. Deemeoma and Spear were part of it too.

THE BEGINNING:
APPROXIMATELY 1950

SPLIT TRUTH

1
IT'S NEVER BEAUTIFUL WHERE YOU AREN'T WANTED

*W*e *Yanomamö only speak our stories. We never mark our words on paper like you nabas. These words from my mouth—if you are seeing them on paper, you must be a naba. Because you are a naba, there are many things I must explain so you can understand the story of my people.*

You need to know that I have lots of names—all us Yanomamö do. But we almost never speak them. If you were a Yanomamö, I wouldn't tell you any of my names, and you wouldn't ask. All my friends know my names, but they never speak them out loud. But to tell a story to you nabas, I have to use everybody's names. One of my names is Jungleman. There. Because you are far away in naba land, you didn't hear me say that; you'll only see it on paper. To tell you my story, I will have to take you way back to when Deemeoma was a little girl. But even before telling about Deemeoma, you must understand the spirit world. No story of my people can be understood without knowing about the spirits. And to tell you about the spirits, I'll have to take you back to when I was a little boy.

No one should be in the jungle alone, especially not a child. But I was, and it felt good. A small log lay across the trail. Instead of stepping over it, I stepped right on it. That's when it happened. The log said, "Why are you stepping on me? Get off of me!" I shook with fear and ran home to my mother.

And when I went hunting, even when I was little, the animals came up to me and said, "Go on, shoot me." I ran home, scared to death. But my mother told me that it was because I was special and I shouldn't be afraid of them.

After I became a young man, everything in the jungle talked to me. When I walked on the trail and brushed the leaves to the side they said, "Why are you pushing us out of the way? What did we do to you to make you treat us like that?" I threw my bow and arrows down and ran home.

"These voices you hear," my mother said, "aren't the voices of animals or plants. You know plants can't talk. They are the voices of spirits that want to have you. They want to help you. Don't be afraid of them. You are special. You will be a great man of the spirit world."

"But I haven't trained to be a shaman," I said. "I haven't taken ebene and asked the spirits to come to me like all the shamans do."

"That doesn't matter. The spirits have already chosen you to be their special one. They are coming to you even though you haven't decided to be a shaman. This is your calling even if you don't like it."

"I don't think I like it," I said. "I'm afraid."

"There's nothing to be afraid of. They're wonderful. As you learn to control them, they will stop scaring you."

"What if I get the wrong spirits? What if I get those bad spirits that I've heard about?"

She said, "Don't worry about them now. You'll be able to get rid of the bad ones later and keep the good."

The next morning I went out early and was about to shoot an ocelot when the cat said, "Don't shoot me. Why are you trying to shoot me?" Again I threw my bow and arrows down and ran home. Later I came out with a group and got my things back. The spirits never said anything when people were around. But when we separated to hunt, I saw a big toucan and wanted to shoot it. The toucan doesn't have much meat, but his beak is big and beautiful and we love those feathers. As I drew my bow it pretended like it had been shot and fell down right in front of me. Then it turned into a rat and the rat said, "Why are you always running away from me? Why don't you stay with me?"

My mother is right, I thought; *this isn't a rat talking to me. It is a spirit that wants to get to know me.* But I was still afraid. I ran.

"The next time they speak to you, follow them," my mother told me. But it was just too scary. One day a bird whistled at me and it sounded just like a person. And there were other birds talking to me. Since they were only birds I decided to follow them. They led me all over the jungle, to places where I heard more spirits calling me. This had happened many times before, but I had always been too frightened to listen or to keep following.

This time as I got closer to the voices it was clear that there were many of them. I was more frightened than I ever thought possible. I was way off the trail and so far out into the jungle that I knew I could never get back. I climbed over a big log. When I slid off the other side, I saw a huge beehive in the log and spirits came flying out of it, more spirits than I ever thought there were. They all came to me and told me to stand still and they stung me. I was about to run, but they all kept saying, "Hold still! Don't run! Don't leave us! We will protect you!"

And they just kept on stinging me until it hurt so bad that I couldn't feel anything. It was impossible to tell if I was being stung by real bees or by spirits in the spirit world. But it didn't seem to matter.

Suddenly I looked up and the jungle turned so beautiful— more beautiful than any Yanomamö has ever seen it. The most beautiful Yanomamö people in the world came toward me. The warriors were perfect. They were tall and their muscles stood out. And the women! They were so flawless. Their hair was long and shining black, and their bodies so clean and perfect. I never thought that a woman could ever make me as happy as I felt just looking at them. And they all wanted me.

There were women laughing and girls giggling and one of the spirits said to the others, "Get out of here. You stink." I couldn't tell where all the voices were coming from, but it was clear that they were fighting to get my attention. When I saw how much they wanted me, the pain from the stings turned to a wonderful feeling.

They took me to Omawa Spirit, the leader of all spirits. Just being near him is the greatest thing that could happen to a shaman. He is so beautiful, with the overpowering smell of the loveliest flower of the jungle. Not even ebene could give such a thrill. They took me all over the entire jungle and even back through time. I saw all those things happen that I had heard my mother and the old people talk about.

I saw Omawa come to the Yanomamö people to help us become the fiercest and most beautiful people on earth. I saw him teach a young shaman to grind up the bones of his relative and stir them into a big banana drink. Then Omawa told him, "This is the body of the one you love. All of you, drink it. Then we will go and kill the person who caused his death." I watched them surround a village and attack through the *shabono* entrance. They killed the man they were after.

Then Omawa helped the shaman in the other village learn how to grind the bones of their relative and they went back to kill someone in the first village.

Each time the spirits returned to me, they showed me more. One time I watched the shaman try to save a tiny girl from dying. When she was almost dead, the enemy spirit sent his hawk to grab her soul. The shaman called for the Ice Spirit and together they chased after the hawk to get the girl's soul back. As they all got closer to the land of the great enemy, it got too bright and too hot, and Iceman covered the shaman with ice to cool him down. Without the ice he would have failed. Just before he reached the land of the great enemy, the shaman grabbed the soul of the child and brought it back to her body.

"You'll do that," my new beautiful friends told me. "We will give you the power over sickness, even over death." *What wonderful spirits these are,* I said to myself.

After the shaman put the spirit back into the child, she sat up and began to talk. The mother was real happy.

The next day the hawk came back for the same little girl's soul. I watched the shaman chase after them again. But this time he was too late. The hawk took the child's soul up through the bottom of the lake into the land of the great spirit. It was too hot and too bright and too noisy for the shaman to stay there. "What is that place?" I asked my spirit friends.

"That land is where the great enemy spirit lives," two of them said at once. "He's the most powerful spirit there is," another said. "But he's unfriendly. You can't get near him. Like right now. He took the soul of that girl and he'll never give it back. He's eating it right now. And we can't get into his land because it is too hot there and too bright. That's why we call him Yai Wana Naba Laywa—the unfriendly enemy spirit. He'll never come out of there to talk to us."

"What about all that noise?" I asked.

"That's all the other beings up there singing to him and celebrating. They're always celebrating something. Right now they are probably celebrating that they got the soul of this child from us."

Soon I was comfortable with these perfect Yanomamö beings. They had introduced me to a world of joy that I never thought was possible. I kept remembering my mother's words: *As you learn to control them, they will stop scaring you.* How right she was.

They were such beautiful people. And the women—I never knew that women could be so perfect and beautiful. I saw one who was stunning, with longer hair than the others. It waved to her shoulders. I saw that she noticed me.

All the women spirits were jealous of each other, crowding around to get my attention. And the special one, the one that was almost too perfect, had pushed the others back in order to get beside me. "We wouldn't want to go there," the beautiful woman said to me. "We're not wanted there. Yai Wana Naba Laywa will never let us go in there."

It made me weak just to look at all that beauty. I stood and stared up through the bottom of the lake. The water was so clear, I could see everything, and it was too pretty to even tell about. "But it's beautiful in there," I whispered, still afraid to look at her.

"Yes, it is. But it's never really beautiful where you aren't wanted," she answered. She was right. She leaned close to me and whispered in my ear, "My name's Charming." Her soft voice made me feel like the wind of the whole jungle had blown through me. Then she looked at me and smiled. The white of her teeth shone against her smooth, brown face. I smiled back.

When the shaman returned without the soul of the little girl, I heard her mother and father let out a wail that came up out of the jungle and around the world. They burned the child's body, then ground her bones in a hollow log. Later they stirred them into banana juice and drank them. I knew all about these things of course, but now I was seeing how it started.

I had always wondered why we never took revenge when a small child died. "That's because the enemy spirit takes the souls of the children," Charming told me. "But grown people are always killed by another person. So for all those deaths we must get vengeance."

After that, I saw that every time someone died, unless he was a baby or an old person, his relatives would grind his bones and drink them and take revenge on a person that the spirits named. If they killed the person that the spirits named, then Omawa's spirits would help that person's relatives grind his bones and come back to get revenge for themselves.

Charming taught me everything, and all the other spirits helped her. "After Omawa taught us Yanomamö everything we need to know," she said, "he went to the world of the nabas to help them learn these ways too."

It was many seasons after I became a shaman that the things began to happen that led to the fight I told you about at the beginning. It all started in a far away village when Deemeoma was a little girl.

Deemeoma's feet landed in a thick layer of dust on the dirt floor as she slid from her cotton-string hammock and scampered after her father, Wyteli. He headed across the center of the shabono toward the entrance. Deemeoma's father walked tall, carried a bow even taller and a few cane arrows even longer than the bow. She was proud to be his daughter and she had to run to keep up. He was the powerful leader of her whole world—the shabono: a huge wall that goes around in a big circle. The wall leans inward so much that every family can hang their hammocks under it and keep out of the rain. There is plenty of room in the middle for all the children to play in the sun, and for the big people to do all their things.

As they walked around the inside of the shabono, they passed Deemeoma's sister's section; Tyomi was old enough to have babies of her own. As she worked, she clutched a baby against her breast to keep him from falling into the fire. In the next bunch of hammocks, her sister's friend worked over a fire with her son Fredi. Both women looked up, smiled and nodded at Deemeoma as she passed. Everyone noticed whenever her father did anything because he was so important. Deemeoma smiled back and wondered when little Fredi would be big enough to play.

They passed many more families and reached the entrance to the shabono. It wasn't dark yet, but the trails had to be blocked before dark to keep enemies and bad spirits from coming into their shabono during the night.

Outside the shabono she couldn't run beside her father or grab his big hand because the trail through the jungle was narrow. The cool, damp trail felt good to her little feet as she followed behind him. Ahead of her she could see the bottoms of his big wide feet as they lifted up from each step.

He piled up brush on the trail and she found sticks and threw them on the pile. He pushed her out of the way and continued piling brush until it was higher than he could reach. No one could ever get over all that, not even the spirits.

Deemeoma followed him back toward the entrance, then down another trail which he blocked the same way. When they returned to the entrance, they met her big brother and brother-in-law, the man who married her big sister.

"We blocked the other trails," they said to her father.

"Good?" he asked.

"As high as we could," they answered.

"I don't like the feeling out there," her father told them. "I'll call my spirits to see if there is any danger."

She watched the men talk, holding their bows and arrows in one hand. These warriors had muscles from their feet up. Her father was the biggest. Each of them had a huge wad of tobacco stuffed into his lower lip. The string around her father's waist was tied to the skin at the end of his penis, holding it up. She had never seen a man with his penis down and wondered what it would look like.

"Do we have any ebene?" a warrior asked. Deemeoma knew that they did. She had seen her brother grinding the plants into powder. He was learning the many ways of the spirits and would soon be a shaman himself.

Deemeoma never liked it when people blew that black powder into her father's nose. Her father always looked so strange when he danced with his spirits. It scared her. He wasn't like himself. She left her father standing with the men and ran back into the shabono and all the way across the center to be close to her mother.

It was almost dark when Deemeoma's big brother squatted on his heels and blew ebene powder through the long tube into Wyteli's nose. He rolled onto his back and grabbed his head as he felt all the pain. But he sat back up on his heels and took another blow. By then the effect of the powder was ready to take him to his spirits. The ebene dripped out his nose and down his chin and he went into a trance, dancing and chanting. By the time the cooking fires died, he came back from his spirits. Then the village gathered around as they always did to hear what Wyteli's many spirits had said.

That night the village heard Deemeoma's father tell story after story of the things he had been doing with his spirits. Everyone was very quiet when he talked; no one wanted to miss a word. "You know that story we heard about the man who just died? I sent my spirits to kill him." The crowd of warriors, women and children were excited to hear it. "Remember those babies that died over in Sandy Place? My spirits and I traveled over there and blew alowali powder all over them. Within a few days they were all dead. We can be happy that we won't have to worry about those babies growing up and coming back to kill us."

Everyone cheered when they heard what he had done to the babies. They laughed when they heard how helpless their enemies were against his spirits. With each story Deemeoma grew happier as she realized how powerful and how wonderful her father was for her village.

The smoke from dying fires drifted across the listening faces as one story led to another. It was late by the time her father lifted her from her mother's lap and carried her to her hammock. She'd been asleep for a long time and missed most of the stories of the people he had killed. It didn't matter. He would tell them all again.

Her people lay in their hammocks with stories of many killings in their heads. It reminded them of their own loved relatives who had been killed. Some had been killed by arrows but many others had died slowly of diseases—diseases caused by enemy shamans in other villages. So no one was surprised when Tyomi, whose hammock wasn't far away from her sister

Deemeoma, began to whimper. Tyomi's husband started to cry too as he remembered their baby that died. Then the family next to them began to cry. They cried even louder. Deemeoma's mother began to cry, then her father. Now everyone was thinking about someone and the crying soon spread around the entire shabono—wails of anguish by women and men alike that split the tranquil jungle air with the horrible grief felt by every member of the village.

Deemeoma jumped down from her hammock shaking with fear and reached up for her father. He pulled her up and held her tightly against him. She felt his chest heave with each breath as he screamed out his anguish. What pain his enemies had caused him! That's why he had killed so many of them.

Even with her hands tight against her ears the screams still got in. The terror was so loud that Deemeoma thought her head was going in a circle and she wasn't even sure where she was.

Only as their voices became tired did the sound gradually fade and the village slowly fall back into sleep. She couldn't remember her father putting her back in her hammock.

"Raiders!" The scream shook the body of every sleeping Indian. It is what every Indian fears the most. The second scream included the shrill voice of all the women in the village. *"Raiders!"* It hurt Deemeoma's ears.

She jumped from her hammock. The whole shabono thundered. She heard a splat and then a thud. She turned to look. Her mother lay flat on the dirt floor. A long arrow stuck from her body into the air. Blood ran from her mouth. Arrows flew in every direction. Her father was already on his feet shooting back at the enemy warriors. Enemies were everywhere, all around the shabono and still coming in the entrance. Women and children ran to find any place to hide. Most of the surprised warriors were trying to escape. But there was no escape.

The bravest, like Deemeoma's father, never ran. He stood by his hammock, shooting arrow after arrow. He hit an enemy, then another. An arrow struck him in the side but he didn't even stop to pull it out. He shot until he had no arrows left. Now Deemeoma saw why men had sometimes called him Hard-to-Kill. It was true.

She picked up an arrow that landed in the dirt beside her

bleeding mother. Deemeoma reached up high and handed it to her father. He shot it as two more arrows pierced his body. She picked up another arrow for him. She gathered more.

While arrows flew, Deemeoma scampered all over gathering arrows out of the dirt and handing them to her father. The enemy was now everywhere and all the warriors who hadn't run were hit. In a raid, Yanomamö never shoot at children. Each time she handed Wyteli arrows there were more in him. She tried to pull them out but couldn't. The village screams were so loud.

He kept shooting. Deemeoma wiped the dust from her eyes with her arm as she reached for another arrow. She kept gathering them, arrow after arrow, for a long time. Soon Wyteli's body was so full of arrows he could hardly pull the bow back. The screams were not as loud now so she thought everyone else must be dead. But not him. He would never die. *So this is what it means to have the spirits!* She handed him two more arrows and, turning to get more, she heard another *thwack.* He'd been hit again. But Deemeoma knew he would soon drive them all away. All he needed was more arrows. . . .

Everywhere she ran she saw her relatives dying. Her uncle pleaded with the attackers for his life. "Don't shoot me, older brother!" he yelled at the warrior whose bow was drawn on him. Her uncle had shot his last arrow. Now he tried to hide behind his hands for protection, begging for mercy. "Older brother, don't kill me!" he kept yelling. They weren't brothers, of course; that's just a name you might call someone you don't know. But the warrior paid no attention and her uncle's hands gave no protection. The arrow pierced his chest and he fell dead with a thud.

Deemeoma ran to one side and picked up an arrow; another came sliding in and hit the pole next to her. She grabbed it from the dirt, ran back and handed them both to her father. But he didn't take them. He was sitting now, in the dirt, held up by all the arrows sticking out of him in all directions. The ground around her father tried to soak up his blood. But she knew he couldn't die. Not like the others! She grabbed for him, but there were so many long arrows sticking so far out of him that she couldn't reach him. She tried to separate the arrows to get in to hold her father. She couldn't.

She started to cry. Wyteli didn't answer. He was gone. He

had done what he always promised not to do. He had left her.

All the yelling stopped; only the cries of babies and children were left. The enemy checked carefully to make sure that every warrior was dead. They lay everywhere—some with limbs stretched out in every direction. Some in a heap. Some strewn across hammocks. Their bright red blood ran into the dirt and mixed with it. Each body held long feathered arrows that pointed toward the morning sky. A few of the arrows moved a little as Deemeoma's relatives breathed for the last time.

She burst out with a long wail. She should have started crying when she saw the first arrow hit her mother but she hadn't had time. Now the tears came fast. Her mother, her brothers, her father, everyone was dead. Even some of the children had been hit and killed in the confusion. Now that the last warrior was down, the enemy turned their attention to the children.

Deemeoma covered her eyes and peeked through her fingers. Her sister's baby sat crying only a few steps away. *If he would just be quiet,* Deemeoma thought. She knew her sister must be dead. A man grabbed the baby by the feet and swung him with all his might. He bashed the baby's head open against a support pole. Deemeoma closed her eyes when she saw the white, wet insides run down the pole. They killed all the babies that way. But the older children, the ones that could run, their heads were too hard for that.

A man stuck his bow in the ground, grabbed Deemeoma's little brother and stuck him, seat first, down onto the sharp end of his bow. He screamed and wiggled. Then he died. Many of the older children died that way.

One child had been stuck through with an arrow point. He pulled the point from his little body, reached out, and handed it back to the killer. Then he died.

Deemeoma's playmate sat in the dirt crying. A young warrior grabbed her to kill her. "Don't kill her!" an old fighter yelled. "We'll keep her." But he did anyway. Because he was a new warrior, he was anxious to get his first kill.

The ground was covered with blood. Deemeoma was still trying to get through the arrows to reach her father's head when the warriors grabbed her. They were just about to kill her when the old warrior shouted, "No! No! No! Don't kill her. Can't you see she is healthy? She will bear us many children."

"Not for a long time," the young warriors objected. They were about to fight. But the old warrior was fierce and respected.

"Only kill the boys and the babies and the wounded," he said. "We have to keep the healthy girls." He was right and they all knew it. They shouldn't have been killing the girls.

Deemeoma sat in the dirt with her eyes closed tight behind her little hands. Finally she peeked out. But the children were still stuck on the poles. Only now they didn't move. All the bodies were still there. The arrows sticking out of them no longer moved. The poles were covered with white stuff from the babies' heads. She wished they would hurry and kill her.

Then the men discovered some women and a tiny boy hiding behind a pile of wood in a dark area of the shabono. It was Tyomi, little Fredi and his mother, and a few other women. Deemeoma's heart jumped to see her sister alive. *Certainly they won't kill her,* she thought. *She's a grown woman.*

They jerked Fredi from his mother's grip. She screamed, "Please! Don't kill him! He's all I have left! He's all I have left!" A new warrior was about to run him through with an arrow.

"Wait, wait!" It was the same man who had saved Deemeoma. "He's healthy. Let's keep him." But they ignored the man, put Fredi on the ground and tried to spear him with their arrows. He jumped between his mother's legs, then out the other side. They poked, trying to get an arrow tip into Fredi's chest. Deemeoma closed her eyes and covered her face so she wouldn't have to watch. "I told you to stop it!" the man yelled again. "You've had enough killing. Leave him alone." Fredi was flying in and out and around his mother's legs like a bird with a broken wing.

"He'll grow up and kill us!" the new warriors shouted back.

"I want him!" the old man answered. "I'll keep him to carry my meat on hunts." While they argued, his mother clutched him against her and hunched over him on the ground. She flung her arms back and forth to keep them from getting an arrow into his chest.

"Leave him alone," another man said. "He will be able to hunt meat for us when we're old." He grabbed Fredi from his mother while the other men held her.

"We'll kill him later," one of the boys said, and they gathered around the men who had grabbed Tyomi. They had already started to have fun with her.

2

YOU ARE SO BRAVE

In the world of us shamans, that morning against Potato Village is what we call a great killing. Because I, Jungleman, am a shaman and the leader of my village—I led that raid. Deemeoma, Fredi, and the women have a hard time on the way home of course, but they'll get used to us. It could take a long time, but they will.

The whole killing was really the fault of Deemeoma's father. We came to Potato Village at first only to kill a person who had caused a death in our village. I knew he had done it because my spirits told me. So we invited other villages to a big feast, drank the ground bones of our dead relatives, and then came to get revenge on the man who caused the death. We listened from outside their shabono to make certain that the man we wanted to kill was inside. Then we heard Wyteli tell all his stories about the many people he had killed in our village. We were soon so angry that we forgot all about that one person we'd come to kill. We knew then that we must kill them all. It was a great victory.

When we are in such a celebrating mood, we do things that are unthinkable at other times. Fathers and sons would never have sex with the same woman. But . . .

That day proved we are the fiercest Yanomamö warriors anywhere. In our killing frenzy we would do anything. We all took turns raping the women while Deemeoma screamed with terror. She wondered if we would try to use her. But with four grown women, we didn't need her. When I finished with one of the women I noticed Deemeoma sitting there crying, cowering in a dirty corner of their shabono and hiding her face. It was her sister I had just used.

Then I went to the next group of warriors and waited my turn for the next woman. There were four groups of warriors, one woman in the middle of each group. We kept on until we could go no more.

After we were exhausted, they were all still alive. So we tied our penises back up and left for the long trip home, taking the women with us.

It took us many days, but with so many stories to tell about our victory, it passed quickly. The women whimpered and moaned at the retelling of every story and we had to hit them to make them stop. Sometimes hitting them didn't help. But we tried. Deemeoma and Fredi had a hard time keeping up and often had to be carried. Each time we stopped, we would all use the four women.

We were crossing a foot bridge which is always hard for the little ones because there is only one pole to walk on and a vine above it to hold onto. Children often can't reach the vine and have to be carried. As we made our way over the noisy part of the rapids, the young warriors grabbed Fredi to throw him in. Fredi clutched the vine with all his might. But it would be easy for the young warriors to get his little hands free of the vine. "You're not throwing him in!" yelled the man who had saved Deemeoma. But with the noise of the rapids, it was hard to hear.

"He'll grow up and try to kill us," they yelled back, and the argument started all over again. Fredi dropped to his feet and clung to the pole. We had killed enough. But these young, inexperienced warriors hadn't been fast enough to get a kill in the big slaughter.

"He'll be mine!" the old warrior yelled back.

The old man wasn't close enough on the foot bridge to stop the boys. They got Fredi loose from the pole and were about to drop him into the noisy white water below. But the warrior who would have dropped him decided he didn't want to face the anger of the old warrior when they got off the foot bridge. He let him go and Fredi crawled the rest of the way across.

When we got close to our shabono I felt my heart become excited. This would be the greatest celebration of my life. It would be as good as taking ebene. No one had been allowed to go ahead with the news.

A flurry of excitement spread around the shabono as they heard us coming on the trail. The women hurried from their fires toward the entrance.

"We killed them! We killed them all!" we shouted as we came to the shabono entrance. The women cheered with delight and everyone began telling his own story of what had happened, while the women looked over our spoils.

"You should have seen how they died when we put our arrows through them!" a number of us shouted, and we made the motions of a person being hit by an arrow and going down. "They ran everywhere, but no one escaped."

The women and children all crowded around, thrilled to see us and so proud of us. The power that comes from being so fierce is the best that can happen. And I am the most powerful in our village. There in the middle of the shabono they heard every detail of all we did.

Our women walked around the four women we had captured and looked at them. They touched and squeezed each of them. We had used them plenty on the trail, but until now we hadn't taken a really good look.

Stolen women are always timid at first and don't like hearing about what we did to their men. But they will get used to us. And they'll have to get used to hearing about what we did to their men. We will never stop telling anyone who will listen about what we did to their men.

"Spear and Jungleman and him and him and . . . ," a young warrior said, pointing to all of us who had killings to our credit, "have some more days of *unokai* to do." We had begun our many-day killer's cleaning ritual on the trail. During those days on the trail and for a few more, we didn't allow our hands to touch any part of our bodies. If your hands killed someone and then touched your body, the dirty blood from your hands would make a sickness on that part of your body. One time a man had touched his eyes during his unokai and he went blind. One killer had touched his skin and he developed a terrible rash that he couldn't stop scratching. It stayed with him for the rest of his life.

The women could see which of us had killed people at Potato Village because each killer had a stick that fit perfectly into the big hole in each ear lobe. When we ate, we took the sticks out of the ear lobe and used them to carefully put food in our mouths, anything to keep our hands from touching us.

A big argument rose over who should get the women. Our relatives from another village wanted at least one of them. "We came all the way from the headwaters of the Ocamo to help you on this raid and these women are as much ours as yours!" they shouted. The four women stood in a group, listening to the argument. Fredi was already the property of the old man. Deemeoma cried again and clung to her sister's leg as if it was all that she had left in the world.

It was true that our relatives from Ocamo had as much right to the women as we did—even more, because some of them had been injured in the raid. But there were more of us, so we kept all the women and Deemeoma and Fredi too. We knew it wasn't really fair, but we knew that they would have taken them all if we had fewer warriors. They went home mad. Their anger would not die easily.

Spear placed the green ebene into the end of a long tube. Spear was my fellow shaman. After such a victory, we would both have many things to say to our spirits. I put the tube to my nostril and he blew the powder into my head. I staggered back and fell on my side into the dirt. He looked as if he were waving in the breeze. It was a powerful mixture, not like that weak ebene we got from those people over by the Ocamo River. I wouldn't need any more. Spear blurred and I saw them coming, the love of my life. They were coming down many trails. Some even came from the sky. They would give me wisdom, power, anything I wanted. Spear was out of sight now, and all the other men. My spirits came into the shabono of my chest and I was happy to see them. We danced and they talked to me.

"Tk!" I clicked my tongue in excitement to Jaguar Spirit. "Didn't we kill off those people at the Potato Village!"

"It was wonderful, Father," Jaguar answered. "You are a fierce warrior. You are wonderful. We love to come to you."

"You are so brave," Charming Spirit told me in her soft voice. She is the most beautiful woman I have known—in the spirit world or the real world. I danced with all my spirits, a dance that lasted through most of the night. It was a wonderful celebration. Some of the other beautiful women came to dance with me. They are wonderful too. My spirits are always dressed so perfectly, with feathers in their hair and beautiful ornaments in their ears and lips. But Charming finally ran them off. She lets them spend only a little time with me and then she returns. She danced me out into the jungle and made love to me until I was weak. This was the great victory of my life.

The next morning we began the long hard task of staying safe from retaliation. We knew that Potato Village had many friends who would come to kill us.

First we built a huge palm wood wall across the front opening of the shabono. We call it an *alana*. One end of the alana is tied tight up against the shabono wall. The other end has a small space between the alana and the shabono wall for a person to walk through into the shabono. We were so afraid that we made the alana go all the way around the outside of the shabono. This would make any raiders take a long path between the outside of the shabono and the alana just to get to the opening of the shabono. Then we closed all the little holes in the shabono wall where family members slip in and out.

Spear took a young warrior out to check the trails and make sure they were well blocked. The warrior was too young to have a name, but I'll call him Shoefoot, a name he got much later. Spear and Shoefoot didn't go far because it is too easy to get ambushed on a trail. While they were out together they relieved themselves. Everyone else would have to do it inside the shabono.

The first day we felt safe. But the next day we needed some food from the garden. We sent half of our fighters with the women to the garden to gather food and the rest of us stayed to guard the shabono. Spear and I stayed in the shabono because we couldn't even touch garden food until we finished unokai.

That night Spear and I were real tired because we hadn't been able to sleep for many nights. So we lay down in our hammocks and got the women to pile firewood around us until it was so high we were hidden from view. This would help us get some sleep while the women could watch for enemies and wake us if they came. They did the same that night for many of the other warriors. It was the first night that we got good sleep, although I'm not sure that Spear did. I heard his hammock strings pulling all night as he rolled around in his hammock. One of the people Spear had killed was a young man. Spear was real close to him when he shot him. The youngster yelled, "Don't kill me, older brother." Now Spear lay in his hammock and wondered why he had made him suffer so much.

In the morning Spear said he slept good but he still looked tired. The women brought us food and we took the sticks from our ears and picked it carefully from their hands. We still couldn't touch them or any of our relatives.

We did the same thing that day—sent half the warriors to the garden to protect the women as they gathered the food. But we couldn't work the garden to make more food so our supply was almost gone. This day all they got was yucca—it's our main food. It would be a long time before we would ever get something we really enjoy, like wild honey.

That night I dreamed that we were all being killed in a raid. When I woke, my hammock was covered with my sweat. But I saw the wood piled high around me and I knew that there had not been a raid. Still I was scared; I knew that if there was one, it would be hard to shoot from behind the wood and it would take me a long time to climb over the pile and start shooting back. I couldn't get back to sleep.

The next morning before it was light, Spear and Shoefoot and I took three warriors and went hunting. We moved slowly down the trail. Shoefoot and I and another warrior searched the jungle for signs of ambush ahead. Spear was in the back, looking for any signs that we might be followed. He covered our tracks as we went. The other two warriors looked and listened for game.

But this was a worthless way to hunt. Animals don't stand and wait for six hunters to come shoot them. "If we don't split up we will never find anything," Shoefoot whispered to me. He was still young and didn't fully understand.

"Remember your uncle," I whispered back. I knew

Shoefoot remembered, not because he ever knew his uncle. He didn't. It was because his mother kept his uncle's bones in a gourd. From the time Shoefoot was little she told him about the people who had killed his uncle, and how Shoefoot would one day drink those bones and take revenge on them.

"That's how your uncle was killed," I said. "He went hunting alone when his village was at war. They ambushed him and filled him full of arrows before he could even get off the trail."

"We'll have to find some safe trails where we can hunt or we'll starve," Shoefoot whispered back.

"After what we did to Potato Village, there is no such thing as a safe trail," I said. "Remember how your mother has been talking to you about revenge for your uncle even though he was killed before you were born? Just the same, the relatives of Potato Village will be talking to their children about killing us. They will talk like that until long after we are dead."

In the distance we heard a wild turkey. You can always tell its sound. It sits high in the trees and hums a little song. We all looked at each other. "This is where we have to be real careful," I cautioned everyone. "It could be a trap. They could be making the turkey sound. And even if they're not, they know we will be coming for the turkey. There might be an ambush anywhere between here and that bird."

Of course Spear knew all about the dangers and what to do. He took two of the warriors and they began to search the jungle in one direction for any signs that an ambush had been set. Shoefoot and I and the other warrior took the other direction. One step at a time we made our way toward the turkey. There are so many places in the jungle to set an ambush that it makes this kind of movement very slow. But with six of us, we knew that at least we could make a good fight.

I felt damp leaves brush off my back as I walked backward, carefully watching the trail we left behind us. "Nothing," I whispered over my shoulder to Shoefoot. But I also knew that quiet in the jungle is not always a good sound. We heard the turkey hum again. We were closer. Shoefoot was looking to one side, the other warrior to the other, and I watched straight back.

Step by step I walked backward, my bow and arrows ready. An ambush can hardly ever be seen in advance. All you can do is be as ready to shoot back as fast as possible. With each step the fear grew. In the distance I heard the chatter of a *howashi*. But it meant nothing. I heard something at the side, jumped and drew my bow. It was nothing. Ahead of me on the trail all five of the hunters had arrows drawn and pointed at the same place. Slowly we removed our arrows and went on.

As we neared the turkey, the hunters in front checked to make sure that the hum was coming from high in the trees. Sometimes a jaguar will sit at the bottom of a tree and hum like a turkey. Then he'll eat whatever comes to eat the turkey.

It took us a long time, but we finally shot the turkey. The boys carried it because Spear and I couldn't touch it. The return to the shabono was not as fearful because we had already searched the trail. But we still had to be very careful because warriors could move in behind us. On the way back, we relieved ourselves in the jungle so we wouldn't have to do it in the shabono. That saved us the trouble of wrapping the solid stuff in leaves and throwing it over the wall. Everyone else was doing it inside and the shabono was getting smellier every day. Lots of bugs had already come.

It was the middle of the afternoon before we returned with the turkey. The women cooked it over one of the fires. Each person in the village got a tiny piece of meat on some yucca. The children crowded around and stared with hungry eyes. There certainly wasn't enough for them to have any. I could have eaten the whole thing myself, but it was gone before I got any.

That night Shoefoot asked his mother about his uncle. "It's just what I've been telling you all your life," she said. "Every day I ask you, Do you know why you aren't happy? It's because you are missing an uncle. If he was here to play with you and take you hunting, you would be happy. But those people from Yoblobeteli killed him. That's the truth. You have seen me mourn for him all your life. But when you are grown into a fierce warrior, we will drink his bones and go kill the people responsible."

"They will be dead by that time," Shoefoot responded.

"That won't matter." she said. "Their children will be grown up. You can kill them. It won't matter who you kill, just so you get revenge. The uncle you have missed all your life deserves that."

We checked all the trails leading away from the shabono and piled brush even higher on them. The boys who stayed awake to alert us of any danger stood by the big wall at the opening of the shabono. They made noises all night so it would sound like there were people awake inside. They laughed and talked and kept their fire going. This made it even harder for us to sleep, but we knew that as long as they were making noise we were safer. The women stacked the wood around us again that night.

The next morning was the last day of our unokai. We hadn't touched our bodies for many days, more than the fingers on a hand. But today would be the end. Our hands would be clean again. In the afternoon Spear and I and the others who were on unokai took our hammocks and our bows and arrows and left the shabono. We stayed in small groups for fear of ambush. I found a hardwood palm tree, the tree that makes the best wood for our bows. Around the tree I tied my hammock, my bow, my arrows, and all my deadly arrow points. Now the tree would take all the bad effects of my killing. I would be able to forget how much I made them suffer. The other warriors found hardwood trees and did the same with their things. All the while, more warriors watched all around us to make sure that we were safe from attack.

That night Spear blew ebene into my nose again and we danced with our spirits. We needed much direction from them for the hard time ahead. The village was so hungry. The children were always crying. Some had already died and my spirits were not able to get them to revive. We needed a spirit that could just give us food in the shabono so we didn't have to go out and get it. But my spirits didn't know of any such spirit.

"What shall we do now that their friends and relatives will come looking for us, to take revenge?" I asked Jaguar Spirit and the others. "We can't grow anything in our gardens. We can't hunt. We can't sleep. We can't even go to relieve ourselves."

"It's time for you to move. Maybe even split up as a village."

"We hear about white nabas in another world," I said. "Who are these people? Can they help us? We need so much, especially now that we can't work our gardens because we know our enemies are coming for revenge."

41

"The nabas are people that have many things that you need. You should go to their land and get things." The thought of going to the naba land scared me so much. How would we get there? What if they weren't friendly? I might be humiliated in front of my people. But my spirits knew all my fears and assured me they would take care of us.

I danced with my spirits for a long time, talking and enjoying the great slaughter of Potato Village. Then I relaxed in my hammock while they hung all around my shabono upside down like bats. After a time I could see again the men gathered around my hammock, and I told them all that my spirits had said. I knew what they would say.

"Go to the naba land?" they reacted in fear. A hush fell over us all. They couldn't tell that I was just as scared. No great fighter ever shows fear. Even when he knows he is being killed, a great warrior will stand and let them fill him with arrows, but he'll never show fear.

When you have spirits as wonderful as mine are, you would never think of ignoring their advice. So we were soon ready to go to the naba village.

In order to keep hidden from our enemies, those who stayed behind took the women and children, left the shabono and split up into many groups. We walked until late in the afternoon when I shot a monkey and we decided to eat and stop for the night. The boys with us quickly built us a lean-to shelter from poles, vines, and palm leaves. We hung our hammocks under the shelter and shared roasted monkey.

I sat on my hammock and chewed the meat down to the bone. There was little talking. In the distance two large trees rubbed and we heard the low moaning sound. We all turned to look. It was nothing, but everyone was scared about the uncertainty ahead of us.

There wasn't enough meat on that tiny monkey and we were all still real hungry. But everyone knows that when you travel you are always hungry.

We traveled through the jungle for almost a full moon. Never before had any of us been this far away from our lands. It was in answer to my spirits' advice to go to the world of the nabas. But none of us was concerned that we were lost. My spirits knew that we would come to a big river and find the nabas there.

Each day in the jungle we got hungrier. One day I shot a turkey. While it roasted over the fire the men asked me, "How much longer?" I didn't know. I never thought it would be this long. Every day we thought, *this will be the day we will reach the big river.* Every day we were disappointed.

"Are you sure we are going the right way?" I asked Jaguar Spirit every night as I lay in my hammock in another part of the jungle that we'd never seen before. Every night he would tell me that we were going right.

Then one night he said, "Maybe you should get another spirit, the one that knows all the directions in the jungle." But my other spirits were certain that we were going in the right direction.

Finally one morning we were making our way along and I was looking up into the trees for monkeys. Before he could stop himself, the warrior in front of me shouted with fear. His eyes had caught a glimpse of something he'd never seen before—big water. Then he was ashamed of the fear he had shown. Maybe we would rename him Afraid-of-Big-Water.

The rest of us were able to hide our fear even though we knew that everyone was scared. We had never seen a river like it. "How do you ever get across it?" someone asked. "I can hardly see to the other side."

"Did you know it would be this big?" they asked me. I knew it was big, but I never thought it would look like this. We were even more shocked when we saw the village of the nabas. We walked into the village with great fear. All around us were great big wooden things that the nabas had made—things so big that people could walk inside of them. They were covered on the top with the same kind of leaves we use on the shabono to keep rain out. *It must be where they live,* I thought. My people knew that I had the power to protect them from any harm in this fearful place. I never told how scared I was.

There were other Indians in the village, but they weren't like us. They were Myc Indians, who did all kinds of work for a naba named Noweda.

The Myc Indians used to live close to us Yanomamö and we had a long war with them. It started when a Myc Indian finally got impatient with a Yanomamö Indian who kept stealing food from his garden. This is not a big offense. We do it all the time. And the owner of the garden is welcome to come get food from our garden too, especially if he can get away with it. But this Myc got mad. He went and cut a breast off the man's wife. Now the Yanomamö man was mad. He returned and cut off both breasts of the Myc Indian's wife. This made the whole village mad, and soon there was a full shooting war between the tribes.

The Mycs could beat us in a straight battle out in the open. But we don't very often fight straight battles out in the open. We attack when everyone's sleeping or we lie in ambush on a trail. But the most important thing for us is that we never end a war. I told you, we save the bones of our dead and grind them to powder like Omawa taught us. We have the big feast, stir the powdered bones into banana juice, and drink our relative. Then we go and take revenge for his death. We've done this ever since Omawa told us how. So once the war started with the Mycs, there was no way for them ever to stop it. Of course we stole their women whenever we could. Their women are huge, so all of us always had a great time with them.

The Myc Indians never could figure out why we kept coming season after season and generation after generation to fight them. Finally they moved so far away that we couldn't go kill them any more. So it became known that you could win a war with the Yanomamö today, but your children's children would pay for it forever.

Noweda, the naba on the big river, was a giant of a man with white skin and no hair on his head. I saw right away that he had some sort of power over the Myc Indians. He ordered them to do whatever he wanted. They cooked his food, hunted meat for him, and did anything else he said. He treated us nice, maybe because we had bows and arrows in our hands as we walked into the village, and maybe because we were Yanomamö and he knew we would take revenge. But none of his Indians had bows, and he hit them with his club whenever he got mad.

"He must have some kind of spell on these people," my brother said to me.

"Yes, I know," I said. "Mycs are brave warriors. These people look like cowards." We were puzzled that they would allow one naba to control them all. But Noweda seemed to fear us and treated us very well. Because I came out of the jungle he started calling me Jungleman. That's when I got this name. Now all the other nabas call me that. We spent many moons with Noweda. We traveled with him on the river and helped him build one of the big wooden things for himself. The nabas call it a house. For this he gave us many trade goods. We got so rich. He had a huge trough which we filled with papaya and every other kind of fruit from the jungle. It would sit there day after day and ferment and they would drink from it all the time.

We traveled to many lands with Noweda and his Mycs, gathering rubber from the trees. Everywhere we went, all the people knew him. He always had lots of women around, but he only kept them until they had a baby. Then he wasn't interested in them any more. Whenever he got the urge to have a woman, he would grab whoever was closest, rip her clothes off, and start in. He didn't care who was around and nobody even told him not to. When I first saw him do it, I began to have a curious feeling about the nabas. Maybe they weren't as smart as I first thought.

Way down the Casiquiare River we found a place where there were more ebene trees than I have ever seen. There was ebene growing everywhere we looked. It was like a shaman's heaven. I jumped out of the canoe to get some, but the old man who owned the canoe said, "Don't you go touching my ebene! If you do I'll shoot you." But there was more ebene there than all the people in the world could ever have used. So I did steal some when he wasn't looking.

One day Noweda said to me, "Come across the river with me and we'll swim and bathe." There was a large lagoon over there where the water was still. "And go get Parrotbeak to come with us." He put on his big belt that holds those metal things that make a loud bang. He had one on each side. I got Parrotbeak, one of his Mycs, and the three of us got into Noweda's boat and crossed the giant river.

The Myc boy acted strange. Noweda said to me, "You swim over there and don't be afraid," and he told the Myc boy to dive in. Noweda stayed close to the bank and so did I because I can't swim. But the boy dived into the water like an otter and swam like an alligator. He made beautiful dives from the top of a rock and disappeared into the water for a long time. Then he'd come up way across the lagoon. I had never seen anyone do such things in the water. One time I saw him dive under and a stinging eel hit him. He came out of the water like a jumping fish. But he climbed back up on the rock and dived again.

Noweda sat on top of the big rock and watched. As he stared at the boy, a funny look came on his face. The next time the boy dived into the water, Noweda pulled one of the metal sticks from his belt and pointed it at the place where the boy would come up. When his head came out of the water, I heard the crack of thunder, and saw a little flame come out of the metal stick. A bloody hole appeared on the boy's face. He sank into the water and it turned red with his blood. I ran in terror. My chest was pounding with fear when I reached the beach of the big river. I ran a few steps along the beach but couldn't get around a big boulder because I couldn't swim into the water.

Noweda let out a huge laugh. "Friend!" he yelled as I crouched under the boulder and shook with fear. "Don't be afraid!" He pointed to the bloody pool, mimicked the boy sinking in his blood, and roared with laughter. Some of his Myc workers had said that he killed people, but I didn't believe them. This killing would certainly start a war with the boy's people.

On the other side of the river they had heard the shot. When they saw us coming back, only two of us in the boat, they knew what had happened. A wailing scream rose from the shore as we got closer. I wanted to get away from Noweda because I knew arrows would be flying.

But he took his metal things out and started waving them around and shouting at everybody, calling them names of private body parts and a lot of other words that I didn't yet understand. And they did nothing for revenge! I knew right then that whatever power I had inside of me that helped me control people, he had more of it. He had so much control over these people that even the boy's relatives did not try to take any revenge.

I called the warriors together and we hurried to leave for home. Noweda had promised to get me one of those metal sticks he called a gun. And I would have loved to have one, but after what I saw, I didn't wait for it. We left richer than we ever thought possible, anyway. We were loaded with axes, machetes, red material for loincloths, and pots for cooking-everything.

The trail home was long and hard even though we now had machetes to help us clear the way. The second morning some of us woke with sore throats, painful eyes, and very hot. I had some ebene so I got someone to blow it into my nose and I talked with my spirits. Again I saw my shabono and the beautiful people I love came to me calling me Father. And they like for me to call them my children.

"The nabas have put an evil spell on you," Healing Spirit told me. "Many of you will die."

Charming whispered in my ear. "I will make sure you do not die. You are my own brave warrior." She is so beautiful and kind to me. I love her.

With Healing Spirit's help, I sucked out the disease and spit it away. But the next day one of our warriors died.

We burned his body, gathered his bones and kept moving on. But the next day everyone was sick except for me and my brother. We couldn't travel the trails very quickly. The next day another person died and the next day another. Each time, we burned the body and gathered the bones before we went on. But they continued to die and my spirits were not able to stop the dying.

There were so many dying that we couldn't take the time to burn them all. We began leaving the bodies along the trail. Every day somebody died; some days, two. Someone died for every finger on both my hands and all my toes. In the end we were too sick to travel and we stopped to wait for the sickness to go away. But it didn't.

After many days we started on even though we were too sick to walk. We crawled on our hands and knees all day and didn't get very far. Two of the young warriors were well; they hunted food for the rest of us. When night came we were not able to get up to tie our hammocks so we slept on the jungle ground. We were too weak to mourn that night for the one we lost that day. We left him on the trail.

The next day was the same. And the day after. More of our men died.

When we entered the shabono, weak and skinny, we began to wail for all the "broken arrows" we had left behind. We hadn't even been able to burn their bodies. All the women joined us and we wailed together for a long time. That night as we slept, the women started wailing for their men. It went on all night. And for many nights after that, the women kept us awake throughout the night with their wailing.

I asked my spirits if we should take revenge. "You might lose too many warriors trying to get revenge," Jaguar told me. "You need the spirits that protect against naba disease. Next time, before you go to the world of the nabas, you must spend much time with us and send us ahead of you to protect against the bad that will come to you in their land."

When we finally got our strength back, I led some men and women down the trail to recover our dead and the goods we had left along the way. We found them by looking for termite nests. Everywhere a body lay, there was a huge termite nest on top of it. All our loincloth was destroyed, but we got the axes and machetes.

Each place we found a body, we built a fire, burned it, and wailed for our loss. It took us many days to find all the bodies and burn them. We returned to our shabono with so many bones.

When we entered the shabono, everyone wailed. Many of our lost ones were friends and relatives from nearby villages who we had invited to join us on the trip. One of them handed his brother's bones to his wife and grabbed me by the arm. He pulled me to the shabono center and stuck out his chest. I stuck out my chest and he hit me across it as hard as he could, and then stuck out his chest. I hit him back as hard as I could and stuck my chest out again. He pounded my chest once more and stuck his out for another blow. We traded blows until he was beaten and tired. He was angry with me. And I was angry with my spirits. We needed a fight like this to help us with our grief.

Then one of his relatives stepped up to take his place and hit me in the chest. I hit him back. He too had lost his brother. After he got tired, another took his place.

There were many more to hit me, but I couldn't hit them back very hard. Finally, I could take no more and fell to the dirt. We spent the rest of the night wailing out our grief. It was a horrible time for me because I had led all our loved ones to die. I knew that I deserved that beating. But that night while I lay in my hammock listening to all the cries of my people, I became angry with my spirits.

"Why have you done this to me?" I shouted at Jaguar Spirit. "Why couldn't I keep our people alive? *You* are the one who sent us on this trip."

"Don't be angry with us, Father," Jaguar Spirit begged. "Please don't throw us away. We are not the right spirits for controlling the sickness of the nabas. You need to get a different spirit for that. You need the spirits that rule naba diseases."

I didn't know what to say to him; I already had more spirits than I had time to talk to. I was angry all night and my spirits kept trying to calm me down. They sent Charming to be with me. She always makes me feel better. But I was still angry.

The next day all the men counseled together to decide if we should take revenge on the nabas. But we were confused. Spear and I contacted our spirits. Even the spirits were confused. "You need to get a different spirit for the naba diseases," they kept telling us.

Our life was better now with all the new things we had from the nabas. But we still couldn't sleep for fear of a raid from the relatives of Potato Village. Spear was so scared when I was gone that he took the whole village on *wyumi*. They hid out in the jungle, looking for food and covering their tracks wherever they wandered.

So we strengthened our shabono and built the alana higher across the opening and longer around the side. This would make it much harder for attackers to get inside and get a good shot at us. Still we weren't safe and we knew it. We couldn't sleep.

3

NOT EVERY SPIRIT IS WHAT HE APPEARS

Deemeoma grows older every day. She stays close to her sister for protection against the other children. But Fredi has no protection and the children always tease him. They say, "We slaughtered your relatives." The experienced killers scold the children. But it never stops them. Fredi always cries.

Spear marries a girl we call Noisy Privates. We call her that because one time she was bathing and making noise with her privates. She hates the name of course, but . . . , When a boy grows to a man, his childhood name becomes an insult and he will fight to keep anyone from using it. But we call the women anything we want. Noisy Privates gives Spear many children.

One of the killers on the Potato Village raid was a shaman like me. Everyone respected him, both as a shaman and as a warrior. He had a son named Shoefoot. Shoefoot was the young man who helped me hunt the turkey. The other village leaders and I discovered that the spirit world had a real interest in this young man. As a leader among shamans, it became my job to train him and to pass our ways on to him.

We built a special place for him in the shabono where no one could see him or talk to him. He could eat only certain things and very little of those. "We need to get you very skinny so the spirits will come to you," I told him.

Day after day I watched Shoefoot get skinnier. He wasn't allowed to talk to anyone except me and any spirits who might come to him. After a long time he was ready. We brought him out. Spear stuffed a handful of green ebene into the end of a long tube and we carefully placed it up to his nostril. I blew on the other end and shot the ebene into his brain. He doubled over on the ground from the pain, then got to his feet as the ebene began to hit him and move him into the spirit world. I danced with him, calling for the beginning spirits that would build a shabono in his chest. This would make a place for other spirits to come and live.

"I saw things like I have never seen before," Shoefoot said to me after he came back from his trip to the spirit world. It was clear that the spirits had taken him to some of the places I'd been.

"I told you that the spirit world is far better than this one, didn't I?"

"Yes, you told me. But how could I have known?"

I knew from the beginning that Shoefoot was going to be good. He would become as good with the spirits as I am.

"You're going to be a great man of the spirit world, friend," I told him. "I can tell that already. You will be a great leader of our people."

Every night Spear and I would take ebene and talk with our spirits to see if there was danger in the jungle around us. Now we began to include Shoefoot in our regular times with the spirits. Even after all these moons we were still not able to go out and work in our gardens for fear of being attacked, and there was not enough food to eat. The children were always crying from hunger.

When we did get something to eat, all the adults were so hungry that by the time we were fed there was almost never anything left for the children.

One night I was wakened from sleep when a trembling hand touched my chest. I leaped from the hammock and grabbed my bow and arrows. "I'm sure I heard something," Shoefoot whispered, his voice shaking with fear. I shook too, but we heard nothing. We crept, one silent step at a time, toward the shabono entrance. The moon and stars weren't out so we saw only black. We couldn't even see each other. Behind us we could barely see the dying embers of the shabono fires. That was all. The silence was stopped by the distant hum of a turkey.

"Boy, I'd love to eat him," Shoefoot whispered. "Let's go out and get him."

"Never!" I whispered sharply. "You know that's where our enemies will be waiting in ambush for us." Just past the shabono entrance we heard a slight movement coming from the jungle in front of us. We both drew arrows to shoot. I was about to release when I heard whispers coming from the brush.

"It's us, it's us," they whispered, almost too late. They were men from our village. They had gone to get the turkey but then got afraid and came back. We put our arrows away.

"It's good you didn't keep going," I said. "There is something out there. I can feel it." We returned to our hammocks but didn't sleep.

Night after night was like that. We hid inside our shabono, afraid of being attacked and afraid to go out and hunt. We would soon die. So we decided to put the whole village on wyumi. "We won't be as well protected wandering out in the jungle," I told everyone, "but we will be harder to find and we can split up and go different places. Maybe we can find something to eat."

Wyumi is always hard. We just wander through the jungle day after day looking for anything that's eatable. When we don't find anything, it is horrible. The children die first because they are always the last to be fed and it is so hard for them to keep up. But nothing could be worse than what we had been going through since the Potato Village raid.

We split in all directions and went deep into the jungle, covering our tracks as we went. Spear and I were in the same group. Shoefoot came with us because I was still teaching him.

We found a papaya tree and got some fruit. I shot a turkey. Everyone knew that the people with me would eat the best because I could always bring back plenty of game. Other hunters stalked their game very quietly until they got real close but then they usually scared the animal off. My way was to climb wildly up a tree and make lots of noise just like the monkeys do. When I got right next to the bird or monkey in the tree, I shot him. My spirits made the animals think that I was just another monkey.

Naturally the jaguars followed me around because I was always where all the game was. One time I was out hunting and found a tree full of turkeys. I left most of my arrows at the bottom and began to climb up to get one, when I heard something tramping all over my arrows at the bottom of the tree. I stuck my head over a branch and looked down. My heart stopped when I saw something black moving up the tree.

If it's a jaguar, I thought, *this might be the end.* Then I saw those huge pads on the bottom of his front paw as he reached up and sank his claws into the bark. On each side of his mouth, I saw the two big teeth that come together. But his eyes were the scariest. The cracks in the middle of his big blue eyes tell you what he's after.

I looked around but there was not another tree close enough for me to jump to. I looked down. He was closer and still climbing.

I climbed to a higher limb where there was more room to move and took the string off my bow. As the jaguar got close, he stayed on the side of the trunk away from me. I could see his paws on each side of the tree. I heard each short breath as he worked his way toward me.

When he reached my level, he moved slowly around the trunk. But I was ready. I stabbed him in the neck with the end of the bow and knocked him off the tree. I screamed with fright. He screamed when he hit the jungle floor and ran. Of course the turkeys wouldn't sit through all that. They were gone.

Each time I went out to hunt, the jaguars followed me. They scared me to death. They were always jealous of me because it was so easy for me to get food in the jungle. One time a jaguar had me trapped and was about to grab me with his claws. But I quickly said to him, "Don't scratch me now. I'm stuck in these vines here. You're taking advantage of me." I don't know why, but he released his claws and sat back in the vines. I shot him in the throat. After the poison point killed him, I tied him to my back and started carrying him home. Then I said, "All right. You can go ahead and scratch me now."

I sometimes wondered if the jaguars I met could be related in some way to Jaguar Spirit, but I never felt that they were. Jaguar Spirit was a Yanomamö with the courage of a jaguar. It was that spirit that made me so courageous. And courage is the only way to face a jaguar.

At night I took ebene and taught Shoefoot more about the spirits. He was a hot-headed young man, but what a great one for the spirit world.

Wyumi was so hard because there were always people sick. This made plenty of work for us shamans to do. Especially the little ones got sick. Many times I would chase the souls of the children up to the land of the unfriendly spirit and bring them back. But many times I couldn't reach them in time and they died. The old people often die on wyumi. We knew that when we all got back together we would have many gourds full of ground bones to drink and much grieving to do.

From that time until now, Spear has never told anyone what happened to him. But he told me.

Spear's father was very old and dying and couldn't keep up with us. But he wouldn't die the way the other sick people did. He just grew older and weaker. We both took ebene and used our spirits to make him well, but it never happened. My spirits told me to leave him. Each day as we moved on in search of food, the old man fell farther behind. Spear and his wife and little children stayed back with the old man to keep him from getting lost and to help him keep up with us. We watched for them, but finally they were so far behind that we lost them in the jungle. "Leave me," the old man kept whispering to Spear. "Just leave me. Let me die on my own."

But Spear couldn't do it. The next day was worse. The old man could hardly walk. Spear went hunting but found nothing. The area was all hunted out and there was no fruit on the trees. In the right season the jungle might make enough to keep a person alive. But in the wrong season, there was nothing.

When Spear came back that night, the old man wanted to talk. He wanted to tell Spear to go where he could find food for the rest of the family and to just leave him alone to die. But his mouth didn't want to make the words. Spear lay in his hammock in the dark jungle. There was much he wanted to say to his father. But he couldn't talk. There was much he wanted to ask him, so many things that he didn't know, especially now. But would he get wisdom from a confused dying man? Spear looked to his spirits to ask what to do.

"It's time," they told him.

The next morning, Spear motioned with his hand to his wife and children. They knew that it meant for them to leave and try to catch up with the rest of the village. They knew that Spear would follow when he was done. He stayed behind with his old father. *He's not even sick,* Spear thought. *Just so old he can't move very well.*

After the others left, Spear tried again to talk to his father. But still he couldn't say anything. He couldn't even tell him that the family had gone ahead to catch up with the group. And there was a lot more. He wanted to say that he didn't want to do what he was going to do; but he couldn't talk about that either. His throat got real hard like a big nut.

The old man looked at Spear. He could see in his son's tired eyes what he was thinking. He wanted to talk to his son, but didn't know how to start. He said nothing. Spear looked into his father's eyes. He saw fear. Despair. Surprise. Hadn't his father meant it when he told him to go on and leave him?

Spear placed the few pieces of dry fruit and nuts on a palm leaf under his father's hammock. He really couldn't spare the food, but. . . . There was nothing left to do, nothing left to stay for, except to say all the things he wanted to say. But he wasn't able to. So he did things, things that didn't need doing. He untied his hammock string, then tied it back, then untied it again. He arranged the fruit and nuts on the palm leaf. He tightened his bow string even though it was already tight. He straightened the arrow feathers. Spear knew he wouldn't hunt today anyway. He couldn't. This would be the most horrible day of his life.

"Where are you now that I really need you?" Spear cried to his spirits. "You never told me how to get through this."

Spear didn't know how to take that first step away from the hammock. Should he back away and keep looking at his father? Should he turn? He couldn't keep a tear from running down his face. *Nothing in my whole life could be harder than this,* he thought.

He took a few steps away from the little palm-leaf shelter that would protect his father's hammock if it rained before he died. Then he took a few more steps and then some more. He looked back. His father's head was bent down out of the hammock. He was watching out from under the leaves of the shelter. Spear looked away fast. Maybe his father hadn't seen him look into his eyes. *I knew I shouldn't have looked back,* he thought as he turned to walk on. He broke into wails of pain. The family heard him and knew that he had finished his job and was following after them.

Spear was furious with his spirits. "Why have you made me do this?" he asked them in anger. "You are worthless! You have no healing power at all! I ought to throw you all away!"

Spear's father listened to the wails of his son until they were too faint to hear. He listened for the rest of the day. But the wails never came back. *I'll be stronger tomorrow,* he thought . . . *maybe. Maybe I'll get up then and follow.* He would have eaten some of the fruit and nuts but he wasn't hungry. He hoped to sleep and not wake up. But he did. He ate all the fruit and nuts and was still hungry and he hurt. He waited for dark. He waited for Spear. He waited for the pain to leave. But it didn't. The pain was so bad that he knew he must be dying and he wished it would happen fast. But it wouldn't. But the *pain* of being *alone* to die was worse than the pain of dying.

We never saw Spear's father again. But I know how he felt because one day we found a man who had been left just like Spear's father. He had been there for days but was still alive. We fed him and he came to live with us. He was so sad he wouldn't talk about being left. One day when no one was around, he whispered into my ear his story of being left on the trail.

When night came, Spear lay in his hammock and wailed. All the family wailed with him. All the rest of us in the village wailed too. It made us remember our own relatives whose bones we have drunk and we wailed all the more. Everyone remembered all the other times we have had to leave an old relative and we wailed for them. The noise of the wailing scared the children and they ran to their parents for comfort. But we had nowhere to run for comfort. After wailing for half the night, our voices became sick and would make no more sound. Spear was left alone with his thoughts. "It can't get any worse than this," he said to his spirits.

He was right. It never did get any worse for Spear than it

was that night. He knew he wouldn't sleep, even after the whole village had been quiet for a long time. Maybe this would help him forget that other worst memory that had been stealing his sleep—that warrior from Potato Village. Spear saw his face again and heard his scream, "Don't kill me, older brother!" Spear tried to change what he remembered and not shoot this time, but he released the string and the arrow flew.

Surely now, with his father's face to remember, he would soon forget the awful face of that warrior begging to live. But how would he sleep? *Other fierce fighters don't have any trouble sleeping after they kill,* he wondered. *Did I do something wrong during unokai? Maybe I touched myself with my fingers and didn't really get cleaned of the killing.*

Now the pain of his father's memory was added to the other. We all knew Spear was in great pain, but he never told anyone how much. After a long time wandering in the jungle, we gathered together again in the shabono.

One night after the fires had burned low and the village was quiet, the families around Spear were startled from their hammocks when a sharp cry broke the stillness. "Older brother, don't kill me!" No one was afraid because there were no raider cries in the air. It was Spear's voice crying out, "Don't shoot me, older brother!"

Fruitboy got out of his hammock and stumbled through the dark to his father's hammock. He grabbed his father's arms as they swung in front of his face in an attempt to protect himself. They were wet and slippery with sweat.

"It's a dream! It's a dream," Fruitboy whispered as loud as he could. He must keep his father from knowing that he had wakened others with his awful dream. His father would be humiliated if people knew that he was troubled about his killing. Spear struggled to free his arms from his son's grip. "It's just me—Fruitboy!" he whispered into his father's face. Spear woke and collapsed back onto his hammock. He breathed a great sigh of relief. Fruitboy went back to his hammock.

The village was quiet again. Quieter than before. People lay awake thinking. Fruitboy wondered how long it would take his father to forget. Spear wondered if he might have wakened anyone else. *They will surely think I'm not a fierce killer,* he thought. Shoefoot's father and Crossedeye's father wondered if they had ever had a dream like that which showed others their fears. *Maybe everyone knows we are not as fierce as we say*, they both wondered. And each one wondered what the other might be thinking.

But we never admit fear.

Like any good shaman, I tried to get the best spirits for Shoefoot. There are always plenty of bad spirits that love to live in your chest in order to make you do crazy things. Any beginning shaman must learn to tell between good and bad spirits. A shaman will never be any smarter or more powerful than his spirits. That's why I was always warning him about Deer Spirit.

"I met a spirit this time that was beautiful," Shoefoot said after the ebene wore off.

"Tell me about him."

"He was able to make himself very attractive to all the women. They just loved him. He could have any of them he wanted. He would just speak to them and they would love him and want him."

"That's Howashi Spirit," I said. "You don't want him either. That monkey spirit is the worst. Please believe me. You don't want him."

"But he was so amazing. He could make a woman want him just by looking into her eyes," Shoefoot argued.

"You have much to learn," I said. "Listen. Not every spirit is really what he appears to be. Howashi is a deceiver. You've seen howashis. They think that every animal in the jungle wants to have sex with them. But do they? That's why the monkey always looks so stupid, why it's covered with its own sperm all the time. Well, that's exactly what that spirit is like. That is just the kind of spirit you don't want. He owns you. You don't own him. Once you get him, you'll never get rid of him. He's nothing but trouble."

"Have you ever known anyone to get stuck with him?" Shoefoot asked.

"We both know someone. Think and see if you can tell who it is."

Shoefoot thought a little. "You mean my uncle, don't you?"

I nodded. "Certainly. Doesn't he think that all the women in the village want to have sex with him? He's completely deceived by Howashi Spirit." Shoefoot knew very well about his uncle. He was the biggest source of fights in the village because he couldn't keep his hands off the women.

The next day Shoefoot took more ebene and tried to avoid Howashi and find new spirits. But somehow he got into trouble again. The spirits led him out of the shabono and down the trail. I chased after. On the trail, they attacked him and hit him over the head with a huge tree limb. He fell to the ground. I was sure he was dead.

I jumped into the spirit world and battled with these new spirits as they hovered over Shoefoot and beat him. My spirits joined me in the fight. It was a hard one. Even I couldn't tell if it was in the spirit world or in the real world. Many times it happens in both worlds at the same time.

Together we fought the spirits off and they left Shoefoot alone. Some of his relatives saw what happened and followed us out of the shabono and onto the trail. They saw me fight for him, but they couldn't see the spirits of course. We all watched as he lay motionless for a long time. Finally he woke.

"What happened?" I asked him.

"I don't know," he said. "You tell me."

"You got some bad ones again. They tried to kill you. I don't know why."

After that I took much more care in training Shoefoot. It was clear that he was special. All the spirits were taking great interest in him. I wasn't surprised to see him fooled a little by Howashi, but I was completely confused that he would find some that would try to kill him. At the end of his life they might kill him, like many spirits do to their shaman when he's old and useless. This wouldn't happen to me of course; I have good spirits. But it shouldn't be happening to Shoefoot either because he was only beginning.

I wondered if it could be some of those women who were jealous because I had ignored them. Maybe they were trying to get even by killing my favorite beginner. There are so many spirits that look good but are nothing but deceivers. We shamans must be very wise and selective.

Shoefoot was making a good beginning. He had the right spirits, the ones that build the shabono in your chest. Now many other better ones should come and live in him. But instead Shoefoot kept getting spirits that he didn't get along with.

One time he was lying in his hammock, sick with malaria, and two spirits came to his hammock with a delicious drink of palm fruit. They were beautiful, just like my own Charming. Shoefoot was so charmed. They wanted to take him away, but he was afraid to go with them.

The next day they returned to steal him. They were too beautiful for him to resist. They led him into the jungle where there was no underbrush and they ran with him at great speed. They took him far from the village. But Bat and Won't-Grow's father chased Shoefoot into the jungle and found him. When they tried to bring him home, he didn't know them and was terrified to see them. It took them a long time, but finally they got him home.

Soon we needed more trade goods, so we made the long trip down to the village of the nabas and worked for Noweda again. This time we worked real hard with our spirits to keep ourselves protected. Noweda always treated me like a friend. We traveled to a place where Noweda's brother lived. His brother must have had some powerful spirits because he was even more cruel than Noweda and the people did nothing against him.

One time we went down the Casiquiare River to the edge of Brazil. A big crowd of nabas were all drinking a drink that makes you act funny. I went into a big house where there was a crowd of people; all of them were naked. We Yanomamö are all naked, of course, but that is only because we don't have any clothes. I could not guess why people who had clothes would want to be naked. They were all tangled together, everyone having sex with everyone else, with no care of who might see. Noweda joined right in.

I clicked my tongue and shook my head. I will never forget what I thought. I thought, *these nabas might have a lot of trade goods and they might know a lot of things, but they are really so much dumber than we Yanomamö. Only animals don't care who is around when they mate.*

4

OUR PAIN IS NOT OUR SPIRITS' FAULT

Deemeoma and the women we captured are finally getting used to us. Tyomi got the man she wanted, but she almost died from being chopped with a machete by the man that wanted her. Deemeoma made such a fuss over it that I almost killed her. But they're getting used to us. Fredi still isn't happy. I keep training Shoefoot. His father gives me his beautiful sister, Longhair. She gives me a son. Spear still struggles with his memory of the raid and his father. Our whole village lives in constant fear. Especially me.

I was lying in my hammock having fun with my spirits when I saw Alligator Spirit pick a fight with another spirit. It was the spirit of someone in our village, but I couldn't tell who. "Why are you fighting her?" I asked Alligator. Then I asked another one of my spirits. "Why is he fighting her?"

"He wants to," my spirits told me. "He's not dancing with you. You don't have time for him. So he has nothing else to do." Alligator took a big bite right through the middle of the other spirit. I didn't think about it because I was dancing with my favorite spirit out in the shabono center.

Later that evening, a little girl in our village became ill with great pain in her middle. Her parents brought her to me. I could see right away that it was a pain from the spirit world and there would be nothing I could do for her.

I was the only one in the village who knew why the little girl died. And I also knew that she wasn't the first to die like this. Many times I had seen Alligator Spirit or Jaguar Spirit take vicious bites out of the spirits of children in my village. That day or the next, the child would suddenly be sick and die before I could help.

I told this to the old man of the village, Crossedeye's father. He was the one who had saved Deemeoma, Fredi, and the women that day at Potato Village. He's a shaman, so I knew that he wouldn't tell the village if one of my spirits had killed one of our own people.

"You've got powerful spirits," he said. "I know those spirits well. Let me show you how to make them do this against our enemies. It is what they really like to do."

I asked my spirits if they could kill other children. "I don't do that," Charming told me, "but I can get you spirits who can." She introduced me to Snakeman. There was no room left in my shabono for any more spirits. But he crowded in and found a place anyway.

"First you find the footprint of the person you want to kill," Snakeman said to me. "Then you very carefully dig out the big toe print and the toe next to it and wrap it in leaves and vines. Then comes the hard part: you find a poisonous snake and get it to bite the bundle of leaves. That will cause the person who left the footprint to get bitten on the foot by a snake and die. You'll see. If you need help with snakes, I'm the spirit you need."

The next day I followed the directions that Snakeman gave me. It was a lot of trouble and dangerous to get the snake. But the results were worth all the work. We later got a message from the village that one of their children had died of a snake bite. So Snakeman became another of my close friends of the spirit world.

Crossedeye's father was right about Alligator Spirit too. I soon had many more spirits who could attack our enemies. And we would soon hear that the person had died.

One day I was lying in my hammock watching a bunch of children playing in the sunlight of the shabono center. One of them yelled, "Hey, you stop that, Barkhead."

"Hey you!" The boy's mother yelled at him. "Don't call him by his name. Those shamans in our enemy villages will hear you and use it to put a spell on him." And she was right. It was one of the jobs of mothers to keep their children from speaking names that our enemy shamans could hear. Barkhead was the boy's name, but he would only use it until he reached manhood.

"What will he do to me?" the child asked.

The children gathered around her as she worked over the fire. The woman lowered her voice to a whisper. "Don't you remember all your friends who have died?" she explained. "Our enemies heard their names. After they know a person's name, they can use the name to put a spell on them."

"Is Jungleman the best shaman there is, Mama?" the child asked.

"Yes," she whispered. "That's why another one of his names is Child-Eater. It's because he has killed so many children in our enemies' villages. You can be sure that they never let their children say their names for fear Jungleman will hear. But he knows all their names anyway because the spirits have taken him to all their villages."

She squatted, placing a chunk of wood on the coals and three pieces of yucca on the wood. She blew hard into the coals and flames jumped up around the wood. The children hoped there would be enough yucca for them tonight.

"Yes," the mother went on telling the children about me, "he certainly is the most powerful shaman we know. When he comes back from hunting, don't you see how much meat he brings with him? Sometimes he will come back with more meat than all the other hunters in the village can get together."

One day a child got sick and I wasn't able to heal him. He died real quick. "I almost caught the hawk that stole his soul, but he got up through the bottom of the lake into Yai Wana Naba Laywa's land just before I could catch him," I told his parents. "This was the work of a shaman in another village." It was the same wound that Alligator Spirit had used to kill that girl right here in our village.

"Who was it that killed that boy?" I asked Alligator Spirit. He took me where there were large open places—no jungle, just grass. I had never seen a place like it. A shaman named Toucan was sending his spirits out from there to kill the souls of children in other villages.

What should we do? I thought. *This village is too far away for us to travel there and avenge our death.*

"Don't worry," Alligator told me. "I'll be happy to take care of the problem for you." I saw Alligator go and take a big bite out of one of their young boys. That night the boy died.

I lay on my hammock that night and with the help of my spirits I listened to the relatives in that far away village wail for their boy. The children were the easiest to kill and Alligator was always anxious to help. I soon became respected and feared as a child killer.

The village in the jungle by the big grassland was responsible for many children dying in our village. Toucan, their shaman, was a fierce warrior who had killed many men. He continued to kill children in our village, and each time I killed a child in his.

One day our son became very sick. At first Longhair wasn't worried because she knew I could heal him. But even after I called on every spirit I had, he just wouldn't get better. Spear tried. Shoefoot tried. But I'm still the best, so I tried the hardest. I took ebene for days and worked over his little body with Sucking-Out Spirit and even got other spirits to help. Charming even helped me, and she never helps with the sick. Finally he began to get better.

The next day, he died.

We grieved so much for our son. "Why have you allowed this to happen to me?" I cried in pain to Charming. "It is so awful. I hurt so much."

"This was caused by the people who live in some villages close to Toucan's village. It is a spell that requires another special spirit to defend against it," Jaguar said. Charming came again, but I didn't feel like seeing her. Another spirit woman spent some time with me and I finally felt better.

"We can get revenge," Snakeman told me. "Get the poisonous snake tomorrow and pull its teeth. We'll blow the powder in the direction of Toucan's village and I will do my work."

The next day I followed Snakeman's directions and soon I had my revenge. It was so much easier than traveling all the way to Toucan's area and trying to kill someone. But the effect was the same. A child in their village died.

I lay in my hammock thinking how nice the revenge was. But I still missed my son so much. All the revenge in the jungle would never bring him back.

The village where my spirits killed the child is called Shooting Village. It's called that because they are always in a shooting war with someone. Toucan didn't live there, but it's close to him, about a day's walk. He visited often because it's his wife's home village.

I have never been to Shooting Village, but I know a lot about what happens there because I have visited so many times in the spirit world when I kill their children. It's just part of a shaman's work.

Toucan's in-laws liked him so much as a son-in-law that they wanted to give him another daughter for his second wife. He was happy to take her, and his wife was happy to have her little sister come and live with her.

Toucan loved her. She was as pretty as his first wife and would help him have many more children. He was a great hunter and knew he could provide for all of them. He would soon be the most powerful person in his world.

But the sister didn't want to leave home and didn't like Toucan. It wasn't right for her not to like him and her sister told her so. But as soon as Toucan left to go hunting, the little sister sneaked out of the shabono and made the long trip home to mother in Shooting Village.

When Toucan returned two days later he was furious. It would take him two days to go get her and bring her back. What a waste! But even after he brought her back, she kept running away every chance she got.

One time Toucan returned from hunting and his first wife told him that her sister had run away again. But this time she had not been gone long. If Toucan hurried, he could catch her soon and wouldn't have to make the long trip to her village.

He took a different path through the jungle and came out on her trail. It was bare of tracks. He was ahead of her. He hid and waited. It was easy to hear her coming because part of the trail was under water.

When she reached the spot where he crouched hidden, he jumped onto the trail and faced her. "Why are you always so much trouble? Why do you give me such grief?" She saw the rage in his eyes and froze with fear. She could see that his patience was stretched far beyond the limit. She was within reach of a killer with a machete in his hand and fury in his eye.

When she turned to run, he lashed out with a blow that

struck her in the back of the neck. She collapsed on the trail. Toucan sat down waiting for her to wake up. He had seen many such wounds in animals and people. She was bleeding heavily, but she would soon get up. They always did.

He sat quietly, waiting and watching her bleed. He sure didn't mean to cut her that deeply. She hadn't moved a muscle since she fell.

He began to cry. *Why did I do it, he wondered? Why did I let her make me do this? I love her. She will be the beautiful mother of many of my children.*

She kept on bleeding and he decided that when she woke he would not hit her again. She had suffered enough. *Now she'll come back and be a good wife and live happily with me and her sister,* he thought. *She'll soon roll over and look to me for help. And I'll give it. I'll take care of her and bring her back to health. When she sees how much I love her, she'll be happy.* He watched her closely, looking for even the slightest movement.

But she never moved again, not even a finger. His machete had cut too deep into her neck. While he thought of all the things he wished he hadn't done and would have done different, and all the things he would do for her when she woke up, she bled until she was dead.

"Why have you done this to me?" he cried out in anguish. "Why?" But the jungle was silent. Not even a bird had seen what he had done. After a long time he rose slowly to his feet. With tears running down his face he took a big step over her body. It had to be a big step to keep his feet from touching her blood. With this on his mind, it would be a long trail home.

"Why did you make me kill you?" he screamed as he trudged back down the trail. "Why did you bring this anger out of me?" He shed great tears his whole journey home. He continued to ask these questions until his voice could no more make the sounds. But there was no one to hear.

Toucan's village grieved for his wife. Shooting Village should have made war over her death. Even though Toucan was my enemy, I would have used my spirits to help him fight the war because I also hated the people in Shooting Village. Then my spirits would have helped the people in Shooting Village to fight back against Toucan.

Instead of waiting to be attacked, Toucan went to Shooting Village and returned the bones to his in-laws. He told them their daughter's death was an accident. No ordinary person would ever return from such a trip alive. But Toucan wasn't ordinary. His fame was everywhere. His spirits had taken him all over and he could tell everyone about places he had never been. He even saw things in the huge villages of the nabas. He saw people get into a big box and a long vine carried it through the air over the top of a mountain and down the other side.

His in-laws grieved with him over their daughter's death and decided that they were not interested in trying to kill him. Even though he escaped death and war with his in-laws, Toucan could not forget his pretty wife. He did everything to try to forget her. He hunted. He fished. He worked his garden. But every night when he lay in his hammock, he saw her face.

He pleaded with his spirits to help him forget her. But it was no use. He knew they wouldn't. They got him into this mess. They encouraged his anger with her. They encouraged him to hit her with the machete. They were his source of fierceness—the reason he was so famous all over the world of Yanomamö and even outside. All we shamans know that the spirits are happiest when we kill people. And we love to show our fierceness by doing it to our enemies. But this wasn't an enemy; she was a woman he wanted.

Toucan was angry with his spirits. He couldn't sleep and they wouldn't help him sleep. He decided not to come to his hammock until he was so tired that he couldn't possibly stay awake. But every time he lay down in it, no matter how tired he was, he saw her face, that terror in her eyes in the moment before she turned to run. She had been a cornered animal without a chance against him.

He knew all about terror. He had learned to live with it because he knew that all our villages wanted to kill him for the many people he had killed. He had put all that same terror on a pretty girl who had done nothing but get homesick. *Why did I have to do it?* he asked himself over and over again.

Each time her face appeared, he heard his angry voice, "Why are you always so much trouble?" He knew every word. He held his ears but it never worked. He heard the next words anyway. "Why do you give me such grief?" And he saw her terror-filled face again. He missed her so much and he thought so hard to remember the good times they had when she had lived with them. He remembered how nice it was to be with her in the hammock. Then the picture of her coming to a startled stop on the trail kept breaking into all the other memories and wrecking them. So to stop them from coming, he had to stop remembering her. And his spirits wouldn't help him forget. They liked the memories.

One morning Toucan went hunting. When his machete sunk into the neck of the crocodile, he saw the blood ooze out. And there it was. The back of his wife's beautiful neck, with his machete in it and her blood oozing out. Even holding the machete in his hand reminded him of that day. So he went without a machete. But he couldn't go through the jungle without a machete.

It *must be that I have not destroyed all her things,* he thought. He and his first wife went through everything in the village to make sure that nothing of his dead wife's was left. They found something that might have been hers and burned it. Still the memories would not leave, even though no one ever spoke her name.

Toucan wondered if it is possible that other fierce men could have this problem. *No one would be afraid of me if they knew I felt remorse for killing,* he said to himself, *especially if they knew it was for killing a woman.*

My people still faced a big problem—all the friends and relatives of Potato Village. We still lived in constant fear that they might raid for revenge at any time. Our only friends left in the jungle were the relatives who live close to the Ocamo River, the ones who came with us on that raid. Now we were even afraid of them. They had never forgotten that we refused to give them any of the women from that great victory.

After many moons they invited us to come to a feast. We were suspicious. Our women cried because they knew that we were going to be killed. They also knew that they could not talk us out of going. "We all know it's a trap," Spear said to us who were the leaders.

"But if we don't go," Shoefoot answered, "every Indian in the world will call us cowards from now until we die." I told you Shoefoot was a hot-headed young warrior—the perfect leader for me to train. He was getting more spirits all the time.

We all knew he was right. Nothing the women could say would talk us out of this feast.

We entered the village at Ocamo in full war paint and with all our arrows drawn. It was a great show of power just in case they planned anything. But things calmed down when they offered us food and drink. We all feasted together. We ate good tapir meat all day and had a wonderful time.

The next day we took ebene together. They had a good supply for all of us. Usually only those of us who are shamans take the ebene, but at festival times everyone participates. One person blew ebene through a long tube into another person's nose. Then the first person got someone to blow ebene into his nose and we continued this until everyone felt real good. We never noticed that whenever it was their turn to get the ebene, they always had someone from their village blow it into their noses. We never thought that they might just be pretending to blow the ebene and pretending to go into a trance.

Both our villages blew ebene and danced around in a trance until we felt real good.

Then without warning it happened. They all had their bows and were shooting at us. There was blood and dirt everywhere. We ran for our weapons but were not able to use them. Many of us escaped into the jungle. But many others didn't. They put our dead outside the front of their shabono so we could get them and carry them back home for burning.

We found out why they tricked us. One of their people had died and their shaman had learned from his spirits that someone in our village was responsible for the death. That is why they had to invite us, to take this revenge on us.

When we got close to our shabono, we began to wail at the thought of the terrible news we had to bring. The women heard us and began to wail. They knew what to expect. We wailed all that night and for days after. We ground many bones during that time.

Now we knew that we had no friends in the world.

Every night I went to the opening of the shabono and made sure that the trails were well blocked and the alana was strong. Now we had the wall built so long that it went all the way around the shabono. Raiders would have to sneak all the way around the outside of the shabono just to get to the entrance. We made our wall from poles of the hardwood palm. It would be impossible for raiders to get through it. Still I was afraid. Spear met me there late one afternoon.

"We are too big and too easy to find," I said peering out the opening and down the trail. "We can't keep on living in this fear."

"I know," Spear told me. "I wouldn't want them to hear us say it, but we can't go on like this."

From down the trail the setting sun made long strings of soft cottony cords of light that landed in bright spots all around us. But I couldn't enjoy the beauty of my jungle when I knew it could be hiding the enemies that were after my death.

Shoefoot joined us. "Shall we ask the spirits for an answer to our problems?" he asked.

"Is our fear that plain?" Spear answered him.

"Everyone knows," Shoefoot said. "We aren't free to go hunting unless there's a lot of us and then we can't protect the women and children. We can't work the gardens. We can't do anything. We can't survive."

Spear and Tigerlip's father and I would never have wanted anyone to know that we were growing weary of the strain of constant attack. A few small fights would be fine. But after what we had done to the people at Potato Village, none of our enemies were interested in a small fight. They would be shooting to kill.

"No one expects you to be able to keep this whole village together," Shoefoot went on. It was good to hear my young shaman speak wisely. *He will certainly be a great leader for these people some day,* I thought.

While we were thinking about splitting the village, a horrible fight broke out between Shoefoot's uncle and many of the other men. "We are sick of you messing with our women!" one of them yelled at him. "You've got your wives and your brother's wives. That's enough women for any man. Keep your filthy hands off my wife!" There were others shouting the same thing. Howashi Spirit always causes fights. They either end with a village splitting into two villages or in someone getting killed. We split.

It is always a sad day when a village has to split, especially if it's not because of hatred. We would get together again, but no one knew when.

Tigerlip's family went toward the Ocamo River where the

sun rises but not close to our new enemies. They became known as Ocamo. The rest of us moved a long way toward the Metaconi River where the sun sets. Longhair and I and a number of other families crossed the Metaconi and moved toward the Padamo River. I wanted Shoefoot to stay with us because he was learning the ways of the spirits from me, but his family wouldn't allow it. The others split into two more villages and made sure that there was so much distance between them that no enemy could attack them both.

Deemeoma, Fredi, and his mother stayed with the group that Shoefoot's family and Spear were in. Tyomi and the other woman from Potato Village were married to men who went with Tigerlip to the Ocamo. So Deemeoma and her sister were finally separated.

We would see each other again. Shoefoot often traveled the long trail over to my village to learn more from me about working with the spirits. Of course Longhair was always happy to have a visit from her brother.

"I seem to be getting all kinds of spirits coming to me now, brother-in-law," Shoefoot told me one time.

"Well, just be sure not to be friendly to the spirit of the deer," I told him.

"Why not?"

"He's the spirit of confusion. He's timid. You know what a deer is like. It runs away at nothing. Well, that is exactly what Deer Spirit does. I knew a man once who had this one. He was so afraid of everything and everybody that finally we hardly ever saw him. He'd run off out in the jungle at the smallest thing and we wouldn't see him for days. If he had any sense, he'd be afraid to be in the jungle alone. But he's stupid. He's only afraid of people."

Shoefoot thought this was very strange. "Why would anyone ever be like that? It's courage we want, not fear."

"Of course," I told him. "And you already have Tiger Spirit. He's the most important. You must not have seen Deer Spirit yet. He'll come around. You'll see."

"But how will I recognize him? How should I treat him?"

"You haven't seen him yet because he is so shy," I said. "He'll come though, as soon as you have been friendly with all the other spirits. You know how more spirits come all the time? The more time you spend with the spirits you know and love, the more others feel welcome to come too." Shoefoot nodded. He was doing very well at learning the ways of the spirits. But he still couldn't give the village what they needed.

Shoefoot's father, also a powerful shaman, could see that their village was in trouble. Even though it was the biggest of all of those that split off from us, there was so much sickness and death that he knew they needed help. "My spirits keep telling me that our pain is not their fault, that there are other spirits we need to help us with our troubles," he said to Shoefoot one morning. "I think we must get help from the world of the nabas. You will have to take some warriors and make the long trip there. Work for some of the naba things we need and try to get someone to come and live with us."

In the early dawn Shoefoot left the shabono with a small bunch of warriors and began walking down the trail in the direction of the big river. They walked many days, as many as the fingers on one hand, before they found it.

"You get the string ready," Shoefoot told some of the warriors, "and I will get started on the bark." He climbed up a yellow-flower tree and made a cut into the bark all the way around the tree. Then he made a cut through the bark straight down to the bottom and another cut around the bottom. Starting at the top, he peeled the bark off the tree in one big long piece. Then they cut each end so they could fold the end up and the water couldn't flow in. With the string they tied the ends up and the big piece of bark became a canoe.

The water was slow moving and peaceful. The thick jungle overhanging the river reflected off the smooth water as it floated by. "What do you think these nabas will be like, Shoefoot?" they asked him.

"Jungleman has always gotten along with them," he answered. "They must have a lot of the things we need. I hope we can try to earn them." There was plenty of time to say their many thoughts as they sat and drifted slowly in the big river.

They came to a wide place and couldn't see where the river went. It looked like it disappeared. So they pulled their canoe to the side and carefully looked over the edge to see. It was a huge waterfall. They climbed down the cliff and built another bark canoe.

The next day they met another river and the two joined to

make a river twice as big. So much jungle went by that they often wondered if they would ever get back. They never knew that the jungle could be this big. Each night they stopped and hung their hammocks in the jungle at the water's edge.

Days later they came to rapids so big and dangerous that they had to give up their canoe again, walk through the jungle around the rapids, and build another canoe.

After many more days floating on the river, they came around a bend and saw something that struck fear into everyone. "What is that!" they all asked, looking ahead to a place where there was water as far as they could see. They were really asking Shoefoot. It took his air away just to look at it. None of these men had ever seen big water before.

One shocked warrior said, "We could not even shoot an arrow across this much water!"

"This must be the river of a very big spirit," Shoefoot said, but he was so scared he could hardly talk. He wondered what would happen when the canoe floated into such a big place. Could they ever get out?

Many more days later they saw strange-looking people on the shore and the same big houses that had surprised me when I first went to naba land. They got the canoe over to the shore, but everyone was afraid to get out. Shoefoot felt like someone was squeezing his stomach real hard. It was the same naba village where I had first met Noweda; the nabas called it Tama Tama. But now Noweda was dead and other people lived there. The white nabas came toward them, but with no weapons in their hands. Shoefoot thought, *They must be friendly.* So the Indians got out of the canoe.

They had been traveling for almost a moon. Shoefoot pushed their empty canoe out into the water. He knew that he would have to walk back through the jungle. As he watched the canoe drift slowly downriver and disappear, he wondered how long it would be before he would see his shabono again.

Then he didn't know what to do and a naba lady he couldn't understand gave him a drink of real cold water. Shoefoot thought this was strange, but it made him very happy.

Shoefoot and his friends worked for the nabas the same as I had done. They earned many things that made them rich. Because he was a shaman, Shoefoot was fascinated by the nabas' talk of a great spirit. But just like me when I first went there, Shoefoot had trouble understanding the naba talk. There is a certain kind of talk that all people use when we trade for things, but it isn't very useful when talking about spirits and other important things. So Shoefoot thought they were saying that this spirit would burn the world with fire.

"Whatever spirit these nabas have," he told his friends, "it must be a very rich one."

"Yes," one answered. "We sure do need some of their things."

They stayed about a moon. Then it took almost another moon of walking through jungle they hadn't seen before. Finally they got home. Then Shoefoot asked his father about the spirit that the nabas said would destroy the world with fire.

"Well, he's already tried it once," Shoefoot's father answered. He was old. He remembered the big fire that burned almost all of our jungle. "But I don't know what spirit he could be talking about. It could be Thunder Spirit or it could be some other spirits we don't know. I suppose it could be Yai Wana Naba Laywa, the unfriendly spirit who eats the souls of our children. *He* might try to burn the world."

"But he's unfriendly," Shoefoot objected. "The nabas couldn't know him."

Shoefoot's village was rich now from the axes, machetes, pots and the other things they were able to get from the nabas. But soon they needed more, so Shoefoot returned to the naba village at Tama Tama. "They said they would send someone to live with us, so ask them again to do it," Shoefoot's father told him as they left the shabono. "We want to know about this spirit they talk about and how to live better. Tell them that we cannot learn these things unless someone comes and tells us."

Again Shoefoot and his party made a bark canoe, walked around the waterfall, made another canoe, walked around the rapids, made another canoe, and finally got there. This time the nabas were beginning to speak much better. Shoefoot asked them if someone could come to live with them and teach them about their spirit and their ways.

"We need much help," he said. "Every moon many people die of diseases that my spirits cannot heal." But no one would come, so Shoefoot got back home with a sad story.

"I still do not understand about this spirit of fire," Shoefoot's father wondered out loud after Shoefoot got home. "It seems like it should be the enemy spirit, Yai Wana Naba Laywa. But how could the nabas know this spirit? Nobody can get close to him without burning up!"

"But his land is so beautiful," Shoefoot said.

"Yes, but we can't get there and he never comes out," his father answered.

"That's right," Shoefoot agreed, "he's so unfriendly—and all our spirits hate him."

But his father really wanted to know about this new spirit and sent Shoefoot back to naba land many times to ask for someone to come live in their village. No one ever came.

"We are too far away," Shoefoot's father said. "That's why they won't come to us. It is time for us to move out to the river."

The village was afraid to make such a big move. But Shoefoot's father was a powerful leader. After the long, hard move, Shoefoot went back again to ask for a naba to come. But none did.

After many seasons, Shoefoot's father said, "We are still too far for the nabas to come. We'll have to move down below the waterfall and the rapids. It's the only way we will ever get someone to come and teach us anything." So they moved again, all the way down to the end of the Metaconi River, where it goes into the Padamo.

When they got there, they found many beehives all over. Everyone feasted and there was even enough that the children were able to get some. From that time we have called them Honey Village.

One day a dugout canoe came up to their riverbank. It was a naba wearing a long dark robe. "Look at all the grey hair on that man's head," Shoefoot's father said, as the whole village watched the man tie his canoe. "He must be very wise. He will sure be able to tell us about this strange spirit of the nabas, this spirit of fire. Certainly he'll show us how to get out of so much of our misery."

But the grey-haired man got out of the boat, handed everyone something sweet to eat, and got back in his boat and left. The village was sad.

5

WE WANT YOU SO MUCH

*W*e see the nabas more and more and are still wondering about
their spirits. I continue my war with the people in Toucan's area.
Shoefoot travels up the Padamo River to visit me and finds more spirits as time goes. I now have another one of his sisters as a second wife.
She gets along well with Longhair. Fredi is constantly tormented at
Honey. Deemeoma is about to become a woman. Her sister, Tyomi, still
lives in Tigerlip's village with the young man who fought for her.

Somehow Tigerlip's village over at the Ocamo got a naba
to come to live with them, an old woman with a bad leg. It
was made of wood.

All the people of Tigerlip's village came to love Granny
Troxel even though she couldn't speak our language. Every day
she hobbled around the village doing whatever she could find
to do that would help people. She loved all the children and
always held a baby in her arms. She gave them colored things
to eat when they were sick, and it helped keep them well.

When she went into the river to bathe she could take her
leg off and leave it on the bank. Tigerlip was just a boy then,
about to reach manhood. One day he and his friends followed
Granny to the river when she bathed. While she was in the
water, they stole her leg and hid it. Then they hid in the brush

and watched her hop around on one leg. She called to the women of the village. They chased Tigerlip and his friends, scolded them and got the leg back for Granny. No one was upset, so this happened almost every time she went to bathe.

Granny finally got sick and it made the village very sad when she had to leave. After that other nabas weren't afraid to come into Yanomamö land and many began to come. Tigerlip trained to be a shaman and became the leader of the village. They called him Tigerlip because he was born with a scar that divided his lip from the bottom of his nose to his teeth. It looked just like a cat's lip.

After Granny left another naba came to Tigerlip's village on the Ocamo. They named him Padre Coco. He lived right in the middle of the village and helped people. He brought cows to the village and tried to get Tigerlip's people to help him care for them. He told them that the cows could make a lot of meat. But who could sit and wait for a cow to grow? And anyway, we never eat pets. He often spoke to the people and asked them to change their ways.

"You Yanomamö need to quit your warfare," he said. "You need to work at making a better life. You need to work to have more food for your children. You have to clean up this village and cut that jungle back from your homes so that you can protect your children from the sicknesses that come from all this filth. You are dying off too fast just from sickness. You'll never survive if you don't stop the warfare." Padre Coco would make this talk to Tigerlip all the time. But Tigerlip was a powerful shaman, and even though he wasn't happy with the wars, he wasn't going to change.

Everyone loved Padre Coco and was happy to have him in the village. He taught the children in a school and showed them how to grow many new crops. And things were good as long as he was there.

They would have done even better if they had not used Padre Coco's cattle for target practice.

Coco went to his garden one day after a short time away and found a huge swollen cow that had been dead for two days. He almost couldn't keep any of his pets alive.

Tigerlip traveled with Coco in the metal bird out to the big village of the nabas. Then they got inside a real big metal bird and traveled for a long time across large water. Tigerlip saw many things there that were so different that when he came back he was not able to tell his friends what it was like.

While he was in Coco's far land, he met Coco's head man. Coco called him "The Papa." The Papa treated Tigerlip kindly and put his hands on Tigerlip's head.

"That touch will be very good for you," Padre Coco later told Tigerlip.

"Why?"

"He has power from the Creator Spirit," Coco said.

Coco was right. The power of The Papa did help Tigerlip. The Papa gave Tigerlip a 40 hp outboard motor which did give him more power back at the village.

Coco also warned Tigerlip and his village that nabas would come who would give things in trade for messing around with the women. "This is something you should never do," he said. But Tigerlip did not know why he said that.

After many seasons, Padre Coco became sick and left the village. Tigerlip and all his people wailed when Coco got into his boat because they knew they would not see him again.

After Coco, many nabas began coming to the village. Just like Coco had said they would, they traded things—fish line, hooks, and lots of beautiful things—for sex with the women. Tigerlip didn't mind as long as they left his wives and daughters alone. Many of them brought cameras and a lot of paper to write on.

One day an Indian came to Tigerlip with a lot of pain in his penis. He didn't want the village to know where he was sick so he didn't tell Tigerlip until the pain was very bad. There was green stuff coming out of it. Tigerlip had never seen anything like it before. He talked to his spirits. "It's a naba disease," they told him. "You'll have to get naba spirits to take care of that."

Later another man came and soon almost everyone had the same sickness. Even the women got it in their private parts.

The new nabas who came were nothing like Padre Coco. They never said the same warnings he did. So Tigerlip's village soon became filthy again like it had been. And the new nabas didn't mind when Tigerlip went to war. Some even liked it and would encourage them to fight. They took pictures. They also took a lot of pictures of the women.

One day someone came to the village and said that Padre

Coco had died. The whole village wailed with mourning. Tigerlip began to remember all the things that Coco had taught him, especially his strange words about the nabas who would trade for sex. *Could it be,* he wondered, *that Coco knew that the nabas would come and spread a disease among my people that my spirits cannot heal?*

Tigerlip was filled with grief that Coco was dead. But he was even more sad that he had not learned from Coco. Once he thought that all nabas would be like Coco, Granny, and the other naba family. Now he knew he had been tricked. These new nabas were no good.

One of the new nabas to come to the Ocamo was a doctor who passed out medicine to sick people, and they got well. One day after Tigerlip and his spirits had spent a long time trying to heal a woman, he saw that they couldn't help. So he sent her to this naba-doctor. She came back a short time later.

"He told me to go to the shaman first," she said.

"What!" Tigerlip yelled. "Does he think I would send you to him if I could help you?" Tigerlip didn't tell the woman, but he knew that the naba just didn't want to be bothered with her. Then Tigerlip remembered how Padre Coco had told him that not all nabas were the same.

Tigerlip and some of his family also made the long journey all the way down the river to Tama Tama, where they worked for the nabas.

There was a whole family of them. The man's name was Pepe. I had met him many seasons before. He had come to visit our jungle and said to me, "I've never seen a Yanomamö. Where can I find them?"

So I had said, "Here we are." He was the first white man I ever saw in our jungle. He had told us he would come back with his family. Tigerlip's brother had a boy named Littlecurl who was too small to be afraid of the nabas; he became good friends with one of the young white boys. The white boy was Pepe's son. Every day they were together in the jungle and along the bank of the big river. They hunted and fished and talked and played. Littlecurl called him Keleewa.

During that time Pepe tried to learn to talk right. He became good friends with Tigerlip. Pepe tried to teach Tigerlip and his relatives about a different spirit, a creator of the spirits. The naba said that this spirit liked the Yanomamö people. Tigerlip listened because he had many spirits himself, and he knew much about the spirits. And Padre Coco had always talked about a great spirit. Tigerlip knew about a great spirit. We all did. Sometimes we called him Yai Wana Naba Laywa, the unfriendly enemy spirit. And sometimes we called him Yai Pada, the most powerful spirit who created everything, even the spirits. Tigerlip didn't like the feeling he got when the naba talked about the great spirit. It bothered his spirits inside him.

When Littlecurl's father left Tama Tama, he agreed that Littlecurl could stay behind so he could spend more time with his little naba friend. "I'll come home with Uncle Tigerlip when he comes," Littlecurl told his father. So the boy stayed. When Tigerlip was ready to leave, Littlecurl tricked him, saying, "My father is going to come back for me."

So Tigerlip left Littlecurl in Tama Tama without any family. Villagers thought his naba friend, Keleewa, was in on the trick and that the boys had done it so they could stay together.

Littlecurl looked deserted, so the nabas took him in. This was strange because the white nabas almost never let Indians into their houses. They probably weren't supposed to. But these nabas were different.

Littlecurl lived with the nabas for many moons. He and Keleewa became like brothers and Littlecurl was happy. Keleewa's mother was happy because she liked to cook the fish the boys caught. The white family treated him just like a son. Littlecurl felt so happy with them that he thought he would stay with them and be happy forever.

After a long time the naba family had to return to the naba land. They got an Indian to take Littlecurl back to Tigerlip's village on the Ocamo River. It was the saddest day of the boy's life. He never found out why the nabas left.

One day as I was talking to Jaguar Spirit, he told me that it was time to take revenge on our relatives in Ocamo Village. They were now our enemies because they had tricked and slaughtered us so bad. So I sent a runner to Shoefoot's father and Tigerlip's father and the others who were attacked on that feast day. I said that we should all get together and invite our enemies to a big feast of our own and try to trick them. Because Tigerlip and his father were both shamans, they knew

Jaguar Spirit. They were already aware of my plans. The thought that we would all be together again taking revenge made me very happy.

We found a man who lived in a village that was friendly with us and also with our enemies. We asked him to go tell Ocamo Village that we wanted to be friends and invite them to a big feast so we could make peace with them. After he told them, they felt relaxed with his words and said they would like to join us in the drinking of our relatives' bones.

"I don't think they believed me, but they said they would come," he told us when he came back. "Their women know it's a trap. They don't want their men to come. So even if the men come, the women might not."

"Of course the men will come," I said. "I told you they'd come. They won't want us telling everyone that they are cowards. But now that the women know it's a trap, we'll have to come up with a trick so we can catch the men off guard."

We all met at a secret place in the jungle to get ready for the big feast with our enemies. We hunted for days, smoking the meat and saving it for the feast.

When our enemies finally came, they didn't bring their women and children, and they came into our shabono with the same fear we had felt when we entered theirs. The moment they came through the shabono entrance, Tiger-Ear, a young warrior, attacked them with an axe. Tiger-Ear's father and another relative had been killed by these people that time when they had tricked us.

Halfway across the center of the shabono our men caught Tiger-Ear, held him back, and took the axe away. Axes had become a new weapon for us. We were beginning to earn them from the nabas on our long trips down river. An axe would kill, but not nearly as good as that magic fire stick that Noweda used to kill people.

When our enemies saw the axe-swinging vengeance in Tiger-Ear's eyes and our people holding him back, they knew that we were serious about wanting peace. We all feasted together like friends and drank the bones of our dead. They were tired from the long trip on the trail, but we promised them that we would all share ebene tomorrow.

We would be generous even with our enemies because we know that stingy people go to the fire pit. My spirits have taught me all about the fire pit. It's the place where stingy people go after they die. And they stay there forever. That's why all of us Yanomamö people share everything we have with each other.

"Sleep well," Shoefoot's father said, to make them feel comfortable. "We'll all have a great time taking ebene tomorrow." Our constant talk of ebene "tomorrow" began to make them nervous. They knew that it was the ebene that had helped them kill us the last time. I saw the fear in their eyes as we talked about tomorrow. We knew they would be on their guard.

"We've had a great feast and shared the bones of our relatives," I said to our new friends. "Why don't you all stay with us here in the shabono tonight instead of going back out in the jungle? Then we'll end our festival tomorrow with ebene." They decided that it would be safe to stay with us because they knew that they would only pretend to take the ebene anyway. They weren't going to fall into the same trap as we had.

So they hung their hammocks among ours all around our shabono and we talked together in small groups late into the night. We began to feel like friends again.

I woke before dawn. It was so dark that it didn't help to open my eyes. I felt for the hard dirt under my hammock and got up slow. I couldn't hear a sound. Our fires had died out. I knew right where all our hammocks were hung so I was able to keep from disturbing any of our visitors as I moved around the shabono waking our men. We all slept with a weapon in hand. We had machetes, axes, clubs, and spears. I put my hand over each man's mouth and shook his head just a little.

I moved one step at a time. It took a long time for me to get all the way around the shabono and back to my hammock. Then I gave the loud whistle of a tapir and each of us attacked the new friend in the hammock next to us. It was so dark we had to feel for our enemy with one hand. The other hand held a killing weapon. Jaguar Spirit was with us that morning, and a scream went up from our shabono that sent a charge of lightning through the body of every one of us. It was a slaughter that we will enjoy as long as we live.

Some of them escaped in the dark, and because we couldn't see, we hid and waited until light to see how many we killed. In the early light of dawn we saw that most of them died in hammocks full of blood.

That night I hung my hammock in the jungle and enjoyed my spirits again. "Tk! Didn't we slaughter them!" I said to Jaguar Spirit.

"You were wonderful, my Father! So wonderful!" he answered. All my spirits crowded around me and we danced and celebrated. It was great.

"You are so brave!" Charming said in her alluring way and I lay back on my hammock to enjoy her coming to me. She was so beautiful. All the bravest fighters wanted her. But she always turned away from their advances and came to me. No one could resist her. In all the world I have never seen a woman stop a man as much as she could.

With her smooth eyes she gazed deep into me. "And you are so handsome, my lover. You have everything we women want. We all want you so much." I felt weak having her with me in my hammock.

Though all my spirits crowded around, they knew that Charming would get my attention whenever she wanted it. The shabono inside my chest grew dark as always, from all the spirits crowding to get toward me. I love them all. But Charming—her I can't describe. What a thrill it is to have such wonderful spirits.

After we celebrated our victory, we went back to our separate villages. There was nothing to eat when we got home, so we went on wyumi and looked for food.

We had hardly begun our first day when my son started crying and in a short time all the children were crying. I knew they were just hungry.

"Where shall we go for food?" I asked my spirits. They led me to higher ground inland from the river. We had been there before but never went back because we found so little food there.

We traveled most of the way the first day and decided to stop for the night. The children were almost too weak to cry any more. My little boy was burning with fever. I worked over him to try to suck the fever out. Snakeman Spirit helped me and his fever got better.

The next day we found some cashew fruit but there wasn't enough for the children. We had to feed ourselves first so we could be strong. All the children knew to do was cry.

✻   ✻   ✻

Shoefoot and Spear, along with their families, finally got what they always wanted—nabas to come live with them. I went to Honey Village often to visit my relatives and Shoefoot and I took ebene and I taught him more about the spirits. "Do you think I'm ready now for the spirits that will take me places to see our enemies?" he asked me.

"Yes," I said. "We'll get you some of those spirits. You may even be able to take some of mine."

The nabas at Honey could barely talk plain enough for us to understand them. They told about another spirit but we didn't know what they meant. Shoefoot needed more spirits. I didn't. My shabono was so packed with spirits that no more light could get in. So I wasn't interested in the nabas, and my spirits didn't like them.

After I left, when Shoefoot and Spear weren't dancing with their own spirits, they talked to the nabas about their spirit and wondered who he could be.

"He could be Thunder Spirit," Spear said.

"Or he could be Fire Spirit," Shoefoot answered. "These are both spirits we don't know much about."

"What about the enemy spirit?" Spear asked Shoefoot. "They keep talking about how their spirit is in a fight with our spirits."

"You mean Yai Wana Naba Laywa? But how could that be? We know that the enemy spirit isn't friendly. No one knows him. If we go close to his land, we burn up with heat. How could anyone know him?"

The next day they talked to the nabas again about their spirit and that night they lay in their hammocks and tried to figure it out. "I think you are right, Spear," Shoefoot said. "I think their spirit is the enemy spirit. I'll ask you something and you try to tell me. Do your spirits come to you at night when you are alone and beg you not to throw them away?"

Spear sat up slowly in his hammock and looked at Shoefoot. "You're getting good spirits now," he said. "You can even tell what my spirits are saying to me."

"So it's true. Your spirits are coming to you begging you

not to throw them away," Shoefoot said. "My spirits do that to me every night. Why would they think I would throw them away? They are all I have. We all know they would kill us if we threw them away."

Spear leaned back and shook his head. "So maybe this spirit of these nabas really is the great spirit, Yai Wana Naba Laywa, the enemy our spirits are so afraid of." All shamans know about Yai Wana Naba Laywa. The next day, Shoefoot explained to the nabas about Yai Wana Naba Laywa, and they soon began to believe that Shoefoot was correct. Their spirit was actually the one we called the unfriendly spirit, because he never showed any interest in us.

"But that's not true," the nabas said. "He is the spirit that really cares about you. He wants your life to be better. But he won't be your spirit unless you get rid of your other spirits. That is why your spirits don't like him."

Shoefoot nodded. He understood. *It's true,* he thought. *That's why my spirits are so afraid. They think I am about to throw them away. And I would if I could find the right spirit.*

Every night for many moons Spear and Shoefoot had the same talk. They both wanted the new spirit. "Everything they say about him is so wonderful," Shoefoot said. "Do you really think that a spirit could be that wonderful?"

"No."

"I don't either. They talk about love and being kind and so many things that seem so nice."

"If the naba's spirit cares so much about us," Spear asked staring at the roof, "why don't the nabas care about us? If this spirit wants our life to be better, why don't *they*? Have you wondered that?"

"That is the only thing I've ever wondered," Shoefoot answered.

"They never share anything with us. My boy asked them for a hook and fish line today and they wouldn't share any with him."

"And they never share the meat they get with their guns, even when we help them get it."

They sat in silence for a while. Shoefoot kept talking. "We know that the worst thing a person can do is to be stingy. But these nabas are more stingy than any Yanomamö we know. At first I thought it was just because they were different and we should give them time. But now they have been with us a long time and they still don't share anything with us. They must see how miserable we are and how much we need things."

"But if this great spirit they talk about is Yai Wana Naba Laywa, then they have the most powerful spirit that there is— Yai Pada. Even our spirits know that."

"Yes, they do," Shoefoot said. "A spirit like that would be wonderful to have, wouldn't it? If I had a spirit like that, I would be happy to be rid of all my other spirits. But if we had that spirit, maybe we would become stingy like them. Then we would go to the fire pit for sure."

Spear was nodding his agreement to everything Shoefoot said. Then Spear decided, "Something is wrong. When we live with our spirits, we become more like them. They dance. We dance. They steal and rape women. We steal and rape women. They fight and kill. We fight and kill. But these nabas don't do what they say their spirit does. They say he's generous. But they're not. They say he's kind. But they're not."

So Shoefoot and Spear kept their spirits and every time I visited we blew ebene into our noses and danced together.

DOESN'T-GRAB-WOMEN

6

THE FATHER EAGLE
NEVER FOUND HIS EAGLET

I still fight with Toucan's people. Fredi has finally gotten used to Honey. Sometimes I wonder if Fredi might make a good shaman. Deemeoma is almost a woman now and has been stolen by a nearby village. So she is finally separated from Fredi and all the others we stole from Potato Village. The nabas have left Honey in disgust because the people don't pay them any attention. When they left they said that no naba will ever come back there. But another white family has gone there. It is Pepe, with his many children and wife. And she is big with another one. One of the children is Keleewa, the boy who played with Littlecurl in Tama Tama. Pepe has built a house and says he plans to stay. So the Indians in Honey are beginning to build their own houses now.

The new nabas tried first to learn the names of the Indians in Honey. But remember, our people don't use names the way the nabas do. Names are often insults, and using someone's name could start a fight. But the nabas didn't know that so they kept asking. They were trying to learn Shoefoot's name when one man got tired of their questions. He pointed at Shoefoot and said, "He's got a mouth; ask him." Like a lot of Indians, Shoefoot didn't have a name except his child name, and no one would be mean enough to ever mention a child name. But he got his first adult name that day. From then on we knew him as He's-Got-A-Mouth. That was his name until he gave something to the nabas in trade for some old shoes. After that he was known as Shoefoot. I have called him Shoefoot from the beginning of this story to make it easier for a naba like you to understand.

Fredi married and went to the village on the Padamo River between my village and Honey, the village that had stolen Deemeoma. This village became known as Forgetful Village. There is a good reason for that name, but no one in the village could remember what it was. They also could not remember why Honey villagers believed that Deemeoma belonged in Honey.

Deemeoma had special value as soon as her breasts started because she had no parents to take care of. It would be like taking a wife without the problems of having in-laws. Now that she had become a woman, there would be a fight for her.

The people of Honey went to Forgetful Village to fight to get her back. Finally they succeeded. So Forgetful Village came to Honey to get her back. In each struggle both sides pulled her until she thought her limbs would be torn off.

Shoefoot had a brother-cousin who lived in Honey and Deemeoma liked him. So she was happy to see Honey come to steal her, and she made it easy for them to get her from Forgetful Village and harder for Forgetful Village to get her back. Finally, she ran away with the boy she liked from Honey. They lived in hiding for many days in the jungle until things settled down in both villages. Then they went back to Honey and began building a house. The nabas showed them how to build it to keep the bugs out. They were right. Things had calmed. But Shoefoot had many brother-cousins who thought they had more right to Deemeoma. One of them forced her away from the one she loved.

The father of the boy she loved was Shoefoot's father-uncle. He wanted her for his son. But the other relatives wanted her too and wouldn't let him have her. The father became so mad that he took his son and all the rest of his family members and left Honey in a rage. He moved to the Ocamo where he joined Tigerlip's village.

He never returned for revenge. But he never returned for any reason. The split between Shoefoot and the other brothers was never healed.

Deemeoma was unhappy living with this new man. One morning warriors from Forgetful Village came and jerked her from her hammock. They dragged her screaming out of the house and toward the river. Immediately she was grabbed by a number of Honey warriors and a fight began. There were so many men on top of her that she couldn't breathe and almost died. She could feel many of them putting their fingers in her private part as they fought. But she wasn't strong enough to stop it.

Finally, one of the men from Forgetful Village took his machete and chopped her a powerful blow in each knee. It cut through the tendons to the bone. "See!" he yelled. "We're done with her! She's no use now. You can have her if you still want her."

Pepe, the new naba, helped stop the bleeding on her legs and close the wounds. Only a few moons before, Shoefoot would have helped her by calling on his spirits. But the new naba told the village that if they took ebene and called their spirits, he would leave the village. And they didn't want the stranger to leave yet. So Shoefoot had stopped taking his ebene whenever the naba was around.

Pepe put medicine and big white cloths on Deemeoma's knees. Every day he put on more medicine and cloths. But it was many moons before she could walk straight again. Shoefoot watched it all happen. It took a long time, but Shoefoot knew that his spirits could never have fixed her legs. Still, he talked to his spirits every night.

So Deemeoma stayed in Honey and lived with the man she didn't want. After a long time she got used to him.

To get revenge for the time we killed many of them, the villages that live close to the Ocamo River began to raid each of our villages separately. And each of our villages returned the raids, tried to steal their women, or kill someone if we could. Mostly they raided Tigerlip's village because it was close to them. But they also raided Honey whenever they could.

My village was the farthest away and we liked it that way. Even with my spirits helping us, we were having a hard time getting our village to grow. Our babies kept dying, and I had a hard time getting Sucking-Out Spirit to suck the disease out of them. Some of them lived, but it was a horrible struggle. War made the struggle hopeless. When we were at war, we couldn't even work in our gardens.

So again we did the only safe thing—go on wyumi. We wandered in the jungle looking for food and places to live where we wouldn't be found. But there was always very little food. And again the children suffered terrible. One time a child cried so much that I killed it.

Finally our enemy relatives moved far away to the big river. They built a shabono at the mouth of the Padamo River, where it joins the big Orinoco. They became known as Mouth Village. Honey was already living at the mouth of the Metaconi with their nabas. They were fierce fighters. They always returned every raid.

More nabas moved into our jungle and many new things began to happen. As one of the most powerful and experienced shamans in all of Yanomamö land, it was up to me to understand these things for my people.

One day visitors came from Honey and told me that Shoefoot had thrown away his spirits. I didn't believe them. "That couldn't happen!" I said.

"It's true. Every one of them is gone," one said.

But I couldn't believe it. "He'd be dead if he threw his spirits away. They would kill him."

But the visitor from Honey shook his head and clicked his tongue. He was just as confused as I was. "He doesn't take ebene," he said. "He doesn't dance. He doesn't chant. He doesn't do anything. . . ."

"But I trained him," I said. "I shared all my spirits with him. I taught him everything about them. He is a wonderful and powerful shaman. He can't do that. Spirits don't just leave!" I was even more deeply troubled by this than I showed. How could a shaman as fierce as Shoefoot had become, ever throw his spirits away?

"He started messing with Yai Pada and his spirits didn't like it," the visitors said.

I went right then to see Shoefoot to find out what horrible thing had happened to him that could make him lose his spirits.

When I pulled my canoe up to the shore at the mouth of

the Metaconi I felt the usual excitement that comes with meeting old friends. But something was very different. *What was it,* I wondered.

"Don't go in here," Jaguar Spirit told me. "There's too much danger here. We are afraid." It was the first time I had ever heard fear coming from Jaguar Spirit, and it made me feel poor inside. My hands began to flutter and I held my bow tight to make them stop.

There can't be any danger here, I thought. *These people are my friends. They have always been my friends.* But it wasn't just Jaguar. All my spirits were crowding the shabono in my chest and making a terrible noise about how afraid they were.

When I saw Shoefoot, I was stunned. "What has happened to your spirits?" I asked him, looking at his chest. I could see they were gone.

"I threw them away, brother-in-law."

"What!" I whispered as hard as I could. "How could you do that? *Why* would you do that?"

"I found the new spirit I was looking for," Shoefoot said. "Yai Wana Naba Laywa—the unfriendly one. You know, our enemy spirit."

"You can't have him!" I whispered in excitement. "It's too hot there and he never comes out!"

It was a horrible visit for me. There was a spirit in Shoefoot's village that I couldn't understand. But it was powerful. That's why my spirits were so upset when I came. I hung my hammock next to Shoefoot and as soon as I lay down they were all there, every spirit I have, crowding my shabono.

"Please, Father!" they all begged together. "Please leave here. It's not safe here. We are terrified." And they were. The new spirit in Shoefoot's chest had them all frightened like I had never seen them before.

He's my friend, I thought.

"He's no friend of ours! We hate him!" All my spirits talked at the same time. "Please, Father! Please don't throw us away."

The thought of throwing my spirits away hadn't even come into my mind. Why would they say that to me?

"He'll want you to throw us away," they said. "You'll see. Please don't listen to him, Father!"

My spirits were right about that. Shoefoot and his new naba friends did want me to throw my spirits away. Shoefoot's new spirit would never get along with mine.

We had relatives who lived in a village close to us. There were two sisters there. The young one is known as Yellowflower, I think because she was so beautiful, and her older sister is known as Sara. I don't know why we called her that. Sara became the wife of a great warrior and hunter in another village. We called him Hairy because there were hairs growing out of his legs and chest. Hairy was the warrior who stood on the grass at Honey that morning and watched.

Hairy's wife, Sara, died. This brought him much sadness. Hairy burned her body and grieved. Then he traveled to her family's village, the village where my relatives live, and asked her brothers if he could have her beautiful younger sister, Yellowflower, for his next wife. Even though he was famous for all the people he had killed, Yellowflower didn't want him. She argued bitterly with her brothers and parents. But they were so excited to keep him as an in-law. "Don't worry," her mother told her. "You'll get used to him. He'll provide plenty of meat for you."

"He already has three children," she pleaded. "I don't know how to take care of them, and I don't want to leave our village. This is my home."

But her parents knew that he would be able to provide meat for them in their old age. "He's a great man," her mother said. "You'll see. You'll soon get used to Hairy and forget your fussing." A man as fierce as Hairy could have almost any girl he wanted. No one was as fierce. No one had killed as many people. No one could protect her as well as Hairy. He was the perfect son-in-law.

Yellowflower knew she was stuck and there was nothing she could do to change things. If only her family would change their minds! She hoped. She begged. She nagged. She fussed. She wailed. She lay in her hammock thinking what it would be like to leave everyone she loved. How could they do this to her? She'd seen her older sisters sent away, but somehow she never thought it would happen to her. Now it was happening. And the hurt of it caught her by surprise.

When the morning came for them to leave, she was still hoping that if only somehow they would just change their minds—if only. . . .

Yellowflower's cries turned to screams when she and Hairy and his people walked out of her shabono and down the trail toward his village. But there was no use in refusing to go. *They'll force me anyway*, she thought, *just like they did the others*.

The trail was long, damp, and exhausting. She had to carry a lot of things and also her sister's smallest child. Damp jungle leaves brushed over her face and onto the child while they made their way into the afternoon. As the day passed she settled down and Hairy began to feel comfortable that she would soon get used to him and his people. But home would never leave her mind.

When they got to Hairy's village, Yellowflower hung her hammock next to his and lay in it quietly. Hairy took her out to the garden and showed her what it meant to be married to the fiercest Yanomamö. He slammed her against the ground. *She's going to make a good wife*, Hairy thought. *She hardly cried at all*.

The next morning Hairy gathered his hammock, bow and arrows, and left on a long hunt to get food for the people who would come to mourn the sister's death and drink her bones.

Things had been very bad for Hairy. He had lost his wife, Sara, and he knew the Hawk people and the Shetaris were planning a raid against him. But Yellowflower didn't care about Hairy's problems. She suffered, but quietly.

After Hairy left, she kept the fire, cooked the evening meal for the three children, and lay down in her hammock early. The fire burned low in the early time before morning. She woke to stir it, quietly untied her hammock twine, and slowly made her way across the middle of the shabono toward the entrance. It was dark and she must not make even the smallest sound.

Outside the shabono, everything was black. She moved one step at a time until she was far enough away to wait for dawn. Then she hurried on down the trail on her long and lonely trip home.

Hairy's face went red with anger when he came back two days later and found his children alone. "Why didn't you stop her!" he yelled at his brother. But Hairy wasn't interested in hearing an answer. His relatives had hardly begun to explain when Hairy left the shabono with bow and arrows in one hand and his hammock over his other shoulder.

When Hairy got to Yellowflower's village and found her,

he wanted to beat her right there in front of her brothers. He knew they would approve. After all, he was a great brother-in-law. But he decided to wait till later to beat her.

I've had enough of this awful woman, Hairy thought while he followed her back down the trail toward home. *What does she think? I bring her meat. I'm going to give her children. I take care of her. I protect her from our enemies.*

Yellowflower didn't care. She ran away again. "He's old!" she complained to her brothers. "He's so old!"

"He is not old," they shouted back. "He's the same age we are. He's got a lot of hunting left in him. He'll be able to bring you meat for a long time."

Hairy came back and got her again. But she kept running back to her family's village. "The next time you come back here, we will beat you," her brother said to her. "Hairy will not be patient with you much longer."

But Hairy was patient. He kept coming back for her. The next time she ran home her brothers did beat her. She lay in her hammock and bled. After that, whenever she ran away, she never went back to her family. She was sad, but she stayed alone out in the jungle. No one could ever find out how she fed herself.

One day some children were playing in the jungle and Trip spotted a hammock way up in the top of a tree. It was hidden in the vines. "It's her," he whispered to his friend. "It's Yellowflower. Go back and get Hairy."

Trip stayed and watched the hammock while the others ran back and brought Hairy. He was humiliated again.

Hairy tied her hammock strings so tight that she could not get the hammock loose. But she ran away without a hammock. Out in the jungle, she gathered vines and made a hammock out of them. She stayed there until Hairy found her. Everyone knew that the day would come when a jaguar would find her before Hairy could. But Yellowflower didn't care.

One time when she was in the jungle, hanging high in a tree, a village came through that area on wyumi. So she joined them. They were all about to rape her when they discovered that some of their people might be her uncles and aunts. So those relatives defended her from the others.

When word came to Hairy about where she was, his

brothers said, "Just go over there and get her and kill her. We don't have any more time for you to be gone all the time chasing that foul woman." Hairy got ready to leave. Some of the women came to him and offered to go with him and to cook on the trail.

"You can't come with me," he said. "I'm so humiliated that when I'm done killing her, I might kill you too."

So Hairy left alone. His brother walked a little way down the trail with him. "Don't kill her," he said before Hairy left him. "We have too many wars now. We can't take a war with her village. If her village joins the others, they'll kill us all."

"I know," Hairy said. "I'd sure like to kill her. And everyone thinks that I will. But I know that we could never defend ourselves if I do."

His brother watched Hairy walk on into the jungle and pass out of sight into the leaves that hung over the trail. He turned back to the shabono. It was a good thing that Hairy wasn't an angry man. *If he gets mad and he kills her, we are all dead,* he thought.

When Hairy finally found the people his wife had joined, he saw that her brothers had joined them too. "We hear that you are sick of her running away and plan to kill her," they said to Hairy. They understood. No man will ever stand for so much trouble from a woman. "We don't mind if you beat her. We already beat her once for you and we'll beat her again if you want. But we can't let you kill her."

"I want to kill her," Hairy admitted. "I really want to kill her. Everyone knows it. But I'm not going to. I need her for my wife. I'll have no place to get a wife if I kill her. So I'm stuck with her." He walked over and stood next to Yellowflower as she lay in her hammock. She got up, untied it, and followed him back down the trail toward Hairy's village. There was nothing else she could do.

Hairy followed Yellowflower along the trail until he was close to his village. He watched her walking along the trail in front of him and grew angrier with every step. Finally he couldn't take it. He grabbed her from behind by the hair and hit her with his fist until she fell on the trail. His anger was still growing as he cut a stout stick.

He pinned her on her back, placed the stick across her throat, and put one foot on each end of it. She struggled against the stick. She knew what he was doing; he was killing her. If she couldn't get the stick off, she never would be able to belong to the man she really wanted. Only the children she played with knew that there was a boy she had her eye on.

Yellowflower's strength swelled up. Every muscle in her body worked to move that stick. But it wouldn't move. She kicked. But there was nothing to kick. Her chest heaved. But no air could enter. Her face screamed. But no sound came out. Hairy was quiet; he concentrated on keeping his weight against the stick. *If I can't have you,* Hairy said to himself while staring into her twisted face, *no one else will have you either.* All that could be heard was the noise of her feet and butt hitting against the trail.

Hairy jumped a little to change his weight and her stomach forced stuff up into her mouth. She got just enough air to smell Hairy's tobacco breath in her face.

Hairy pressed down on the stick for a while and then it was over. He had choked the last breath out of her. He stood over her without moving, staring down at her body. He threw the stick as hard as he could out into the jungle. It flew, and while he picked up his hammock and bow and arrows, he heard it settle into the jungle vines. Then he walked on down the trail toward home. At the first bend in the trail, he turned a little for his last look at her. Not a muscle had moved. She lay limp and flat on the damp trail. In the distance he heard the call of a turkey. But except for him, Hairy was alone. He paused only for a moment, then went on.

His down-turned head shook with regret as he walked. *She's not pretty now,* Hairy thought. *I've had all the female fussing I can take. This world is made for us men. When will they ever learn? Women are here for us, not us for them.*

Hairy felt as if his mind might break with overcrowded thoughts while, he stumbled on down the trail toward home. On any normal day he would have gone after that turkey. But he had enough of killing for this day. *What will become of me now,* he wondered? *What good is it to be the fiercest warrior and the best hunter if you have no wife to care for your children? And now even her village will become our enemies. They will certainly come and make war on us.*

Close to the village, Hairy met Trip and some other children playing. "I killed a sloth back down the trail," he said.

"Go on down there and get it." Trip and the kids couldn't remember when they had last eaten.

"Let's go," Trip said. "We'll roast it and eat it right there on the trail." The children ran into the jungle looking for a furry animal and a meal.

What Trip saw filled his whole body with fear. Everyone else stopped behind him.

"I'm not going any closer," Trip said. And they all turned and ran back toward the shabono.

When Hairy entered his shabono, he was met by the women. They wanted to know where Yellowflower was. He saw the fear fill their eyes when he said, "Don't cry for her. She's down there on the trail." He motioned. "And don't bring her back here. I don't want the smell of her smoke in our village."

The women shook their heads. They knew that Yellowflower's village was the only friendly village they had. As great a warrior as Hairy was, they knew that he could not protect them from all the surrounding enemy villages if they lost their last friends.

Hairy's brothers shook their heads. "What did you do that for?" they kept saying. "Why have you done this to our village? What excuse do you have?"

The women hurried back down the trail toward Yellowflower's village in hopes of finding the body before anyone else did. They burned her body right there on the trail so Hairy would never have to see the smoke. They stayed for a long time, until the fire cooled.

"What will we tell her brothers?" they asked each other while sifting through the ashes for her bones.

"Let's say that our enemies blew the magic powder on her while she returned home with Hairy. We'll say that the spell worked and she died." The women agreed that it was the right thing to do.

"If they join our other enemies, we will all have dead husbands," one said, and she was right.

They sent the story to Yellowflower's brothers. The brothers returned to hear it straight from Hairy. They walked into the shabono and gathered around Hairy's hammock. But Hairy never said a word. He listened to all their questions. But he never answered.

Finally Hairy got up, picked up the dark red gourd that held Yellowflower's crushed bones, and handed it to her brothers. But then he lay back down in silence. They stayed around his hammock for a long time asking what had happened to their sister. But Hairy never spoke.

When Yellowflower's brothers left the shabono, Hairy's people knew that they would see them again—in war paint.

Hairy came back from hunting one day with a small monkey and a turkey. It was enough for his children even though his sister had to cook it for them. He sat in his hammock, tired, sad, and full of fear. Around him was a village of his relatives who depended on him for their protection. But there weren't many left. Sickness or spirits had already taken many of their children. And now they weren't even safe from Yellowflower's village. Hairy didn't have enough young warriors to help. And his young warriors hadn't done any killing yet. He must get a wife for more children. But where? His enemies weren't going to give him one. And he wouldn't be able to protect her anyway. He couldn't even protect what little he had.

Hairy leaned back in his hammock and imagined what it would be like to jump up and shoot his arrows at a band of warriors flooding into the shabono opening. He looked over at the opening. How many could get through there at one time? He looked at his big bow and long arrows and saw himself leaping from his hammock and snatching them into action. He imagined how many of the men he could hit as they came through the opening, saw each one as they hit the dirt with his arrow sticking out of their bodies. Of course he would have to pull many arrows from his own body, and he pictured his daughters gathering more arrows for him to shoot. His body was overcome with all those feelings that come with a killing frenzy—anger, so much anger, and fear, and hatred that cannot be stopped.

His sister had some turkey ready for him, but he was no longer hungry. His older brother was almost as good a killer as Hairy, and his younger brother was getting better every day. Still, Hairy saw little hope for his village. And now their last friends would be lost unless they believed the women's lies.

For many moons, Hairy worried constantly about where he could find a wife. One day a group of visitors came from a far village. Hairy knew about these people even though he didn't have any relatives living with them. Their leader was well known as a shaman because he had been trained by me, Jungleman. He called himself Shoefoot and the naba, Pepe, was with him. It was some people from Honey.

After the ceremonial exchange of greetings and food, Shoefoot told Hairy that they wanted to stop their fighting. Hairy was so shocked, the wad of tobacco almost fell from his mouth. The Honey people were known to be fierce fighters. Stopping fighting is not the way of the Yanomamö.

Hairy was so confused by the friendly visit that for a long time he didn't know what to do. When his oldest daughter got big, he decided to take her to the new friendly village and try to trade for a wife. After spending some time there, Hairy picked a girl that he liked and gave his daughter to one of the young men of the village in exchange. The girl he chose liked Hairy and happily went home with him. Just as he planned, he left with a daughter and returned with a wife. It was the beginning of a long and peaceful relationship between Honey and Hairy's village.

Hairy loved his new wife and he loved her village. He had never seen another village like it. They had so many healthy children. Hairy and his wife visited often. Sometimes his entire village would visit with him, and they began to intermarry. He enjoyed seeing his grandchildren and bringing his children to see their grandparents. The naba, Pepe, had boys who sounded exactly like Yanomamö.

Even though they didn't fight, this village was important to Hairy's survival. It is very important for your enemies to know that you have friends and relatives somewhere who will be upset if you get killed.

When his oldest grandson was about to become a young man, Hairy's village got ready again for the long trip to visit Honey. Hairy's younger brother decided not to go. He was an experienced warrior now, but because he was sick, he stayed behind with his two wives. For safety they stayed away from the shabono and hid in the jungle.

While the village was away, the relatives of Hairy's dead wives came and found the shabono empty. His first wife's death was not the problem. But when her sister, Yellowflower, also died and Hairy wouldn't answer their questions, they needed to settle the problem. They searched the jungle and found Hairy's brother. For many seasons they had looked for this chance to get revenge for Yellowflower's mysterious death.

They beat Hairy's brother with clubs that day. If he hadn't been so sick, he might have driven them off, even though there were many of them. His wives tried to nurse him back to health, but by the time his village returned, he was dead from the beating.

Hairy's village knew now that they had no more friends. Hairy and his older brother were joined by the other warriors and the women in grieving over their loss. They called on their spirits, ground their brother's bones, stirred them into banana juice, drank them, put on war paint, and traveled the familiar trail back to the village of Hairy's first wives. Hairy knew her brothers well, one especially. He was the one who beat Yellowflower one time when she ran away. Hairy remembered the suspicious look in his eye the day that they questioned him about her death. *He'll be the right one to kill,* Hairy thought as they walked the trail toward Yellowflower's village. When they got there, they killed that brother and their grief was satisfied.

Hairy's dead brother had two wives. They moved their hammocks next to Hairy and became his wives. Now three wives' hammocks hung within his reach. *These women must be happy to have me,* he thought. *And things have been much better for the village. Now if we can get more visits from the nabas at Honey, maybe things will keep getting better.*

Hairy got up from his hammock and saw that the whole village was asleep. He walked to the front of the shabono and out into the jungle to be alone. Leading this village had always been a big weight on him. Hairy didn't know why he would leave the shabono alone, but as he got further away, he suddenly found himself in a life-and-death struggle with a jaguar. He grabbed a stick and held it across the jaguar's neck and pinned it to the ground. He placed a foot on each end of the stick to hold it down.

If I let go of this stick, he will kill me for sure, Hairy thought. The jaguar's eyes popped out. Its tongue stuck out. While Hairy held on as tight as he could to save his life, the cat's face turned into the face of a woman. And Hairy heard his own voice say, *If*

I can't have you, no one else will have you either. She smiled and he thought she said, "You'll never forget what you did."

Hairy jumped from his hammock with a cry. He looked around to see if his nightmare woke anyone. *My people will lose all respect for me if they think that I have nightmares over killing a woman.* He lay back in his hammock. It was wet with his sweat. How much longer must I have these horrible nightmares? Hairy asked himself. *I thought this would end after they killed my brother. Certainly, after we took revenge for his death, all this should have been put behind me. But I still can't sleep in peace.*

He tried to get back to sleep, but he didn't want to sleep for fear the dream would come back. So he lay and thought about Yellowflower. *Why did I have to kill her?* He saw the horror in her eyes as he strangled the life out of her. He knew everything that would happen in perfect order. It never changed every time he remembered. Next her tongue stuck out. Then her body stiffened and shook all over. Hairy tried to take his weight off the stick to change the memory. But he couldn't. *I'll never sleep again,* he thought. *Her spirit has come back to rob me of my sleep.*

One day a young runaway girl stumbled into Hairy's village. Hairy and the other men looked at each other. But Hairy shook his head. "Look at her," he said. "She's almost dead. If we rape her, she will die for sure. And right now we need more women for our village."

So the men didn't rape her. Instead they gave her a hammock next to Hairy and his wives. Over the days that followed, Hairy's nephew, the one who needed a wife, began to bring her food. He would leave the shabono early in the morning hoping that he could shoot enough to be able to bring her some meat to eat by noon. Sometimes she would see him leave and it made her feel so good that someone would do that for her.

When she got healthy, she moved her hammock next to his and became his woman. He called her Shecoima. Everyone could see that she had much sorrow from missing her family. But no one would help her return because they knew how badly Hairy's nephew needed a woman. After she became big with a baby, Shecoima was happy.

When their baby boy was old enough to try to walk, he became very sick. The shamans called on Sucking-Out Spirit to work the disease out. He was always the best at sickness. But this time they were wrong and didn't know it. Sucking-Out Spirit couldn't always recognize when he had a problem he couldn't solve. So he'd always try anyway.

"He'll get the sickness out," her husband told Shecoima. "He is a powerful shaman. I've seen him heal many sick babies." But he was wrong. Their baby didn't get better.

Every day the shaman took more ebene and worked with his spirits to get the illness out of the boy. "Sucking-Out Spirit says this is a real hard sickness," the shaman told them when he came back from one of his times with his ebene. "We'll try again though, and we'll get it." But the boy wouldn't get better.

It should have been clear that this was the result of a lost spirit. But they couldn't see it. Finally, when the baby got even sicker, another spirit told the shaman that the baby's eagle twin had been lost. Every Yanomamö male has a twin eagle and every female a twin small bird. Their baby's twin, an eaglet, had been separated from its mother and was slowly dying. This is why their baby son was sick. He would soon die unless Shecoima and the shaman could help the eagle parents find their lost eaglet.

It was, at last, the correct answer to the sickness. But Sucking-Out Spirit, though he was good at healing, often couldn't tell the cause of a sickness. That is why we shamans needed so many different spirits.

Now that they knew the right cause, the shaman could easily get the right cure. In the jungle they built a huge platform high off the ground. The platform was shaped like an eagle's nest. Shecoima put her baby on the ground and covered him with leaves. He looked exactly like a lost baby eagle.

Hairy's nephew held a large palm branch in each hand and then ran around the jungle flapping his wings and making the sounds of an eagle looking for its baby. After flapping around for a time, he fanned the leaves and uncovered his real baby. Then he swooped down, picked up the baby and placed him up on the platform, back in his nest where he belonged.

At last the shamans had done the right thing for Shecoima's baby. A family of eagles in the spirit world had lost an eaglet. Hairy's nephew's mock search for his baby would allow the father eagle in the spirit world to find his lost eaglet.

"When he finds it, your baby will get healed," the shaman said to Shecoima.

But the father eagle in the spirit world must have never found his eaglet because Shecoima's baby died. The shaman said, "This time I couldn't catch the hawk before he took the baby up into the enemy's land."

During the following seasons, Shecoima had many more baby boys. But all of them died just before they could walk. Finally she gave birth to a daughter. "I'm so afraid that the same thing will happen to her that has happened to our sons," she said to her husband. "Our shamans have never been able to help us at all."

"What are we doing wrong?" he asked her, sitting on the hammock with her and the new baby. "My people are saying that you have done something that is causing this. I know about your hard life. But tell me more about why you had to run from your family's village. Maybe we can find out why this is happening and save our baby girl."

"It will make me cry to tell you," she said lowering her voice to a whisper. "It will remind me of my mother and father. I'll have much pain. But I'll tell you." They sat in the hammock together and watched the smoke curl up from her cooking fire.

"When I was a little girl," Shecoima started quietly, "my parents promised me to the oldest man in the village. I was terrified of him. Every time he brought my parents food, I cried because I knew he was doing the things he needed to do to become their son-in-law. They forced me to go to his hammock and he tried to get in me. But I was too little and he never could. I was always crying from the pain.

"Every day he watched me to see if I was bigger. He was so jealous that one of the other men in the village might be the first to get me. He guarded me all the time, and if I ever talked to another boy or man he would beat me.

"After I got a little bigger he came and took me into the jungle. It was what I had dreaded all my life. I was still green. My breasts weren't even started yet.

"When we got a long way from the village, he grabbed me and threw me to the ground. I was so terrified. I screamed so loud that it probably scared him. He hit me real hard right here in the stomach to knock the breath out of me. Then he forced his thing in me. There was blood everywhere. All the way back to the village, he never helped me even though I was bleeding so much. I thought I would die.

"I decided that day that I would rather die than ever let him have me for his wife. Death could not be any worse than what he did to me.

"As soon as my young woman rites were finished I looked for any chance to escape the village. We were getting ready for a big bone-drinking feast so all the men went hunting. We knew they wouldn't be back for days. It was my only chance, so I ran away. I spent many days and nights alone in the jungle before I finally came to Wabu's village. I knew that nothing these people could do to me would ever be worse than the old man. I was wrong.

"I was starving when I entered the village. There was a lot of commotion when they saw me and many warriors went out and followed my trail to make sure that I was really a runaway. Then they fed me and gave me a hammock. I fell asleep with the most wonderful thoughts of my life. I would stay there and be happy forever.

"Late that night my beautiful sleep was suddenly stopped. Two men jerked my arm so hard I flew from my hammock to the dirt. I saw nothing but the grinning faces and wide eyes of strange men. It was a big village. There were so many of them. They dragged me out of the shabono and raped me. One after the other they raped me—some of them twice. I screamed until I had no more strength to scream with. Then they left me there to die. But I didn't.

"I stayed in that village for a long time after that and got stronger each day. The men came by my hammock to see how soon I might be healthy enough to try again. So before I was healthy enough, I ran away. That's why I was so sick when I finally got here."

Her husband was heavy with sadness when he heard her story. He felt the same sadness as when he mourned over a death. He stared into the fire and his eyes watered. Maybe it was the smoke from the fire that made them water. He had never before thought about what village rape was like for a girl. It had never seemed sad like this when he and his village had done it.

So when the shaman heard, he knew right away why they

had lost all their children. "They are being killed by the spirits of the old man you ran away from," he said to Shecoima. "You should have told us about him earlier." The shaman was right. The man was killing her children for revenge.

Shecoima was very sad. "What's the point of having children," she asked her husband, "if they are all going to die anyway?"

When their little girl was about to walk, she became very sick and got real hot. It was time for Shecoima to suffer again.

When the baby was about to die, visitors came from Honey. There was a naba with them who felt the baby and said she was too hot. He stuck her in the arm with a tiny metal stick, and that night she wasn't so hot. The next day he smashed some little white stones and gave them to her to drink. He left some of the little stones behind and told Shecoima how to give them to the baby.

After the visitors left the village, Shecoima asked her husband, "What is the name of that white naba who talks just like us?"

"Keleewa," he said. Her eyes filled with happy tears. Maybe at last the spell of her first husband would be broken. Hairy went to his hammock that night wondering if finally his nephew's child would live. The next morning Shecoima ground up the little white things and gave them to her daughter. Soon she got well again. Shecoima had more children. Whenever people in the village got so sick that the shaman couldn't help them, Hairy sent someone to Honey and the nabas would come and give them things to make them better.

One day Shecoima's husband began liking a woman in another village. He wanted her for a wife. Shecoima was angry and nagged him all the time about it. "Don't worry," he kept saying to her every day. "You will always be my favorite." But she did worry and all her fussing finally made him angry. He left and went to his new wife's village to do his son-in-law duties, hunting and bringing food for the woman's parents, and other favors. Shecoima and her children grew hungry waiting for him to come back.

Each moon that passed she became angrier. She had no parents to care for her while her husband was away getting his new wife. Hairy gave her some food, but he had too many wives already. Finally one of the older boys in the village began to bring Shecoima some of the food from his hunts. After many moons everyone said that her husband would not come back, and she liked the boy, so he moved his hammock next to hers.

But her husband's brother, another one of Hairy's nephews, was furious. "If my brother doesn't want you, you become mine," he said to Shecoima the next day.

"You already have a wife," she said. "And the whole village knows how jealous *she* is."

But he was even more jealous of Shecoima. The next morning before dawn, he slipped from his hammock, grabbed his machete, and slowly and quietly made his way around the shabono to where Shecoima slept. With one chop at her hammock rope, he sent her crashing to the dirt. As she got up, still half asleep, he used the machete on her.

"If you don't want me, you won't have anyone," he said.

She felt his machete slice through her scalp and hit her bone. Again and again he hit her, trying to disfigure her. She ran screaming into the jungle.

The boy who liked her followed the trail of blood and found her hiding in the jungle. "Will you help me get to Honey?" she begged.

They walked through the jungle for three days. When she stumbled up the bank at Honey, Shecoima's ears were hanging, her head was large, and her wounds smelled. Keleewa and his wife and sisters took her in and stuck her in all her wounds with the tiny metal stick. It made her cuts feel funny—thick, like they weren't even part of her. Then he cut off all the smelly parts of her wounds, and sewed her cuts back together. And it didn't even hurt. He was even able to sew her ears back on.

7

BLINDED BY LIES

S pear has thrown his spirits away too. Hairy's village and Honey are now close friends. Deemeoma is settled in Honey and finally happy. Her sister is still at Ocamo. I still fight with Toucan's people. I lose another son this season.

When Toucan visited his in-laws' village he learned that a family of white nabas had come there to live. They confused him and his spirits didn't like them, the same as my spirits didn't like the nabas that came to Honey.

Sometimes these nabas would make the long trip to Toucan's village. They had the ability to make the people well that even Toucan couldn't heal. So he thought it was worth it to try to get along with them even though they had that same spirit that all our spirits hated and feared.

One day a mysterious shaman walked into Toucan's village. As soon as Toucan saw the shaman, he knew that this shaman had come back from the dead.

He could see the trails of the spirits in the man, trails that led to the shabono in his chest. But the trails and the shabono were empty just like they would be if the man had died.

Toucan was excited to talk to him. He wanted to hear about life in the spirit world on the other side of death. But the mysterious shaman said, "I'm not dead. I'm very much alive."

"But I can see in your chest." Toucan said, confused. "I can see the trails of all your spirits leading to your shabono, and they have all left you. You have to be dead."

"But I'm *not* dead," he answered. Toucan had never seen a shaman like this before.

"Then why have your spirits left you?" Toucan knew what we all know—spirits never leave anyone until he's dead. Sometimes they kill a person so they can leave. "Where have they gone?"

"I threw them away," he said to Toucan. "I follow their enemy now, Yai Pada, the one who *made* the spirits we follow." Of course Toucan knew all about Yai Pada, Yai Wana Naba Laywa, the unfriendly spirit.

"That's what I mean," Toucan answered. "That's why you must be dead. If you threw them away, they killed you, and now you're back as a spirit. Tell us what it is like on the other side."

"No, I can't tell you because I haven't been on the other side." The stranger took a gourd of banana drink and they watched to see if he could drink it. It disappeared into his mouth. *Well, he sure isn't a spirit,* they thought. So they were even more confused.

"Are you a naba who has died and come back as a Yanomamö?" Toucan asked. But he knew that couldn't be. Nabas can't talk plain, and the stranger talked exactly like Yanomamö.

"No, I'm not a naba. I'm a shaman who has come to tell you more about the great spirit we have always feared—Yai Pada."

"But that spirit never comes to us Yanomamö," Toucan argued. "Is that the spirit that these nabas talk about?"

"That's right."

"But the nabas follow the unfriendly spirit," Toucan objected. "The distant one—the one who eats our babies' souls."

"That's right," the strange shaman said, and he sat down on a hammock just like all Indians do. "But he is not unfriendly like our spirits told us. We *think* he steals our baby's souls, but we haven't ever *seen* him eat them, have we?"

Toucan was more confused. He clicked his tongue in

amazement. Leaning back in his hammock, he thought for a moment. "You are a dead man come back alive. I just know it. I can see your empty shabono. That's how I know you died. But now you're alive."

"No. I'm a Yanomamö shaman just like you. I used to do everything you do. I took ebene and raided and stole women."

"I know all that," Toucan explained all over again. "That's how I know you have come back from the dead because no one can get rid of spirits. Haven't they ever come back to hurt you?"

"Some shamans have tried to get them to return to me, but they never have."

"What's it like having your shabono so empty of spirits?" Toucan asked.

"I can tell you in one word—peaceful. You can't know how peaceful! We haven't had a war, and we've always been known for our wars. Now we've made friends even with our enemies. We can work in our gardens without fear, and go hunting and fishing. And what's best—we are never afraid."

The stranger stayed in Toucan's village for a few days. All during that time he never caused any trouble, never fought with anyone, or tried to get their women. They soon named him No-Trouble.

After No-Trouble and his friends left, Toucan had many feelings of confusion, more than he had ever felt before. *He looked like a Yanomamö,* Toucan thought. *He talked like a Yanomamö. He acted like a Yanomamö. But he never messed with our women.*

Then Toucan learned that his father had traded with No-Trouble's father. *He really is a Yanomamö,* Toucan thought. *Then why doesn't he mess around with the women?* He was surely the most different Yanomamö that Toucan had ever met.

That night as Toucan lay in his hammock his spirits came to him very upset. "Don't leave us, Father," they said. "Please don't throw us away." It took Toucan a long time to calm them.

After that he thought often about No-Trouble and the many strange things he had said. But every time Toucan thought about it, his spirits would always get upset, and he'd have to calm them down.

My spirits did the same thing every time I went to Honey. One time I walked up the bank at Honey and met Keleewa, the young naba. When I looked into his eyes, I saw his spirit shudder. And my spirits shook with fear at him. It was a war of our spirits. Any shaman could have seen it. The hair at the back of our necks stood up, like two jaguars meeting in the jungle. I didn't speak to him. But the air around us was thick. My spirits ran away. Later I talked to him and he talked just like a Yanomamö. I didn't know nabas could do that.

The people at Honey have always been good to me. And this visit was no different. Whenever I saw something I wanted I said, "Give me that and I'll tell my spirits to keep you safe on the trail." They knew that I could heal people, but even more, that I could make people sick and even kill them. So they always gave me what I wanted.

Now they were becoming rich because of the nabas living with them. It made me want to visit often. And my wives always enjoyed visiting their brother, Shoefoot, and other relatives.

But the next time when we visited, the Honey villagers wouldn't give me everything I asked for. "Whatever has made you people turn so stingy?" I asked them.

"We're not afraid of your power any more," Shoefoot said. It was shocking. Shocking! I taught this little big mouth all he knew about the spirits. How could he say that to me?

"You're crazy! *You are crazy!*" My face bulged out at him. "All of you are crazy! Don't you have any respect for the things we've always done? Don't you remember that stingy people go to the fire pit? And you people have given me nothing!"

"That's not true, brother-in-law," Shoefoot said. "We have given you almost everything we have—all out of our fear that you would use your power against us if we didn't. And you are welcome to come back any time. But now that we don't fear your power any more, we won't be giving you all our things like we have at other times. We are working hard here to live better. It's not right for you to take all we've worked for. Even now we share our food and homes with you."

I was furious. I couldn't believe it. I got my wives and children together to leave. The whole village was there at the river bank to say farewell.

"All right!" I told them all. "This is it. Because you have been so stingy with me, I will send Jaguar Spirit to call all the jaguars in the jungle. They will lie in wait on all your trails. Every time you hear the turkey sing up in the tree and go after it, you will find a jaguar sitting there making the sound. He'll be waiting just for you. And I'll send Armadillo Spirit to get all the armadillos in the jungle. They will burro under all your houses till they fall flat. And do you know whose will be the first? Pepe! His family will be the first with a flat house."

I knew that he was the one who had caused all the trouble. I still remembered my first visit to the village after he came, when my spirits were afraid of him and begged me never to come back. "You will see," I told them all, and my wives and children got into the boat and we left.

The village soon ran out of food. I knew they couldn't go out and hunt. My Jaguar Spirit would place a jaguar to wait for anyone who tried. Jaguar Spirit loves to do that.

Just as I knew they would be, all the men of Honey were in fear of me. They were more fearful of my curses than they were of warfare. In warfare they knew that they could shoot back. But when my spirits were after them, the only way they could fight back was with their spirits. And my spirits were more powerful than theirs. Even as good as Shoefoot was with spirits, he only had the ones I gave him—except for that new spirit from the nabas. But that's only one spirit and he doesn't fight anyway.

After one of them dies, I thought, *they will know that they need their spirits to help them fight me. Then they will recognize my power again.*

They were even afraid to work in their gardens. It wasn't long before the children became weak.

Finally Pepe went to talk to Fastman. We called him that because he was so fast that no one would hunt with him. You would get on the trail of an armadillo, track him until you found his hole, and there you would find the ashes of Fastman's fire. He'd already been there, smoked the armadillo out, killed it, and left. So whenever we hunted with Fastman, we made him go on the other side of the river alone.

"Why did you throw your spirits away?" Pepe asked Fastman. By this time almost everyone in Honey had thrown away their spirits like Shoefoot and Spear.

"Because they never did me any good."

"And you know that Yai Pada made all the other spirits anyway?" Pepe went on. Fastman nodded his agreement. "So what are you afraid of?"

"You have no idea how powerful Jungleman's spirits are," Fastman answered. He almost shivered with fear.

"You say your new spirit is stronger than his. You say that even his spirits know this. Then why don't you go hunting? Your new spirit will take care of you." It was good talk, but Fastman had seen my power. He knew that no one would be safe on those trails.

"Why can't this new spirit make some game come out here so we don't have to go down the trails?"

"Do you think Yai Pada will make a tapir walk into this village and lie down in front of you?" Pepe asked him.

"No."

"Well then, get your bow and arrows and get out there and get some meat for your people!"

Fastman was not used to having anyone wonder about his courage, and never a naba. No one was expected to be this brave. He might be walking into certain death. But he wouldn't be called a coward. So he went.

Fastman's wife, Sofia, cried when she watched him disappear down the trail heading out of the village. She was Shoefoot's sister, my sister-in-law. It was the first time in many days that any of the men had ventured out for a hunt. Why did her husband have to be the first to go? Why had he listened to Pepe? Who was this naba anyway—this man with a different spirit? She had begged Fastman not to go, but it was no use. Now she stood watching the empty trail he went down, and wondered what would happen to her when she lost him. Who would take her as a wife and hunt for her and the children?

Sofia kept crying. She thought about her brother who died. She cried even more, thinking of her husband meeting that same certain fate. She wasn't sure how long she had been sitting on her hammock inside her leaf shack staring at the fire and crying, when she heard a stir of excitement in the village. *It must be about Fastman*, she thought, and ran to find out the awful news.

He was back. He had shot a tapir. "How could you ever have done it so fast?" everyone asked him. She felt her insides turn from anguish to the most pleasant feeling she had ever felt. Fastman was suddenly the most important person in the village.

"It was right down the trail there, waiting for me," he said, like he had done nothing.

All the men ran down the trail, and soon the whole village was sharing and cooking fresh meat and celebrating like it was a feast. But before they started eating, they did something strange. They talked to their big spirit. Shoefoot told them all that it was Yai Pada who had helped Fastman stay safe on the trail and find the tapir.

"The nabas say that when someone does something very nice and it makes them very happy," Shoefoot said, "they have a word that they say to that person. The word makes the other person know that he has made them happy. Remember how we used to think that the nabas always slept a little before they ate their food? Well, they weren't sleeping. They were saying that word to their spirit. It's a word that we don't have. But even though we don't have the word, we should also tell our new spirit how happy we are for the fresh meat we are about to eat. This will become a part of our new ways."

Then Shoefoot talked to his new spirit and the whole village ate. They even fed the children first.

Sofia didn't really care about all the spirit talk—she was so happy just to have Fastman back safe and the children fed.

When I heard the story, I was so mad. "What have you done?" I screamed at Jaguar Spirit when I found out what had happened. "You've betrayed me!"

"Please don't be angry with me, Father," he pleaded. But I was angry. This had never happened before.

"I'm the most powerful shaman I know!" I yelled back at Jaguar. I yelled at all my spirits. But Jaguar was my most powerful spirit. If *he* couldn't kill the people at Honey, none of them could. "What went wrong?"

"Please don't throw us away, Father. There's nothing we can do against this spirit at Honey. We told you when we were there that we can do nothing against this spirit." Now they were all pleading with me, just like they had when I was at Honey. "Please don't throw us away, Father," they all repeated.

It almost became a chant. But how could I? They were my whole life. Especially Charming! They pushed her to the front of the group. But I was so mad that I didn't want to see her.

She knew it. "Please don't hate me," she whispered soft in my ear. Just her whisper made me feel so good. She knew how wonderful I felt about her.

"Even if I throw the others away, I could never throw you away," I told her. I held her close. All the other spirits left and she calmed me for a time. We sat in the hammock together for the rest of the day. Finally the other spirits returned.

The next morning I was still upset about Honey. My spirits hadn't done anything about it, and I wondered what my people would think of me if they ever learned this.

Over many moons we shamans learned that Honey was a place to stay away from. It was just too troubling to our spirits. One shaman whose wife went there often to visit family members would not even get out of his canoe. His family would stop and visit for a while, but he always stayed in the canoe facing the other side of the river. All the time his relatives visited, he would never turn and face the village or talk to anyone. That is how much our spirits had come to hate that place.

My enemy shaman, Toucan, was also being bothered all the time by his spirits. They knew what he was thinking. His spirits came to him as he lay in his hammock at night and pleaded with him not to throw them away. It was just the same as my spirits had pleaded with me. But Toucan wouldn't listen to them. He followed the advice of the strange visitor, No-Trouble, and threw his spirits away.

One day Toucan went to visit another village and met a confused shaman who looked into Toucan's chest and said, "I can see the trails of all your spirits leading to your shabono, but they have all left you. Why? Where have they gone?" Toucan remembered that he had used these same words when he first saw No-Trouble. It made him think that maybe he was becoming a little bit like No-Trouble. The thought made him happy.

Toucan soon noticed that he had lost those horrible memories of killing his wife. Now he began to remember the good things about her. He could use his machete without seeing it sink into her neck. Most wonderful of all, he could sleep again. He became known as Laughing-Man.

For many seasons Toucan didn't kill anyone in my village. So I stopped killing people in his village. And he stopped traveling around in the spirit world because he didn't have the spirit that took him places any more.

One day Tigerlip tied his canoe at the Honey bank for a visit. He needed help from his old friends against new enemies he had at the Ocamo.

"We aren't interested in raids any more," Shoefoot told him.

"What!" Tigerlip said surprised. "My spirits have told me to take revenge. I have to."

"We don't have those spirits any more," Shoefoot answered.

"What!" Tigerlip whispered. "You've turned into cowards!"

When Tigerlip left Honey, he went back to the Ocamo, stopping at Mouth Village on the way. He couldn't wait to hear their laughter at the stories he told of Honey. Mouth Village had been an enemy of Tigerlip's village for a long time. But Tigerlip was sure that because Honey refused to go on raids, Mouth Village would become his friend against them. He was right.

"It doesn't matter to them if you get their footprint," Tigerlip said to Cloudy and the others at Mouth Village. Cloudy had gone on the first raid at Potato Village. "They don't think that getting a footprint will help cast a spell." They all laughed at Tigerlip's words.

"Well, let's get one and teach them a lesson."

"They don't even care if you blow alowali powder on them," Tigerlip said. They laughed harder.

"They're crazy!"

"And the funniest thing is, they say they won't fight and kill any more," Tigerlip said. This time they roared with laughter.

"Let's go get their women!" everyone shouted. And they began planning it.

After Tigerlip's group left, Cloudy took some warriors and went against Honey to steal women. But they were beaten with clubs by the mysterious village that didn't fight! As the Mouth warriors ran from Honey, they took up positions and waited in ambush. But no one chased after them. They went back to their own village, blocked all the trails, and got ready for a revenge raid. That night every warrior was ready with his arrows and clubs. No one slept. But nothing happened.

"They're smart," Cloudy said. "They're giving us time to relax. But we won't." And they didn't. They blocked all trails carefully every night. They built a high alana across the opening of the shabono and far around to the back. It took days, but they knew it needed to be strong. They always went together on hunts, and when they worked the gardens they had the women stand all around and watch the jungle for anything suspicious. A warrior kept guard every night. Even with the warrior guarding, the village didn't get much sleep. But Honey never came.

They must raid us, Cloudy thought. No village with any pride would ever allow themselves to be attacked and not raid back.

Finally Mouth Village could no longer stand the fear. "Let's go attack them again," Cloudy said. "It's better than just waiting for them to attack us."

Again the warriors of Honey drove them off with clubs and again Mouth lived in constant fear of a revenge attack. But none came.

Cloudy began working every day with his spirits to put spells on the village that had beaten him. Nothing worked.

In Honey the people worried all the time and talked to Yai Pada, their new spirit. They wanted him to help them fight off their attackers. One morning Spear got out of his hammock at the first light. He couldn't sleep. He had been talking to Yai Pada all night because he was so afraid of Mouth Village. As he stepped from his house onto the wet grass, he saw that Honey Village was surrounded by people, warriors maybe; he wasn't sure. But there were so many of them, big beautiful people in bright white shirts that went down to their feet. Spear could tell that Yai Pada had sent them to protect Honey from all the attacks. But after the sun came up, they were gone. And no one in the village had seen them. He asked Pepe if Yai Pada had people like that. Pepe said, "I've never seen them, but his book says that he has them and they can protect you."

One day Tigerlip came with all his warriors from the Ocamo into the shabono at Mouth Village. Their heads were covered with dried blood. Cloudy knew they had been to Honey. "Did you win anything from them?" he asked Tigerlip.

Tigerlip clicked his tongue and shook his head. "Nothing. They chased us right into the river. And now we have to go back to our village and get ready for their revenge."

"We have attacked them often," Cloudy said, "but they never come for revenge. They're cowards. But they always beat us. And I can't get any of my spells to work on them."

"It's that naba who lives with them," Tigerlip said to Cloudy. "He's a shaman. He only has one spirit—the great spirit, the enemy spirit. That's why our spirits shake with fear every time we go to Honey. Nothing works against Honey because of that spirit."

Over many seasons every shaman learned that Pepe was a shaman with a powerful enemy spirit. We all tried spells against his village. Nothing worked.

One time a Mouth warrior told the Honey people that they were going to find one of their footprints and take it to Cloudy. Once they had a footprint, they could make sure that the spirits would be able to kill them. So one of the Honey people stuck his foot into some soft dirt and said, "There's mine. Take it." But Cloudy's spirits couldn't hurt anyone with it.

Cloudy decided to take his wife and children to Honey for a friendly visit. Because his wife is Shoefoot's sister, the village received them and they had a nice visit. He stayed with his old shaman friend, Spear. It was strange being treated so good in a village he had raided. He went back many times for friendly visits. And sometimes to raid. But he was always beaten when he raided.

On friendly visits he lay in his hammock in Spear's house. "We don't understand your village," he said to Spear. "Are you cowards? Have you stopped being Yanomamö?"

"We're not cowards," Spear said. "We're still Yanomamö and we still try to be brave. We're not going to let you take our women. The only difference is, we have chosen not to follow our old spirits any more. We have learned that those wonderful spirits who used to send us off on all those raids, like when we slaughtered Potato Village—those spirits tricked us. Your spirits shake with fright when you come here, don't they?"

"Tk! They sure do!" Cloudy said, but he was full of wonder. "How did do you know that?"

"Because they did that all the time with us before we threw them away."

"They do that because our spirits hate your new spirit," Cloudy said, "and your spirit hates our spirits . . . and us."

"That's the exact place where we have all been wrong," Spear answered before Cloudy could finish. "It's true that he hates them and they hate him. But here's the really big truth—you can take it from a lifelong shaman and I know every one of your spirits because I had them all." Spear sat up in his hammock to say every word carefully. *"Our spirits hate us—Yai Pada loves us."*

Cloudy could not figure it out. "Are you sure?"

Spear laughed. "It's confusing, isn't it? Because our spirits have told us all our lives that Yai Pada is the unfriendly one. What could we do but believe it? We Yanomamö are caught in the middle of these two powers—one good and one bad. Each one telling us that the other one hates us. Each telling us the other is lying. And the decision is left to the wisdom of the Yanomamö."

"Does everyone in this village follow the great spirit?" Cloudy wondered.

"No. But all of us shamans have. We were blinded by lies. But not any more."

"Has anyone tried the great spirit and then gone back to Jaguar Spirit or Healing Spirit?"

Spear paused. He wasn't sure how to say it simply. "Look around our village. Do you think anyone here would ever go back?"

Spear leaned back in his hammock and watched a cockroach crawl along his palm-leaf roof. Cloudy knew he was remembering the old days. They had gone to Potato Village together for a great slaughter. It was only when Spear wouldn't let him take any of the women from the raid that they started being enemies. He and Spear were known for many killings. No one was more fierce than Spear. But his voice cracked with the sound of grief and pain when he said, "There is nothing you could give me that would ever make me go back to that."

Spear clicked his tongue. "Nothing."

8

A VERY NICE WORD

I stop fighting Toucan's people. I have no old shaman friends left in Honey, but they still welcome me. Deemeoma is happy there. Tigerlip and Mouth raid them often, but they don't want my protection. Honey always drives them off but never goes after them. Tigerlip and Mouth are learning that their spells don't work against Yai Pada of the naba. And there is something else new in the jungle. I don't even know what it is. Maybe a naba. It started way up the Ocamo River at Shetary's village.

Some of our people moved and built a new village many days' travel up the Ocamo River. After a time, everyone in their village got sick and many of them died. All around their shabono were the special fires that burn the bodies of the dead. The few who weren't sick gathered bones from the ashes and tried to keep the rest alive. People just lay in their hammocks and got hotter and hotter until their bodies shook and they died.

Finally their shaman learned from his spirits that it was the smoke from the fires of the dead that was spreading the disease. "We'll have to begin hanging them out in the jungle," he told everyone.

One boy who lay sick had just finished becoming a young

man. He was now ready to begin his useful time as a hunter of meat for the family. So his father and mother did everything they could for him to get well. All day every day they cared for him, hunted for him, brought him water, got the spirits to help. He was all they cared about. So his father, Shetary, had a lot of pain when the boy's body began to shake and he died. The shaman said that this disease was so bad that the spirits just couldn't help.

Because of the disease, Shetary couldn't burn his son. Instead, he took long slats of wood and wove them together with jungle vines to form a large wooden mat, a *heeheeka*. Shetary laid his son's body in the middle of the heeheeka and wrapped the edges up over him and tied it tight around him. He wailed with grief. His tears kept falling onto the vines as he tied them in knots to make sure that nothing could get into the heeheeka to bother his boy. His wailing got louder when he carried him in the heeheeka past the shabono opening to hang him out in the jungle. The heeheeka would protect him from animals while his son's body fell from the bones. As he walked down the cool trail into the jungle, Shetary was thinking about the person who would have to come out later and do the awful job—scrape the rest of the flesh off his son's bones to make them clean for grinding. The thought made him wail even louder.

A safe distance down the trail from the shabono, wailing friends helped Shetary stick two leaning poles into the ground. At the point where they crossed, they tied them together with vines. Three steps away they tied two more poles together. High in the air between these four poles, they tied a pole going across. While Shetary wailed for his son, they lifted the heeheeka and tied it to the cross-pole.

"We'll have to do this with all the rest of our dead until the disease leaves us," the shaman said. And there were more.

Many days later an Indian came running into the shabono screaming, "Shetary! Shetary! Someone ruined your heeheeka!" The whole shabono was too shocked to speak. Shetary ran down the trail toward his son's body. Only a few days before, he had seen the heeheeka there just as he had left it. The villagers followed, talking excitedly but trying to be quiet to respect his grief.

When he got to close, Shetary saw that the heeheeka had

been cut down to the ground and opened. What he saw would change his life forever. There were maggots everywhere covering his son's shoulders and chest. But there was nothing above his shoulders. Everything inside Shetary's chest turned into a tight knot. He fell to the ground wailing with grief.

"My son! My son!" he screamed. "Who could do this to us?"

The men behind him felt the terror in his screams. When they got close enough to see, they could not believe what they saw. "Who would ever do a thing this bad?" they all asked each other.

"Our worst enemy would never do this," one man said.

Another said, "No Yanomamö Indian anywhere would ever do anything like this."

They found a yellow cloth in the bushes nearby. There were nabas from far away who came into the jungle and squirted fog all over to kill mosquitos. The mosquito nabas all wore yellow and had yellow things. So they decided it must be those mosquito nabas.

Then they found two rubber things that looked like they might fit over a hand. They were confused. The whole village went into panic. Shetary ran back to the shabono and grabbed his bow. "It has to be the nabas!" he shouted. "No Indian would ever do this. I'll kill them!"

With a small group of warriors, he ran to his canoe and paddled down river. At the first village they stopped and asked if the people had seen any nabas. "Yes, we saw one," they answered. "He had some Indians with him. They came by here real fast in a motor boat. They didn't stop to say a word."

Shetary and his friends jumped back in their canoe. "When we find him, we'll kill him!" he shouted as they left. They paddled down to the end of the river, but they never found a naba.

"I'll kill any naba I ever see," he said on the way back home. They stopped in the villages on the way and Shetary told everyone that he would kill the next naba he saw.

The government of Venezuela heard about what Shetary said. After that they wouldn't allow the mosquito people to go into that part of the jungle.

Shoefoot went far up the Orinoco River to visit some of our relatives who he had never seen. He didn't know if they were still alive. He wanted to see if he could find them and tell them about the new spirit he had found.

He came to many villages, but found no one who knew any of his relatives. Finally, far up the Orinoco where the Mavaca River joins, he entered a village and met a man named Turkey. After they talked all morning, Shoefoot thought that maybe they had the same grandparents or were in the same family. But this is always hard to tell because we Yanomamö will never speak the name of the dead.

After much talk Shoefoot said, "I'm sure you are my relative, but I must know. May I whisper my grandparent's name in your ear?"

Turkey wanted to know too. "And I will whisper in your ear."

Very carefully Shoefoot put his lips next to Turkey's ear and cupped his hands around his mouth. He whispered so quietly he could not even hear himself speak. Then Turkey did the same to Shoefoot.

It was true. They were so happy to know that they were related. Shoefoot spent many days visiting with them and went back many times. He told them about the nabas and the new spirit he had learned about from them. Turkey had seen many nabas, but none had ever actually lived in his village.

"We have had a long war with the people over at the Siapa," Turkey told Shoefoot. "If we could have some of the weapons of the nabas, we could really kill them."

"It won't help to kill them," Shoefoot answered. "Their children will come back after you, and then their children's children. The only way to end killing is to stop killing. You need a spirit of peace."

Turkey hadn't heard of a spirit of peace. "What use is that if they keep coming to kill us?" he asked.

"If you stop killing them, they will stop killing you."

Turkey thought for a little. He had never heard anything like it. It was too simple. "If you keep killing them," Shoefoot kept talking, "they will sure keep killing you."

"Can this possibly be true?" Turkey asked Shoefoot. "It sounds too good."

"It's true. All the people in our village who are just now starting to have children have never known what it is like to kill people. And we never have anyone trying to kill us."

Jungleman and author.

Slothtail, Mique, and dinner for the whole village.

If it moves, it's eatable—even this anaconda.

Won't Grow and Shortman.

Deemeoma.

Kaobawa (left), friend and informant of Napoleon Chagnon, was first seen displaying Yanomamö fierceness on the cover of Chagnon's best-selling book.

*With the village on wyumi, the shabono is cleaned out. Notice the
unfinished roof-line to the right of the entrance.*

Yanomamö warrior.

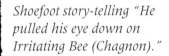

Shoefoot story-telling "He pulled his eye down on Irritating Bee (Chagnon)."

Shetary's village

Shoefoot and family.

Fierce killer, Hairy, strikes the Yanomamö pose that shows he has no fear of the white naba or his camera.

Trip (standing), author and Spear.

From left, author, Spear, Fruitman (standing), Shoefoot, Jungleman, and Keleewa translating as the Indians tell one story after another.

On one of his many long trips, Keleewa demonstrates that traveling the headwaters of the Orinoco is exhausting as well as beautiful.

"What we need is a naba to come live with us and teach us the way you have at Honey," Turkey said.

"How long have you been in the war?"

"As long as anyone can remember. My father was fighting it when I was a baby. Many of our women were stolen from them. And they have some of ours. But we have sure killed more of them than they have killed of us."

The enemies Turkey talked about lived by the Siapa River. I had seen them many times when I traveled in the spirit world. I knew their people and I knew that they were tired of the wars with Turkey's village. They too had heard about nabas who were coming into the jungle. But they would have to go through Turkey's area to be able to find the nabas. And that would be far too dangerous.

One day these enemies at the Siapa were visited by the strangest Yanomamö man they had ever seen. He came into the village from the Orinoco trail, so he should have been an enemy. But he had no weapons.

"He *looks* like a naba," Swampfish said when he saw him.

"No. He's not a naba," their shaman answered. "You can see that he is a shaman. He's a Yanomamö."

The whole village argued about who he was. He should have been an enemy, but he carried no weapons and wasn't interested in chest pounding.

"That's why he must be a naba," Swampfish said. But the most mysterious thing about him was that he never grabbed the women. They had never before had a visitor that didn't grab after their women.

"He's a shaman," their shaman said after he left, "but he sure doesn't have Howashi Spirit." All the men liked him because he never tried to do anything with their wives or daughters.

"How does a person get like this?" one man asked. "It can't happen."

"This is the kind of man we would like to get for a son-in-law," another man said. The village gave the mysterious visitor the name Doesn't-Grab-Women.

Their shaman said that the visitor must be a Yanomamö who had been able to spend much time with the nabas outside the jungle and had been able to get other spirits from them.

"We must move closer to the nabas," he said.

Even little boys like Shortman and Hairylip knew about the strange visitor. And for seasons after, they heard their parents talk about him. "Doesn't-Grab-Women was a Yanomamö like none we have ever known," they would always say. "One day we will escape to the world of the nabas and find out how he did it."

After many more seasons of wars with our relatives in Turkey's village at the Mavaca, the people at Siapa finally decided that they must move their village. "We can't fight this war forever," their shaman said. "We have to get closer to the nabas. And we have to find out what it was that made that visitor so different from us."

Even though it would mean a long move that would take many moons and much suffering, the whole village agreed that they must do it. They traveled along the Siapa River for many moons, almost a whole season. It was the most painful time of Shortman's life. Every day he and his friend Hairylip cried because they never had enough to eat. Finally they came to a large place where there was no jungle, only tall grass. Whenever villages travel, they always keep their children close for fear of their enemies and the spirits and the ghosts of the dead. But even though they were watching closely, one day two of the children disappeared.

The whole village looked everywhere but they could not find the children. It was an easy area for searching because there was no thick jungle. But they knew that large cats hunt there and their boys might have been eaten.

Then the shaman's spirits told him what had happened. They had been stolen by unfriendly spirits.

When the people heard this, they stopped their travel and hunted for the children for days. Every day the shaman spent much time with his spirits, getting directions for places to look.

The first day they found fresh tracks of two children. The tracks wandered as if the children had been led by spirits. The people moved out of the grassy place and into the jungle so they could block the trails and get better protection from the spirits. For many days they searched and each night they listened to the mothers weeping in their hammocks.

Then one evening just before dark some fresh tracks were found. All the men ran ahead on this trail and took places in hiding and waited for the children to come. The shaman told them that this might be their last chance. The children had been with the spirits for so long already that they would no longer want to come back.

As they hid on the trail, many were filled up and over with fear. Finally they heard many voices coming down the trail talking together. But they were speaking a language the men could not understand. By now it was so dark that they couldn't see anything. When the voices came to the place where the men hid, they all jumped onto the trail and grabbed for anything they could in the darkness. Mostly they caught each other, but in the confusion, they also caught the missing children.

All the way back to camp the boys kicked and screamed, trying to get away. The shaman was right. They were already used to living with the spirits. Back at the camp in the light of the fire, they saw that the children had been painted with a paint that has never before been seen in the jungle. It had to be a paint that the spirits use. And they were decorated with flowers from the jungle. They were horribly skinny and huddled close together by the fire. They sat there crying for their parents to come and get them. But their parents were right in front of them.

"They're crying for their spirit parents," the shaman said. "The spirits stole them to be their own children. If we hadn't got them when we did, we would never see them again."

Early the next morning, the whole village packed everything and left the horrible place. The men spent much time to be very careful to hide the trail. They placed special clues along the trail that would make it look like the everyone had gone another way. This would confuse the spirits if they tried to follow and get the children back.

For a long time the boys tried to escape. The village took turns guarding them day and night. They cried all the time for their parents. But after days of eating good food, they got their strength back and recognized their real parents. Then they could not remember their time with the spirits. All they remembered was being called out into the jungle by their family. They had followed the call, but when they got there, they found no one. They had been drawn by deceiving spirits.

After this, all the children began to behave. But this happening split the village. Moving was becoming much harder and many wanted to turn back. "We are far enough from our enemies now," they said. "We should stop and live here."

"My spirits are angry with me that we are going so far," one of the shamans said. "They tell me we should settle here."

"That's true. My spirits are angry too," another shaman said. "But I don't care. We have to get to the nabas and find that strange Yanomamö who visited us long ago. I think my spirits are just jealous of the spirits I might find there."

"Well, I'm not making my spirits any madder," the first shaman said. "They won't go any farther."

So the village split. Half of them, led by one shaman, settled on the banks of the Siapa River. The others, led by another shaman, kept going toward the Casiquiare River. Everyone was angry because the village couldn't stay together, but the two shamans refused to come to an agreement.

By the time they reached the Casiquiare River, two seasons had passed and too many people had died. Then they were struck with grief when they learned that they were still very far from the nabas. They settled on the banks of the Casiquiare and called it Banks of Nowhere.

Finally the shaman sent a few men up the Casiquiare to the Orinoco to see if they could find the place called Tama Tama. After a time they returned with canoes that had loud motors on them. There was a white man with them called Dye. The naba put the whole village in his canoes and moved them to Tama Tama. He found a deserted village close by, and he bought it from another Indian tribe. They settled there and began to grow new gardens.

When Dye began to teach them about a new spirit, the village shaman knew that his thoughts about his spirits had been right. They did not like Dye's spirit. "This is why my spirits wanted us to turn back," the shaman said. "This new spirit must be the spirit of that stranger who visited us long ago."

The whole village was happy they had found what they were looking for. They liked living near Dye at Tama Tama. And they were free of war. They became known as Sahael.

But one day Dye left and never came back and his friends at Tama Tama never visited or taught them anything. So the village began to watch for the other nabas who traveled up and down the Orinoco River. They met a merchant with the biggest boat they had ever seen. He agreed to give the village an outboard motor if they would clear the jungle for him and plant a big garden. They were never so happy.

They cleared a garden so big that it ran for two and a half bends of the Orinoco River. They planted watermelon and other plants, and the man returned many, many times to fill his big canoe with plantains that he sold downriver in the huge naba village.

When the harvesting season was over, the merchant gave them some of the plantains and promised that he would come back with the motor after the crop was planted for the next season. The whole village worked another season for him, and again he gave them some of the plantains and promised that the motor would come after the next season's harvest. This happened for five seasons.

It turned out to be a bad thing for that village, but the nabas after him were worse. Many nabas thought that all Yanomamö women craved them. They walked into the village, pulled out their penises and waved them at the women. In one village, a naba went up to a woman and whacked her with his penis. Her friend said, "Ooh, that almost went in, didn't it?" He couldn't talk Yanomamö so he didn't know they were laughing at him.

"These fools cut part of their penises off and then they think we crave them!" She laughed while they watched him wave his thing around.

One Indian said, "I'm going to have my machete ready for the first naba to pull his penis on my wife—I'll whack the ugly thing right off!"

Hairylip became a teacher at the naba school. But he became angry when he was told to dress in the old loincloth and the children had to come to school naked. "We want to have better lives," he told the padre at the school. He quit and began practicing to become a shaman.

Hairylip's childhood friend, Shortman, had no parents now, so he left his village and traveled all around to many other villages in Yanomamö land. After many seasons, he came back to Sahael. Hairylip was happy to see him again. They remembered together the pain of their childhood and the long trip out from the Siapa.

"Where have you been for so many seasons?" Hairylip asked him.

"I've been a lot of places," Shortman told him. "But now I live in Honey and have a wife there. It is a wonderful place. Remember that mystery visitor, Doesn't-Grab-Women?" Of course Hairylip remembered. He was the reason they made the big move. "Doesn't-Grab-Women is the leader in Honey. We call him Shoefoot, or sometimes He's-Got-A-Mouth."

"Tk!" Hairylip clicked his tongue. "Doesn't-Grab-Women," he remembered. "Can I come talk to him? Is he still as mysterious as they said he was? Doesn't he ever grab women?"

"Come with me to Honey and you can talk to him," Shortman said. "A lot of people in Honey don't grab women. And yes, he is still mysterious. One place where Shoefoot visited, they named him No-Trouble. The whole village is mysterious. We don't have any war there, and we have some nabas who live right in the village with us." Hairylip didn't believe that a naba would actually live in a village with Yanomamö. "I know you don't believe it, but it's true. We even go into their houses and talk to them."

"They must be pretty dumb nabas if they don't know that they should keep us out of their homes," Hairylip said sarcastically. "Any naba knows that."

Hairylip went with his old friend back to Honey. As they walked through the village, Hairylip saw so many changes that he could not believe that they were Yanomamö. "This is what we have always wanted for our village," he said to Shortman. "But no one wants us to have it."

"I know," Shortman answered. "Those nabas that come into Sahael just want us to stay in the same misery we have always lived in. They make so much money taking pictures of our naked women and writing stories about us. Do you know of one village anywhere that wants that kind of naba to come live with them?"

"We'd like for a naba like you have here to come live with us," Hairylip said.

"Of course. Every village would."

My sister-in-law was about to have a baby but it wouldn't put its head down and come right. I did all my usual things to get Healing Spirit to help the baby come but nothing helped. I did much more than usual because she was my brother's wife. And he was a shaman and she was a shaman. Almost no women ever became a shaman. All three of us struggled with all our spirits, but this one was a hard one. When her water came, we took her to Honey for help.

Our relatives there came running when they saw her. They began, as they always do, to wail and talk about all the other women this had happened to, and how quickly they had all died and what it was like to grieve for them and how sad they would all be if anything happened to her.

Pepe, the naba I fear, had moved his family to another village at that time, but the other nabas who were there tried to help her get free from all her visitors. Finally they took her into their own house so she could relax.

But all our relatives followed her in and continued to fuss about how sick she was and how awful it was that they were about to have to grieve for her, and wondering if they could at least save the baby. The nabas begged them to leave. They believe that quiet will make people better.

My niece, Juanita, wouldn't leave. She is so close to my sister-in-law that Juanita calls her Mother. Juanita is married to Spear's son, Fruitman. When the nabas finally got everyone out of their house, Juanita sat in the grass under her mother's window crying loudly. In her arms she held her nursing baby.

This girl will listen to nothing but punishment, the naba thought. He picked up a small stick and began to hit Juanita on the legs to make her leave and go home. As she jumped to get away, she dropped the baby.

The village got mad. They were all standing at the river bank when Fruitman came home from working in the garden. They all tried to tell him at once, "The naba beat your wife and she dropped the baby."

Fruitman didn't need to hear any more. His axe was in his hand, and it was all he would need. When he got to the naba's door, it didn't matter that it was locked with the naba inside. He took a swing at it with his axe. Then he hacked it again and again. With every blow his anger grew.

Shoefoot and Spear ran toward the naba's house when they heard all the noise. "It's all right. It's all right," they both said. "No one's been hurt bad." Then the naba's wife came from the little hut where they relieve themselves. She saw her door being chopped down.

"Fruitman, no! Fruitman, no!" She didn't know of her own danger. The village watched to see if he would do what everyone expected and give the naba's wife a blow that would make up for what had been done to Juanita.

"It's all right," Shoefoot kept saying. "The baby is not hurt. Juanita is not hurt. You've already destroyed his door. It won't help to hit his wife with your axe." Spear tried to get in his son's way so he couldn't hit the woman.

But Fruitman knew it *would* help. It would feel so good. His whole body told him how much he needed to take one swing at her head with the blunt side of his axe. He could see her on the ground, blood all over her head. It would teach everyone that it didn't matter who you are or where you're from or how light your skin is, you don't mess with Fruitman's wife.

For a reason he didn't understand, Fruitman dropped the axe and went back to his hammock. *I'm not a coward,* he told himself, staring up at his palm-leaf roof. *It sure wasn't just for lack of courage that I didn't hit her. Then why not? She sure deserved it. In my old way I would have bashed her head in. It would have been great. Why does this different spirit of the nabas want us to change so much?*

Late that night, the baby came. A few days later the naba came to talk to Fruitman. He said that it was a bad thing that he had done to Juanita; he had no right to hit her, and he wished so hard that he had never done it. He said that no such thing would ever happen again. He said he didn't blame Fruitman for smashing his door; he deserved it; he deserved even worse. He said he was very happy that Fruitman didn't hit his wife.

Fruitman had never heard this kind of talk. He didn't know what to say. It gave him a strange feeling he had never felt before, a good feeling. He lost his urge to hit the naba's wife with his axe. Then the naba fixed his door and never talked to Fruitman again about the damage.

Even the leader of the white nabas came in the airplane all the way to Honey to talk to Fruitman. He said, "This naba that lives with you is new here and doesn't understand your talk or your ways yet. So it was easy for him to do something that was really stupid. It was a bad thing he did and he knows it. And he feels very sad about it and says that it will never happen again." It made Fruitman feel very important. The naba leader said his name was Dye.

So Fruitman said to Dye, "I shouldn't have been so fast to get mad because I knew that he doesn't know us." When Dye left, Fruitman watched the airplane go across the grass and up into the air. He walked back to his house. He was surprised at how all this talk made his anger go away. It even made him feel good about the naba who had hit his wife.

He laid back in his hammock and looked up at the palm leaves and was still thinking about all the nice things that the nabas had said. They even said that they have one special word that they use that means the same as all the things they said to Fruitman. They said that they almost never use the word because it is a very hard word to say.

But Fruitman stared at his palm roof and thought, *it must be a very nice word.*

9

PULLING HIS EYE DOWN

The problems from nabas get bigger as more of them come. Honey still likes their naba. Turkey's village at the Mavaca has nabas nearby, but Turkey wants one to live right with them. Shetary hates all nabas. He waits every day for his chance to kill one. Someone has started to talk about the missing head. But no one knows where this talk is coming from. Shetary's village isn't the only one of our people who had much grief from white nabas. I lose a daughter this season.

For many moons all our other relatives in Turkey's village longed for a naba to come live with them. They were like me. They wanted all the trade goods that the nabas have, but they were frightened by the spirit of Pepe, his son Keleewa, and other nabas.

A naba lived in a village across the river from Turkey. They called him Fish because he had no hair and it made his head look exactly like a fish. One day he came to Turkey's village with a new naba, a huge man. This man couldn't talk to us because he had just come from the naba country. Turkey's village liked it when Fish came for a visit and to trade. So they were friendly to the new naba.

After many days, Fish taught the new naba our talk, even though all nabas talk like babies. One day the new naba came to visit Turkey alone. "Why do you listen to the things Fish tells you?" he asked Turkey. Fish was always telling the people that they should stop killing and raping and following spirits, all the same words that Padre Coco had said to Tigerlip. "You don't have to listen to Fish," the new naba would say.

These nabas aren't as smart as I thought, Turkey said to himself. *Fish can't even tell his friends from his enemies.*

The next season the new naba stopped his boat at Turkey's village. "I'm going to live with you to learn more of your ways," he said. Great excitement rushed through the village. At last Turkey would get some of the things his people needed so badly.

But Turkey was a little disappointed when the naba didn't try to teach them anything. Most nabas would call the village together and teach things about how to live better. Still, everyone was happy that they could trade with the naba for his good things.

A few days after he came, the naba got up in the morning and took his clothes off, wore only a loincloth like we do, and began taking our ebene. The village gathered around and watched in amazement.

"Look at this wise white man, will you?" Turkey whispered to a brother-in-law. "Is he crazy? Does he think we're naked because we like it? Can't he see how much we want to have clothes to protect us from these terrible bugs?"

It was a funny sight watching a white person who knew so much, act so stupid. But no one could laugh. For many seasons they had dreamed of getting a naba to help them improve their lives. Now they stood and watched their dream squat naked in the dust blowing ebene up his nose. "The man we thought would teach us, is imitating us," one man said to his brother-in-law as they walked sadly away.

Turkey lay in his hammock and looked across the shabono at the naba. *I've already got enough miserable people,* he thought. *Now I've got a big one with white skin and he talks like a baby.*

The next day the naba began asking people in the village about their dead. Of course no one would tell him anything. As long as he lived with them, Turkey and his people never knew why the naba would be so mean. It was all he ever wanted to talk about. He treated them like animals by continually asking about their dead.

Finally, one warrior told him if he asked any more

questions about his dead relatives, he would kill him. So he asked other people and gave them pots and other trade goods each time they told him something about the dead. So of course they didn't like him. They named him Irritating-Bee because his name sounded a little like the word for that honey bee that always buzzes around your head.

While Irritating-Bee was still with them, another naba came. He brought trade goods and that made the village happy. But he didn't teach Turkey's people anything. Instead he stood and watched them and made marks on his paper.

After he learned our talk, this second naba began traveling to other villages on the river. The boys of the village went with him to help and were able to earn many valuable things in trade for their help. He also played "howashi" with them, grabbing them by the private parts and sticking his fingers up their butts.

One night they were in the jungle on the upper Orinoco. Everyone was away from the shelters hunting except the naba and a boy named Lizzard. The new naba came to Lizzard's hammock and sat on it with him. He began a little playfulness. When Lizzard had enough, he said, "Stop it! I'm getting out of here." But the naba kept him in the hammock. Lizzard became angry. He struggled with all his might to get out of the hammock and out of the naba's grasp. But he was not full grown, and the more he struggled the more the naba seemed to enjoy it and he got stronger and wilder.

Lizzard would have screamed, but there was no one to hear. He felt his whole body fill with pain and then rage when the smart white man jammed his dirty old penis into his butt and jerked just like a wild animal.

"I'm through with you," Lizzard sobbed when the naba got up. He had never before felt so much shame. He was horrified at the name he would certainly get if anyone found out. "Don't you ever turn your back on me because I'm going to have my arrows always ready and you'll be dead."

"Don't be angry," the naba said. "That little radio you got was great pay for your use and you know it."

"I'll never travel with you again," Lizzard said. Now he understood why he and all his friends had suddenly become so rich.

The next morning Lizzard whispered to a friend. He would

never tell what happened to anyone unless that person had also been used by the naba. He soon discovered that almost all the boys were keeping quiet about the same thing.

"He'll never get away with anything like that with me," one of the boys said when he heard the other boys' stories. But the naba did.

"I told you he treats us like women," Lizzard said to his friend later. "He stuck his filthy thing in you, didn't he?" But the boy had too much shame to answer.

When the story was told in the village of Turkey's enemies they laughed and laughed. "Turkey's village finally got a smart naba to help them and he thinks he can reproduce himself from the back-end of boys?" the leader yelled, doubling over with laughter.

"We really have a lot to learn from them," another said, and they laughed even harder.

"Where do these smart white people learn these things?"

"That's what they teach themselves," another answered. They laughed so hard.

But there was no laughter in Turkey's village when the leaders heard the story. Lizzard's father was the village chief. He drew back an arrow, pointed it at his son and ordered him out of the village. "I will not have a son of mine acting like a woman," he called after him as his son backed out the entrance to the shabono.

"Yes. We thought we were stupid," he muttered after his son left. "This man was our hope to get out of our misery. Now I have more misery because I've lost a son." The leaders went back to their hammocks and were sad.

That's how the naba became known as A.H., meaning Ass Handler. Lizzard never traveled with him again.

Runner was a warrior who traveled with A.H. and became a good friend. He was a full grown man and a good hunter too. A.H. never tried to treat him like a woman.

But A.H. got mad easy and often hit the young boys who traveled with him. One time Runner told him to leave the boys alone.

"You're not any different than them," he said to Runner. "They're with us to do the work. I'll hit you too if you act like them."

"Go on, hit me," Runner said. "I can't wait. Just be ready to be hit back."

Days later they found a herd of capybara. It's an animal that looks like a giant rabbit, even bigger than a man. And we love the taste of its meat. A.H. shot a couple of capybara and they decided to make a shelter and enjoy eating them. The boys cleaned the game and started working on the shelter we always made when we spent the night in the jungle.

The boys found a bunch of trees perfect for hanging hammocks. They picked four trees, one at each corner of the hammock area. These became the four corners of their shelter. With the help of his friends he cut four poles that joined the four trees. Across the four poles they strung many poles that formed the roof of the shelter. Over the poles they tied a network of palm leaves, arranged just right so that the underneath was safe from rain.

While some of the boys built the shelter, another boy cleaned and cut up the game. One boy built a rack and made a fire underneath it for smoking the game. But he left the head of one capybara in the canoe. All this time A.H. lay in his hammock telling everyone what to do. He said to the boy who had prepared the meat, "Go down to the river and get that head out of the canoe and get it on the smoke rack."

But the boy told A.H., "No, I'm tired. I'll get it later."

A.H. went into a rage and hit the boy. "I won't have any more of this!" he yelled at all of them.

Runner was way down in the river bathing, but he could hear the fighting. He too had very little patience left. "Leave them alone," he called up to A.H., which only made him angrier.

"All right," he yelled back at Runner, "you bring the head up! And right now!" The boys stood still to listen. They knew that A.H. hadn't got his thing into Runner's butt, so he wasn't going to take too much bossing off the naba.

"You want that head, naba," Runner called from the water, "come on down and get it yourself."

A.H. yelled back, "You get that head or I'll really get mad!"

"You're already mad!" Runner yelled back. "I've already cleaned your capybara and now I'm done washing up. If I carry that bloody head all the way up there, I'll have to wash all over again. So . . . I'm not doing it."

A.H. kept yelling and threatening. Finally Runner called out, "You listen to this. You either close your mouth or I will take this head and throw it in the river."

"You do that and I'll clobber you!" A.H. yelled back, and there was silence. It was the end of the talking part. When the boys heard the quiet, they ran to the top of the bank to see what Runner would do. He stood up from the water and walked slowly over to the canoe. Without looking back, he lifted the bloody head from the canoe bottom and threw it as far as he could out into the river. It splashed. The water slowly turned red. The blood drew the piranha and started them into their mad feeding. The tastiest part of the capybara was ruined.

A.H. ran down the bank, so mad his eyes bugged out. He hit Runner a great blow in the face. No one was more surprised than A.H. when Runner gave the blow back twice as hard.

A.H. almost fell to his knees. "You're dead!" he screamed, running up the bank. "I'm getting my gun and you're dead!"

"Hurry and get it!" Runner yelled back. He bent down and picked up his bow and arrows. "I can't wait for you to get that gun in your hands, naba!"

It was the end of the fight. A.H. and Runner got along after that. The naba always treated him different than the others.

In one of the villages A.H. began to pay the chief so he could have his daughter as a wife. The village was excited that they had a naba who would really become one of their own. He learned to chew tobacco the way we do. We shared our ebene with him and he even tried to call our spirits. But the village became upset when the naba started to mess with another woman who was not his. So he went to her brothers and asked what he could give as a trade for the use of their sister.

"Go on, use her," they said. "Then bring us a machete."

When the same thing happened to other young girls, many of the people got upset. After A.H. had sex with a girl, he would not be interested in her again. After a while they noticed that he only wanted girls who had never before had sex. These girls are very hard to find and always very young.

When Pepe left Honey, he moved with his family to a village at the Mavaca River, the same village where A.H. lived right across the river from Turkey's village. It was many days paddling on the river. One day the children of the village got into A.H.'s house while he was away and stole as many of his things as they could get. When a Yanomamö steals something, he will often give it back, even if it is many seasons later and the thing he gives back is not the same thing he stole. But the chief of the village knew that A.H. would be real mad. He knew that A.H. didn't know about how we steal and often give back. So the chief went to the children and made them give him the stolen things and all the food that they hadn't eaten. When A.H. came back, the chief gave him his things.

But this was not enough to stop his anger. A.H. went into a fit of rage and yelled at everyone in the village. When A.H. got like that, he said many words we didn't understand. He screamed at everyone and said he would beat the children.

One of the men lay in his hammock, arms folded, one hand over his mouth, watching A.H. scream at everyone in the village. He saw A.H. pause.

"Do it," he said calmly.

"Sure, do it," another father said, leaning on his club.

Another one said, "My girl needs a beating real bad." His bow and arrows rested between his chest and folded arms. "You're probably the best one to give it to her, naba." They never called him A.H. when he was close enough to hear. Everyone gathered to see what A.H. would do.

He thought for a moment. "Youngbird is the one who started all this trouble," he screamed. "I'll beat Youngbird!" Youngbird was a good choice for A.H. He was from another village and had no relatives to care what happened to him. The fathers with the weapons wouldn't get into a fight over a person who wasn't a relative. And Youngbird wasn't a warrior yet. He had barely become a young man.

"Somebody go get Youngbird and I'll beat him good," he yelled.

But Youngbird had made a good friend of Pepe's son, Keleewa. "You'll have to beat me too, then," the white boy said without thinking. "Youngbird was out hunting with me when your stuff was stolen and you know it."

"Yeah, you're his friend. You protect him," one of the Indians said to Keleewa.

145

"If you want to beat someone, beat him," Keleewa said pointing to the chief's child. "Everyone knows he stole your things."

"Yeah," everyone said, imitating Keleewa and daring A.H. to raise his hand against a child. "Everyone knows he stole your things."

The whole village was on edge. A white boy was siding with an Indian boy against a full-grown naba? Everyone watched A.H.'s face turn dark red with anger.

A.H. didn't get to beat anyone that day. But everyone knew it wasn't over. For many days after that, Youngbird and Keleewa stuck together. Finally A.H. left the village to go on a trip.

Some time later A.H. came back in the middle of the night. He tied his boat and entered the village so quietly that no one was disturbed. He knew exactly where Youngbird slept, in a small hut outside the village. A.H. slipped into the hut and stood over Youngbird's hammock. Except for the crackle of a few dying fires, the village was quiet.

Youngbird's peaceful sleep ended when his face was filled with the sharp pain of a savage beating. He screamed. The quiet of the sleeping village ended. The whole village jumped from their hammocks and ran through the blackness toward the screaming. But when he heard them coming, A.H. ran to his own house and locked the door.

"A.H. beat me while I slept," Youngbird said to everyone. "He ran just before you got here."

Keleewa ran back to his house and got his gun. "You put that thing away," Pepe ordered. "We'll take care of him in the morning."

The next morning Youngbird's eyes were swollen so big he couldn't see. A Venezuelan medic was in the village at that time. He had spent a lot of time with nabas. He went with Pepe to A.H.'s house. Keleewa wanted to go too, but Pepe wouldn't let him.

They got into an argument and A.H. threatened to throw the medic into the river. The medic was one of those large Myc Indians. And he was real big—as big as both of the nabas together. He drew back his huge finger. "You!" he said with a sharp poke to A.H.'s chest, "are going to throw me?" and a second poke, "into the river?" and a third. A.H. stumbled backward with each finger-punch. He decided not to. He left the village and didn't return until Pepe and the medic moved away.

A.H. went further up into the headwater of the Orinoco where nabas almost never go. But even in that far away village, there was a naba named Padre Gonzales who was helping our people learn better ways of doing things. Just like Padre Coco had done, he was always telling them that many of the things they did were evil and they should stop doing them. But he also said that many of the things that nabas do are evil too.

After A.H. was in the village for a time, an Indian went to Padre Gonzales and told him why the boys were suddenly getting so many new things.

Padre Gonzales stopped A.H. in the middle of the shabono. "What are these boys doing for you that is worth all you are paying them?" Gonzales asked.

"What does this matter to you?" A.H. answered.

"This is my village," Gonzales said. "I'm trying to help these people, and I want to know what's going on here."

"This isn't your village. I have just as much right here as you do."

"I hear you're paying the boys to use them for sex."

"That's a lie! Where could you have ever heard a thing like that?"

"From this boy right here." Gonzales motioned to the Indian standing beside him.

"He's lying," A.H. shouted. Everyone saw his face fill with anger.

Padre Gonzales turned to the Indian. "He says you're lying. What do you say?"

"I say he's lying," the Indian answered. By this time there was a crowd around the two nabas. They all backed up the Indian's story.

"Why don't you just get out of this village and stay out?" Gonzales said.

"Who are you to tell me that!" A.H. shouted back, sticking his finger into Padre Gonzales' face.

"Nobody needs you here teaching these people your filthy ways," he answered.

A.H. put his face real close to Gonzales' face and shouted, "And who made you the judge of what filth is?"

"Even these ignorant savages know more about right and

wrong than you," Gonzales answered calmly. "You leave this village and don't come back."

A.H. had heard all he could stand. He pulled back his fist and hit Gonzales in the face.

But Gonzales didn't move. "You better not do that again," he said, and A.H. hit him again as hard as he could.

We had never before seen nabas fight. We always hit in the chest and never in the face. And we always fight fair; first you hit his chest, then he hits yours. We also thought that Padre Gonzales had a spirit that didn't fight because he was always telling us to stop our wars. Maybe Padre Gonzales forgot, because he hit A.H. so hard it almost knocked him to the dirt. A.H. stumbled, then hit Gonzales a few more times, but he didn't seem to feel the blows. Then Gonzales hit A.H. two more times in the face. A.H. fell to his knees and then spread out flat in the dust. It was the shortest fight the Yanomamö had ever seen.

A.H. lay motionless with his face in the dirt. Padre Gonzales turned and walked out of the shabono. Everyone stood waiting for A.H. to move. He didn't.

"He's dead," a woman whispered as if she was not sure that white people died.

"What are we going to do with his body?" another asked. They thought they had a big problem. Then they noticed that he was breathing, and a little later he woke up. A.H. never went back to that village as long as Padre Gonzales was there. All the women were happy.

In another village, A.H. gave the chief a few machetes and things in exchange for the use of his daughter. The trade worked good and the chief's daughter treated A.H. as her husband. But when A.H. went to the world of the nabas and didn't come back, the chief's girl was left without anyone to care for her. So the chief gave her to another man.

When A.H. did finally come back, he wanted his girl again. But the man who had her was no longer afraid of the naba. After they said some angry words, A.H. reached for his gun. Before A.H. could blink, the Indian's club hit him on the arm and side and knocked him to the ground. The other men of the village moved in to make sure no one would be killed. A.H. went out to the world of the nabas to have the bone in his arm fixed.

"What happened to your arm, naba?" an Indian asked when he saw him with the huge white bandage that is hard like a rock.

"I fell off of that foot bridge," A.H. told him.

"Yeah, we heard all about her," the Indian said, snickering to his friends.

The leaders of the villages in Turkey's area got together to decide what to do about A.H. "Why don't we just kill him?" one said. "That will take care of the problem."

"Sure it will. And then the nabas will come and kill us, the way they did in that other Yanomamö village far from us."

"He travels to all the villages," Runner said. "They'll never know who did it if we just take him into the jungle and don't bring him back."

One of the young men he had used like a woman said, "I agree. Let's kill him and be done with it."

"We can't get along without his trade things," one said. "He's not like us. We pay for a wife once and we keep her— mostly. He has to pay us something every time he wants to use a woman. As long as his thing keeps working, we'll stay rich."

But Runner said, "There are better ways to make money. I don't need to stick my rear out for his penis in order to get paid. In Honey Village they pay people to do things that are useful, like building houses. You go to work for *him* in the morning and you end up stroking his thing until he squirts all over you. It's filthy. After you do that a bunch of times, you get a little radio or tape player."

"Our village cannot be without all the things we have gotten used to from him," a few others said.

Runner shook his head and clicked his tongue. He could see that there wasn't complete agreement. "He could never do this if we weren't so poor," he said. "We're trapped. We're backed into a spot with no escape."

The chief whose boy had been raped was madder than anyone. His neck bulged when he yelled, "How long will we let someone turn our boys into women? How will our people ever reproduce if they start on that habit? I say we kill him!"

The ones who wanted to kill him met later. "How can we kill him now?" one said. "The others will tell the nabas who did it and we'll be in big trouble." As much as they hated him, they were afraid to act.

Runner was sad. He wanted more than anything to stop traveling with A.H. But he was trapped. He needed the trade goods so bad. At least he wasn't pretending to be a woman, although he often wondered how much more trade goods he might be able to get if he did. *This smart white man's workers get nothing but bigger butt holes*, he thought.

When Keleewa became a young man, he went to the world of the nabas to get a wife. As soon as they were married, he came back with her to the jungle and lived in one of our villages. We were all anxious to see if she would like us.

Before he left his new wife to go hunting, he took her outside his leaf house and handed her a little gun. Then he hung a papaya on a tree trunk across the village. He told her to shoot it. She pointed the gun and shot the papaya three times through the center. A cheer went up from the village. "The white girl can shoot," all the women yelled. "We'll be safe now when the men are gone." They were so surprised, they didn't notice how surprised she was. Keleewa and the men left for a long hunt.

Two days later all the women of the village ran yelling and screaming into the naba's house, almost breaking the door. They jumped over tables and chairs in a race to hide behind Keleewa's wife. Some were even trying to get their heads under her skirt. Because Keleewa's wife couldn't understand our talk yet, she thought it was a raid.

Then the naba, A.H., appeared and stuck his head in the door. He saw the women hiding under things and behind the white girl. The women hoped that A.H. wouldn't bother them when there was another naba around who wouldn't be afraid of him. He could see that they weren't as interested in sex as he always was. He left without getting any.

During the season that Pepe lived at the Mavaca, a very funny thing happened. Of course, we Yanomamö could tell at the beginning that Irritating-Bee didn't like the nabas who tried to help us change our ways. This was easy to see because when the helpful nabas weren't around, Irritating-Bee would say things like, "You don't have to listen to them," and, "The spirit they talk about is no better than yours." But Fish and Pepe didn't know that he said these things.

One day Runner, who was a shaman, and another shaman named Kaobawa became upset because Pepe had been teaching them that the great spirit would some day destroy the world with fire. They came to Irritating-Bee and asked him if it was true. "They tell you lies about the spirit world," Irritating-Bee said to Runner and Kaobawa. "Don't accept these lies. You have all the spirits you need. And the naba spirit they tell you about, the one they call the great spirit—there is no such spirit. All nabas who have learned a lot more than them, know that there is no great spirit. Come, I'll prove to you that there is nothing to fear from their spirit. Get your ebene." And he started taking his clothes off. "You, Runner and Kaobawa, will help me call the spirits."

The whole village suddenly filled with excitement. And they got more excited when they watched Runner and Kaobawa paint and decorate the big white naba. Then they got quiet when he squatted on the dirt floor of the shabono with almost no clothes on and stuck the long ebene shaft into his nose. Runner blew the ebene into Irritating-Bee and he danced and chanted, calling to the spirits to come to him, just like all of us shamans do. Everyone in the village sat and watched to see if any spirits would answer him.

"Coming, coming, they're coming, coming," Irritating-Bee chanted again and again as he danced around and his arms floated into the air. Kaobawa and Runner danced with him and the whole village stared and wondered. They knew that Runner's and Kaobawa's spirits would come. But would our spirits come to a naba who knows about the great spirit, the one who is unfriendly to us?

"Coming, Periboliwa, Fereliwa, Lahacanaliwa, coming, coming," he kept calling and naming them while the village sat, watched, and looked at each other, then looked back at the naba. Finally he called out to Kaobawa, "Look! Here they come. Here they come." And then Irritating-Bee shouted to the whole village, "Wadubaliwa has come into my chest." Everyone took a big breath and looked at each other. Wadubaliwa is the spirit of the buzzard. He's famous for being one of the most violent of all the spirits. I did not have this spirit, but Kaobawa did.

"Tk!" one woman said. "The naba has Buzzard Spirit! He'll be as fierce and powerful as us now." And a hiss of excitement went through the village. Everyone knows how harmful Buzzard Spirit is. So as Irritating-Bee's arms got wilder, the Indians grabbed and held their things to keep him from breaking them.

As he danced, Irritating-Bee said to Kaobawa, "Buzzard Spirit wants to go to another village and kill a child there."

"If you do that," Kaobawa told him, "they will have to take revenge against our village."

"He really wants me to do it," Irritating-Bee said. "So I'm going to." So Buzzard Spirit went with Irritating-Bee to that village and ate the spirit of that child.

Just as the dancing and chanting to the spirit reached its highest excitement, Pepe walked into the shabono. The village went real quiet. They all knew that Pepe had a powerful spirit too. Now he was about to see the naba doing just the same thing Pepe always told us to stop doing. Every Indian in the shabono saw the surprise on Pepe's face when he saw the decorated white man, almost naked, jumping up and down in the dirt.

Pepe stuck his face into Irritation-Bee's and said, "Irritating-Bee, you're a disgusting fool." Then with three fingers he pulled down on the skin above his cheekbone and showed Irritating-Bee that little pink part under his eye.

The whole village went wild with laughter. "He pulled his eye down on you!" all the women yelled. And they started mocking him like they do, all going at the same time, saying things like, "He just gave you the worst insult ever! What are you going to do about it?"

"So Pepe's spirit isn't real and you've got the fierce Buzzard Spirit, the most fierce of all. And he just pulled his eye down on you and you can't do anything."

"You know all about that naba spirit, don't you, Irritating-Bee! What are you going to do about that insult?"

While Pepe walked out of the shabono, Irritating-Bee called to him, "You're the disgusting fool because there is no great spirit." But the women kept going.

"Yes, that's a real fierce spirit you've got there, Irritating-Bee."

The women kept imitating Pepe's eye-pulling, everyone trying to show the others just how he did it. They pointed and mocked, "All those big spirits can't even keep him from pulling his eye down. And you can't do anything." It was the funniest ending of a spirit dance that they had ever seen.

The people went back to their work. They wondered what kind of spirit Pepe had that he could pull his eye down on a person with the powerful Buzzard Spirit. For a long time after that the people would tell the story that always ended the same way: with Pepe pulling his eye down.

10
WE CAN HAVE BOTH WAYS

still love my spirits and talk to them every night. It has now been a long time since I have had a reason to send any of my spirits to fight with Toucan's people. We hear more talk about Shetary's missing head. Like we thought, it was a naba that took it. Some warriors saw him do it. But no one knows who they are. And they'll never admit that they let him do it. Keleewa has brought his new wife to live in Honey. Deemeoma still lives there; her daughter married Won't-Grow. They are about to have Deemeoma's second grandchild. They are still happy, but my spirits are still afraid there.

"She's starting! She's starting!" they yelled to Deemeoma. Everyone knew she was the best at helping babies to come. Deemeoma had told everyone they should get her at the first sign that her daughter, Anita, was about to give birth. She had always helped everyone. She felt so much sadness for people in pain that sick people always asked her to come help them. This morning she was about to see her second grandchild.

She could still feel the early dew on the grass as she ran to her daughter's house. Anita was in the middle of a birth pain when Deemeoma entered the opening in the mud wall. It was dark and it took her a minute to see. Deemeoma could feel her heart jump with excitement as she saw her grandchild's head.

"Relax a little bit," she said to her daughter. "One more push and it'll be here. I think it'll be a boy." She was good at babies.

But she was only half right. With the next push the head came through, then the rest. It was a girl. But when Deemeoma looked close, she saw that it didn't matter that it wasn't a boy. Half the baby's face was covered with a thick black mark. The room turned quiet and Anita knew that something was very wrong.

"What is it? How's the baby?" she asked. Deemeoma could see that this baby was no good. She knew what she had to do. She would take care of it for her daughter.

"Hush," Deemeoma answered. "Don't bother me about it now. You'll have more babies later." She wrapped the baby in a cloth, picked up a machete, and went outside.

News of the bad baby had already passed around the village, and outside the house a curious crowd had gathered, wanting to know her intentions. "It's not right to let her grow up and suffer," Deemeoma said in tears. "I will save her all the trouble right now." Everyone looked at the baby, but no one would touch it. Once you touched the baby, it would become a real person that you would have to care for. The mark was huge and ugly.

"It wouldn't be right to kill a baby," Shoefoot said, so quietly that hardly anyone but Deemeoma could hear. Even if he was the village leader, he didn't interfere any more than he had to.

"She will do nothing but suffer," Deemeoma cried. "Think of what she'll go through when she's grown. She's a no-good. She's ugly." Everyone said everything all at the same time. But usually the village agrees with Shoefoot.

Right then Won't-Grow, the new father, came back from hunting turkeys. "She wants to kill your baby because of her face," they said to him. Won't-Grow took the bundle, unwrapped the baby, and saw the ugly mark covering half its face. How he had wanted a son! This was so different from what he expected.

"Leave the baby alone," he said. "Yai Pada gave her to me, and I'm going to love her no matter what she looks like."

"She's going to suffer so much," Deemeoma cried. "They'll laugh at her. They'll make so much fun of her. She'll be different. She won't belong. I know." There was a pause while everyone remembered what Deemeoma knew. All her suffering had been at their hands. Spear was there. He remembered when they killed her family and stole her. He knew every detail behind Deemeoma's "I know." She had known nothing but suffering.

Deemeoma's husband, the grandfather, spoke. "Leave the baby alone. The men are still going to want her. The mark is on her face, not on her vagina. That's all we men care about."

Keleewa had been standing quietly outside the circle listening to the talk. Shoefoot turned to him. "What do you say?"

He stopped and thought. He knew that Deemeoma had suffered all her life. He knew that it was her great concern for the baby that made her wish to end its life before it became a her. Keleewa motioned to the baby and asked Deemeoma, "Is the baby alive?" She nodded.

"If you take her out in the jungle and kill her, will you become her killer?" She kept nodding.

"Then will you have to go through unokai?"

She stopped. Everyone stopped. Killer rites. They hadn't forgotten—all those rituals they went through every time they killed. It had been many seasons since that word "unokai" had even been heard in their village. There was silence.

Finally Deemeoma's husband spoke again. He was old. He knew all about the old ways—unokai, revenge, rape, child killing, spirits, everything. "I already said leave the baby alone. I'm not going to repeat myself. That is the end of it."

Keleewa's wife took the baby to her house, wondering if they might be the ones who would have to raise her. She cleaned her up, wrapped her in a pretty little blanket, took her back to her mother and said, "Anita, do you want your baby?"

Anita said, "Yes." And her father turned out to be right. That was the end of it. They called the baby Yaiyomee.

Toucan traveled all day to Shooting Village to meet the nabas and learn more about his new spirit. It had taken him much of his life to learn all about his old spirits and now he wanted to learn more about his new one. The first nabas were gone and many new nabas had come.

When he finally got there, he entered their house and called to the man. "Hello, friend. Come out and talk to me."

The naba was in the back part of his house looking in

books and called back, "I'm too busy right now. Go talk to my wife." Toucan didn't want to talk to the man's wife. He wanted to hear more about the new spirit, the one who was the enemy of us shamans.

Every time he visited his in-laws, Toucan would make the same request for the naba to come out and talk. But each time he was too busy.

This made Toucan feel like a woman being pulled by two villages. He didn't like it when the nabas ignored him. It was *their* spirit he had taken. Now when the people in his village got sick, he couldn't call on Healing Spirit for help. And the nabas weren't coming any more to give medicine.

Every time disease would start and people began to die, his whole village begged Toucan to call on the spirits. It was their only hope. Finally he agreed. He took ebene and floated into a trance, calling on the spirits. But they didn't come. He begged. He pleaded. He took more ebene. Not one of his old spirits ever came back to him.

So Toucan became like many other shamans; he pretended. He did all the right things. He took the ebene. He danced. He worked his hands over the sick. He gave them that same old the-enemy-spirit-got-him-before-I-could-save-him explanation when a child died. But he was only pretending to be a shaman and none of his spirits ever returned or did anything for him.

He went on a shooting raid with his village to kill enemies. He was afraid because he knew he didn't have his spirits. But he got so sick on the way, he wasn't able to get there and fight. He had been known as the laughing man. Soon he stopped laughing.

Many moons later, Keleewa and his Indian friends were traveling far up the Ocamo and the Buto Rivers and came to the trail that led to Toucan's village. Keleewa remembered the first time he met Toucan, how he had shivered inside when they first looked at each other. This time when they met there was no such feeling.

"I threw my spirits away," Toucan said. "But now I would like to get them back and they won't come back to me. I want to learn about the great spirit, Yai Pada, but the nabas won't teach me about him."

"Come back to Honey with us," Keleewa said. "It's a long trip, but you can learn all about Yai Pada there." Toucan thought about it for a long time. It was the only thing he could do.

When they were on the river traveling back down the Ocamo, Keleewa heard Toucan telling his new Indian friends about the mountains they would see around the next bend.

"I didn't know you'd been down here," Keleewa said to Toucan.

He looked down, like he was ashamed to say it. "Well, I haven't really been here," he said quietly. "I used to come over this part when I was in the spirit world visiting other places like Jungleman's village. I haven't been able to do that since my spirits left me." When they got to Honey, Toucan met Shoefoot. He recognized him right away as that mysterious Shaman he had called No-Trouble. Shoefoot said, "See, I'm not dead." Toucan began to learn many things about his new spirit.

One day I traveled with my wives to visit their brother, Shoefoot. And there he was—Toucan. Before this I had only seen him in the spirit world. But when I saw him, I knew who he was. I could see that he was the shaman I had fought with for so long. And he could tell who I was too. But I wouldn't mention the fighting to him.

"So you are the one I have known for so long," I said. "What has happened to all your spirits? I can see their trails leading to your shabono, but they have left you! Why?"

Toucan thought. My words were the same words he had used when he first saw Shoefoot's empty trails. "They all left me when I got Yai Pada, like the people here at Honey have."

We talked until late into the night—Toucan, Shoefoot, and I. Shoefoot told us about how Omawa had tricked us Yanomamö with all the things he taught us about drinking bones, killing for revenge, stealing and raping women—all the things we do.

"So Yai Pada became a Yanomamö himself," Shoefoot continued. "He came as a baby, grew up, and showed us a completely different way to live. Even though he knew he would be killed in the end, he did it all anyway. His death was a death for all of us Yanomamö."

I could feel myself and my spirits getting angry at what he was saying. Even though it was comfortable to rest in Shoefoot's house and enjoy his wife's food, the unrest in me always grew every time I heard his words.

"But he is Yai Wana Naba Laywa," I argued with him, "the unfriendly spirit. We all know that his land is beautiful. It's the happy land—plenty of food, plenty of game, and no sickness. It's where he takes our dead children, and eats them. Of course we would all want to go there. But he himself is not our friend and never has been. He is our *enemy* spirit!"

Shoefoot explained some more. "Because he was Yai Pada, he was able to come back from the dead. That's how he cut the trail to where he lives. So he really never was unfriendly to us, but he is the enemy of the spirits we get from Omawa. He is the friend of any Yanomamö who hangs his desires on him."

This was the same story he told each time I visited. That night as I lay in my hammock in my old friend Spear's house, my spirits came to me again. They were so upset. "Don't throw us away, Father!" Jaguar Spirit begged. And Charming—she cried and wailed. The story of the death of Yai Pada and the trail to his land drove them to such panic. It was easy for me to see why some shamans would not even get out of their canoes here. If it wasn't for how friendly my relatives here are, I would never come here myself.

I'm not going to throw you away, I said to Charming and the other spirits, but not so Spear or his family could hear. *You know I've always hung my desires on you. I'll never hang them on anyone else.*

I don't know why I would always let these talks go to the point of making me so mad. But I did. The next day, I asked Shoefoot, "What do you mean, that his death was the death for all of us Yanomamö?"

"You know how we put our bow and arrows on a tree after we are done with unokai?" he answered. I nodded and clicked my tongue. It brought back a lot of memories. "And the tree takes our killing tools and makes our hands clean so we can touch ourselves again. That's what Yai Pada's death did. It changes us from being his enemies and makes us his friends so we can follow his trail to his land."

That was all I could take. The talk of Yai Pada's death was more than my spirits would stand. I went into a rage. I jumped from my hammock and stamped my feet in the dirt all the way out his door. It would take a long time to settle my spirits now.

I came back after a long time, but all night I had to listen to that same terrible don't-leave-us talk from my spirits that bothers me so. But even though I didn't like the people at Honey, they were still good to me. Shoefoot's family was always happy to see his sisters.

During that time there was a big feast way down the Orinoco River; even a long way past Tama Tama. Many of the nabas were there, and they invited all the Indian tribes to go and show the white people how we live. The Yanomamö Indians who weren't afraid of the white people went. It was a great festival and at the end they planned a big shooting contest. We were sure that our people would win over all the other tribes.

Most of our people who went were from the Orinoco River so they had seen lots of nabas. Littlecurl, Tigerlip's nephew who had lived with the whites in Tama Tama, was there with Tigerlip and their friends. They stayed in a special shabono with the other Yanomamö where all the nabas could visit and see how we live. It made Littlecurl feel very strange having so many white people walk around staring at him and his friends.

After they had been there a few days, a man came along who was a mystery to Littlecurl. He was sitting in his hammock with Tigerlip and the man came around and talked to all the Indians. He looked just like a naba but talked and acted like a Yanomamö. And all the Indians treated him like a Yanomamö. *This Indian has been with the nabas so long,* Littlecurl thought, *that he's turned white like they are.*

"Who is that man all of our people are talking to?" he asked Tigerlip.

"That's Keleewa," Tigerlip said, and he yelled at him, "Hey! Keleewa!" The man came over to their hammocks. Littlecurl still didn't know if he was a naba turned Yanomamö or a Yanomamö turned naba. But as he talked to the man he remembered; he was the same one he had played with as a boy. They spent long hours talking of their childhood together.

"I have killed so many that now almost everyone is trying to kill me," Littlecurl said to Keleewa.

"You've become a great warrior then?"

"Yes. But it's not as great as anyone said it would be. I never sleep. How can I when they are all after me? These few nights we have been here in the village of the nabas are the first time I have slept that I can remember."

"Have you heard about our village?" Keleewa asked.

"Honey? Of course. We all know about Honey. How we wish we could be like that. I am so tired of war. The only quick and easy end to it is for the ones who lose. That will be me some day. Did you hear what the nabas did in our village?"

"No. Tell me."

"When we first got a naba to come live with us," Littlecurl began, "we were so excited and listened to everything he said. He didn't teach us about a great spirit like you talk about, but he did give us medicine that we needed bad for our children.

"Then one day the naba decided to have a big feast with the whole village. My father was against the feast and told the people not to do it. He was afraid of the cans of drink that the nabas drink. He knew that it would make us do crazy things. But Father was old and no one listened to him.

"The more we drank the more fun we had, and soon everyone was mock fighting with clubs. It was all for fun, but you know it always goes too far. My youngest brother died that night from a blow to the back of the head. We all knew it was an accident. And no one grieved more than the one who had clubbed him. But you know we have to pay back for every death. It is the way of our spirits."

"Yeah, I guess I know about that," Keleewa answered, shaking his head.

"So the next morning my older brother said he would kill our brother's killer. And we all knew who it was. It was my son."

Keleewa shook his head. He knew the story couldn't possibly have a good ending.

"I kept telling them that it was the naba who caused this thing. 'Let's kill him,' I said. But my father and the rest of the village sided against me. I couldn't let my son be killed. So I took all my family and escaped way up in the headwaters. My son said, 'Shall I go through unokai, Father?' I told him certainly not. 'The naba is guilty of this death,' I said. 'Not you.' No one felt worse about it than the two of us.

"I wonder if any naba will ever come to us that will not just make our miserable lives even worse. They aren't even decent enough to bring their own wives. Instead, they use our women."

162

Keleewa didn't know what to say to his childhood friend. "Come to Honey and bring your family," he said.

"I can't run away," Littlecurl answered. "They'll call me a coward. I have too many enemies to fight. Now it's not just other villages, but my own family hunts me."

When it was time for the shooting contest, the Indians wanted Keleewa to shoot as a Yanomamö because he grew up with us and could use our bow and arrows. He was certainly more like us than he was like the nabas. But the nabas wouldn't let him shoot because he was too white.

Anyway, when the whole contest was finished, it was a Yanomamö warrior who won. But then the Myc Indians, our old enemies, claimed that he was a Myc because, even though he was raised Yanomamö, his father was a Myc. So they claimed that they won. After a long argument, the nabas decided that we won because he used a Yanomamö bow and arrows.

One day a naba visited Honey. He was a good friend of Keleewa's brother and taught the naba children at a special school in Tama Tama. Slothtail, Won't-Grow, and some other Indians from the village went hunting with them. When they came back, they sat in Keleewa's house and talked. The Indians talked quietly among themselves as they often do when Keleewa has a visitor who doesn't understand their speech.

When Keleewa overheard the Indians use the word "howashi," he left his conversation in the naba language to find out what they were talking about. Howashi means monkey, of course, and is the name of that awful spirit. But it is also a very bad name that is used on someone who is always looking for sex.

Slothtail said to Keleewa, "Who is this naba you're talking with? What spirit does he follow?"

"He's a teacher at the mission school. He follows Yai Pada, just like the rest of us."

"No, he doesn't," Slothtail said.

"*What?*" Keleewa's mouth fell open. "*Slothtail!* How can you say a thing like that about a person who believes the same as we all do?"

"Because he doesn't," Slothtail answered.

"What? You've never seen this person before," Keleewa scolded. "You've never talked to him. You couldn't if you wanted to. You can't even speak his language. How can you make judgments like that about other people?"

"We don't have the same spirit. My spirit has no connection with his spirit."

"You can't say that when you hardly know him," Keleewa answered. "What sort of spirit do you feel from him?"

"He has Howashi Spirit," Slothtail answered.

Keleewa's shock turned to horror. "*Slothtail!* How can you possibly call another person such a filthy name when you don't know anything about him? That is terrible!"

"Because I know the spirits. And I can see his being. He has Howashi Spirit. Look at him. Can't you feel it?" They looked at the naba as he sat at the simple kitchen table talking with Keleewa's brothers in the naba language. "I know Howashi when I feel him, and that's him. That's why I feel no treaty of spirit with that naba. Do you?"

Keleewa wasn't sure he wanted to answer. He remembered that Slothtail had been chosen to become a shaman. But he had thrown his spirits away before he became experienced with them. *What could he be seeing,* he wondered? Keleewa let the talk stop.

A month later the mission school had big trouble. The nabas there learned that the teacher was trying to play howashi with one of the children. It had been happening for a long time.

Keleewa was confused when he heard of it. "How did you know?" he asked Slothtail, the only one who wasn't surprised by the story.

"You could see the dirty spirit. You could feel him. Just like with A.H. I'm the one who should be confused that none of you nabas saw him."

"But he follows Yai Pada, like all of us," Keleewa said, still wondering.

"I know some things about the spirit world, but I'm not a master in these things," Slothtail answered. "If you say he follows—maybe. But when our shamans decide to follow Yai Pada, we have to throw our spirits away. There is no other way. This man must be a Yai Pada follower who has not yet thrown away his Howashi Spirit. But I don't understand how that can be."

Keleewa had gone to the naba schools that teach the book about the spirit world. He wondered if he should try to explain it. He thought a little and started to say something, but he could tell Slothtail wasn't going to understand. *Maybe Slothtail's "confusion" is clearer than my learning,* he thought.

Slothtail and his wife, Catalina, had a daughter named Falenci. She was a beautiful girl, but still very little. There was an old man, a relative of Fruitman's family, who wanted Falenci for a wife. Even though the relative lived downriver in Mouth Village, Honey's longtime enemy, Slothtail and Catalina agreed to let the man become their son-in-law. He began working for Falenci, doing all the things that any good son-in-law would do for a wife. He brought them meat to show that he was a good hunter and would make an excellent husband and a provider for them in their old age.

One time when he was visiting Honey, the son-in-law came and wanted to take Falenci to his hammock with him. But she was too little and Slothtail and Catalina wouldn't let him take her. Fruitman came to the man's defense and insisted that they let the man take the girl.

Slothtail was convinced by Fruitman. "We have to," he said to Catalina. "If we don't, we will lose this son-in-law."

Keleewa knew about the problem that had come between Slothtail and Fruitman. He tried hard not to get in the middle of it. But when it was clear that they would give her to the man, he could not hold his tongue.

"You will not give that beautiful little daughter of yours to that man!" he told Slothtail, as forcefully as he could. "Her breasts haven't even started yet. And she doesn't want him."

"We cannot refuse," Slothtail objected and Catalina agreed. "We are related to Fruitman and the whole family. There will be trouble if we refuse. Anyway, we want him for a son-in-law. He has already provided us with many things. We cannot refuse him now."

Slothtail's white friend had known him all his life. They grew up together, learned to hunt and fish together. There was no one else Slothtail trusted and listened to like Keleewa. He could give Slothtail strong words that no one else could. And he did.

"You can't give her," he said slowly. "It is wrong! You know it!"

It was clear from the look in his eyes that Slothtail did

know it. So did Catalina. They loved Falenci. They knew how much Keleewa loved little children. He was there when Falenci was born. He had bounced her on his knee. She had grown up with his children. And now, every night he listened to her crying at the thought that she would be forced into the hammock of a grown man.

Slothtail was caught. There was no way he could refuse to give his daughter to the new son-in-law. No Yanomamö man would ever give in to the cries of a little girl and be able to keep any respect from anyone anywhere. And the son-in-law had been paying for her. He *had* to give her.

"Keleewa will interfere and take her away from the man," Slothtail told Catalina.

"He's your friend," Catalina answered. "You grew up with him. You'll figure out how to handle him."

"We'll wait until Keleewa's out of the village," Slothtail said. "He'll never know."

So the next time Keleewa was away, they told the old man to come and get the girl. Falenci screamed that evening when the man came to Slothtail's house to take her away. Just like Hairy's wife and Toucan's wife and almost all other wives, she was terrified. But she knew that her screams weren't going to help. She had no power to do anything except face what was ahead for her. She went with him. She cried. But there was nothing to be gained by struggling.

Because the old man was related to Fruitman, he always hung his hammock in Fruitman's house when he visited. So the whole village knew right where Falenci was and just what was happening.

That time can be very hard on a village at first. The screaming is so common for the young girls. Even in Honey, with all the separate houses, the sound of Falenci's cries passed out through the palm-leaf roof and carried over the whole village. But everyone knew that after many moons she would learn to like her new life.

Many in Honey wanted to help her, but they didn't want to start a fight. So they lay in their hammocks and listened to the screaming and wished that Keleewa were there to stop it. Finally Keleewa's sister went to Fruitman's house and took the girl away from the old man and gave her back to Slothtail.

But the next night the old man came back to Slothtail's

house and took Falenci again. This time Keleewa was in the village. Everyone knew that he liked Falenci too much to listen to her suffer all night. They were right. As soon as he heard the screaming he got up from his hammock. *I'm sick of talking to these people and then never interfering when they don't listen,* he said to himself. *This time I'm interfering.*

He walked straight to Fruitman's house, grabbed Falenci out of the man's hammock, and took her away. If Keleewa had been a Yanomamö man, there would have been a fight right there.

Keleewa took Falenci to a tiny house that they used when people need to be treated with medicine. Slothtail came running to see what was happening. When he threw the door open and ran in, Keleewa knew he would have to defend his right to interfere.

"Listen to me!" he said to Slothtail. "I gave this girl medicine when she was a baby. I've sat up all night with her when she burned with fever. So I have just as much right to say what happens to her as you do and I'm not going to let you do this to this girl. You don't deserve to be called her father!" Her little private part was covered with blood. The sight of it made them both ashamed. "You don't deserve to have a nice little girl like this. She's a real person. How would you like it if this happened to you?"

"I know it's wrong," Slothtail said, "I know it's wrong. I know you've been right from the beginning. I know it. You know that I know it's been wrong—what I've done to her." He wanted to cry. "But Keleewa, it's only in this one thing that I'm wrong. Only this thing. Can't I be wrong in just one thing? I do right in everything else! There is no way I can keep peace with Fruitman and his family if I don't do this."

Keleewa just looked at him. "Your family's connection with Fruitman means everything to you and Catalina right now, doesn't it?" Slothtail nodded. "So even though you're right about everything else, on this one thing which you say is the most important, you are willing to do wrong?"

"I'm only doing wrong in just this one little thing," Slothtail answered. "Just this one time."

Keleewa was silent for a little. Then he said, "Does Falenci think this is a *little* thing?" There was more silence. Keleewa handed her back to Slothtail and he noticed the blood from her bottom on Keleewa's arm.

"Every time a Yanomamö kills for revenge," Keleewa said, "it's just one thing, just one time." He walked out.

Slothtail carried Falenci back home. He knew she would never understand how much shame he felt.

Fruitman was furious. He and his father, Spear, and the whole family were humiliated that they could not get even one little girl from Slothtail for their relative at Mouth. They traveled downriver to Mouth and complained bitterly.

"The nabas of Honey have interfered and kept us from getting the girl we want," Fruitman told their relative who had tried to get Falenci. All the people of Mouth were glad to see Fruitman and Spear side with them against Honey.

"Let's go raid them and steal the girl." They all agreed. "We'll take some other women while we're there too. They have a lot of healthy young women." But Fruitman wasn't sure that he wanted to go against his own village.

Not long after, Fruitman was invited to eat dinner with a small bunch of nabas in their house on the Orinoco. It was a great honor. Nabas never invite Yanomamö into their homes, especially not to eat around their table. So Fruitman felt the power of being a very important person as he walked, just like a naba, into their home and sat down to dinner.

He was greeted kindly by A.H. and Irritating-Bee and another naba he didn't know. Like all of us Yanomamö, Fruitman knew all about A.H. and Irritating-Bee. We call them antros—people who watch us, make marks on paper, take pictures and are thought to know a lot of things in the white world. We think that antros have become well known from the books they have written about us. They were liked by some Indians, but Fruitman knew that most of us despised them.

Fruitman ate and drank all he wanted of food and importance. "Have you had all you want to eat?" the smart nabas asked when they were through. Fruitman nodded.

"Do you like our naba food?" they asked. He nodded. They knew we all loved naba food.

"Your ancestors didn't eat like this, did they?" Fruitman shook his head. So then they got to the reason they wanted to talk to Fruitman.

"We know you love your people and your ancestors. So why have you stopped being like them? You're a Yanomamö.

Why don't you quit listening to those nabas over in Honey and go back to your old way of doing things? If you have enemies, we'll help you get together with them and you can pound chests and settle your differences the way you always have. Drink bones with them. Do the feasts you have always done, all the things that have always made you so special—the body paint, the chants, the dances, the raids. Go back to being a real Yanomamö the way you always have been."

Fruitman listened to the talk. He hadn't heard talk like this for a long time. It felt good to be thought of as a Yanomamö again, and to sit at dinner with nabas and have them talk so nice about the Yanomamö ways. He hadn't heard such talk since he listened to his shamans. This was the same thing they said: "Go back to the old ways, the old beautiful ways of our people."

And these white nabas who were feeding him were right. Fruitman thought about the problem with Falenci. Falenci's mother, Catalina, was Fruitman's sister. Falenci was Spear's granddaughter. Their family had a right to say who she would marry, and to use clubs to do it if they had to. It was the nabas there who caused that problem. If Keleewa hadn't interfered . . .

Fruitman thought about it.

There were other Yanomamö there at the dinner, friends of the nabas. "We have all the good things from the nabas," they said, "but we still have our old ways too. We still have our spirits and take ebene and steal women and go on raids. These good white people have never asked us to give up these ways. These are the things that make us Yanomamö, and we're not going to give them up."

"How can your village live better if you hold on to your old ways?" Fruitman asked.

"We can have both ways," they answered. "If you hadn't thrown your spirits away, you could be a Yanomamö with us again. You can still be with us again."

Fruitman thought about it for a long time. "I do want to be a Yanomamö again," he said. "I really do. There is a girl right now at Honey that should be given to my relative. And the old man has done all his son-in-law duties. He has earned her for our family. And now the nabas have told her father that he can't force her to go with us."

"See," they said. "That's not the Yanomamö way. Go get her

the way you always have. Don't ever stop being a Yanomamö."

"I know you're right," Fruitman answered. "I shouldn't give up our real ways. How did I ever let things get to the place where we don't even have control over a little tiny girl?"

"Well, go back and settle it the way you always have. Steal her. If they don't like it, you'll just have to bash some heads."

Fruitman went back ready to fight. Spear and the rest of the family agreed with him. Even though Spear had given up his spirits long ago, he was mad enough to try some old ways. And it was just the encouragement that Mouth Village needed. They were still angry over the women they didn't get from the big slaughter at Potato Village, generations before.

When Fruitman got back to Honey, he found even more to fight about. There was another girl that he and his father had planned to get for his brother, Monkeylip. Now she had been given to Trip. Trip had been visiting Honey from Hairy's village. He became a good hunter from spending so much time with Hairy. And he kept coming back to Honey because of a special girl there. He hoped she would notice how good a hunter he really was. When he discovered that she liked him, Trip did many things for her parents to win the right to be their son-in-law.

But Fruitman and Spear had wanted her for Monkeylip since she had been a baby. They had more right to her. They had made arrangements with her parents so that Monkeylip could get her. But the girl didn't want Monkeylip. She liked Trip, and her parents let him have her. She and Trip ran away together and spent some time in Hairy's village.

When Trip came back to Honey with his new wife, Fruitman and Spear were ready to get the girl back. There was a big argument. Monkeylip tried to end it when he said, "If the girl doesn't want me, then I don't want her either."

But Fruitman said, "No, no! We can't do that. What will everyone say about our family if we keep losing every little girl we want even when we have a right to her?"

Hairy just happened to be visiting in Honey at that time. He ended all the talk when he said, "We're going to keep the girl in our village no matter what you do." He meant, *Talk is over; make some noise with something other than your mouth!*

Monkeylip knew that there would be a fight, so he said to Trip, "The girl doesn't want me. You're going to take her even though I want her. Fine. Let's just settle it by exchanging clubs. That way I can at least say that I made you pay a price for the girl."

Trip said, "Good. I'll take a blow for the girl and the rest of our villages won't have to get into the fight." Trip walked to the center of the village, leaned on his club to stick it in the ground, and held his head out to Monkeylip. Monkeylip pulled his club back and brought it down with all his might, thwack! right on the top of Trip's head. Blood poured and Trip staggered. He pulled his club from the ground to take his turn. But Monkeylip refused to hold his head out. He ran back to the women.

Hairy and many of his friends at Honey raged at such cowardice. They all grabbed their clubs. Shoefoot jumped into the middle and yelled, "No clubs! No clubs!"

When they were quiet, the girl's father walked to the middle of the grass and everyone stopped to hear him. Even though he had lived in Honey for a long time, he had never changed from our true way of doing things. He had never listened to the nabas. Of all the people in Honey, I liked him the best. They call him Fierce-One. Very few Yanomamö ever get that name. And he deserved it. Fierce-One was famous for his ability to take a club blow to the head—and to give one.

He said to Fruitman, "This fuss is really just between you and me. It doesn't need to involve anybody else. You are the problem here. You have started this whole thing. I'm happy with Trip. My daughter is happy with Trip. And Monkeylip is satisfied. That just leaves you." Fierce-One stuck his club in the ground. "Here," he said sticking his head out. "Club me. You can club me three times. Then I'll club you three times."

Everyone got real quiet when they heard Fierce-One's talk. Three blows at once; no one ever did that. Fruitman knew it would be foolish to accept such a challenge.

"The naba, Pepe, told me long ago that I have an illness and that I might die if I don't give up fighting," he said. Everyone knew that he could never survive three blows to the head from Fierce-One. So Fruitman turned to another brother, Leadeyes. "You're young and strong. You can take three blows." And he pushed Leadeyes out into the middle toward Fierce-One, who was still holding his head out waiting for anyone with enough courage to club him.

"And when I'm done chasing you into the river," Fierce-One called, still holding his head out, "you'll never come out."

Leadeyes knew he shouldn't. But all the women were calling him and his family cowards. He couldn't get out of it. So he drew his club back. But the people of Honey had no idea how cowardly he was. Leadeyes swung his club from the side and landed a brutal hit just above Fierce-One's ear. It was the most cowardly blow they had ever seen. Club hits must always land on the top of the head. Anyone can kill with a club to the side of the head. Only a coward would club a person in the ear. It was a let's-have-a-war blow.

But Fierce-One didn't move a finger. Blood gushed from the side of his head. Before Leadeyes could pull his club back for another swing, Fierce-One's brother-in-law put a revenge hit on Leadeyes' head. The blow was so fierce that his hardwood club flexed over the top of Leadeyes' head and cut him open from the front of his hair, across the top, and down the back of his head. You could see his head bone.

Leadeyes fell to his knees. He got up. He fell again. He got up again and fell again.

Clubs flew everywhere. Fruitman's family ran. Shoefoot screamed, "No clubs! No clubs! You've already hit them enough! You've made them suffer enough!" Some of Fruitman's family were ready to jump into the river to get away.

Leadeyes finally staggered to his feet. "Get revenge for me!" he yelled at Fruitman. "Get revenge for me! I've been injured!" Fruitman saw the huge lump on the side of Fierce-One's head. But Fierce-One looked like he had only started to take blows. Fruitman knew he couldn't take a blow like that. And he knew that Fierce-One could hit back twice as hard as Leadeyes.

Fruitman silently shook his head. Blood ran down Leadeyes' face and down his back. He was furious. "Get revenge for me!" he screamed. Fruitman couldn't look at it. He just looked down and shook his head.

Leadeyes walked to the river and got into his canoe. His head was still pouring out blood all over him as he paddled out into the river and headed toward Mouth Village. For the rest of the day he would paddle in the hot sun to find someone to help him get vengeance.

THE END: 1982

NOBODY'S THAT STUPID

11

THEY THINK WE'RE ANIMALS

So now you know the story behind the fight that I told you about at the very beginning when I said that a long story goes before every fight. As soon as Leadeyes gets downriver to Mouth Village, they will all come back and settle the problem with clubs, maybe even bows and arrows. And that will be the fight that I told you about at the very beginning. Now I'm ready to tell you the rest of what happened that morning on the Honey grass. And I'm very happy about it. I'm happy because my spirits are happy. My spirits are happy because our old ways of the spirit world will finally meet with the new ways of Honey. But this time it won't be a meeting like we always have at Honey when my spirits get so upset and I get so angry. This meeting will be the way we want—clubs, maybe even bows and arrows. Today is no ordinary Yanomamö war. Today is a war between fighters who want to keep the old ways and peace-lovers who want to end them.

When the Mouth warriors stood in a half moon with clubs ready, it looked like a normal Yanomamö fight over two girls. When Legbone, a fighter with much experience, approached the center and Won't-Grow stepped from the Honey half moon, it looked like ordinary revenge to be fought out. But everyone knew that the need for revenge went back genera-tions, all the way back to the raid on Potato Village when our relatives at Mouth didn't get any of the women.

Deemeoma, now a grandmother, stood with the other old women and watched her son-in-law, Won't-Grow, deliver a quick bunch of bloody blows to the experienced warrior's head. She'd been watching these fights since she was a little girl. She watched Won't-Grow and wondered if this day would bring back all her pain. She was too old now to be able to suffer that kind of pain again. She remembered her mother's body lying in the dirt and her father sitting in his blood. Even in her dreams, she still couldn't reach him through all the arrows.

Tears came.

I could feel in my spirits that there was so much more in this battle. Even though I wasn't there, I could feel it all. It was the old ways against the new. It was our old spirits, the ones Shoefoot had thrown away, against their new one. Mouth Village had many of my spirits. How could our spirits who love to fight ever lose against Honey when their spirit, Yai Pada, doesn't like to fight?

We'd fought before, but not like this. This time Spear and Fruitman and their whole family, who had thrown away our spirits, had returned to the old ways. Only Leadeyes was missing. He was still sick with his injuries from two days before.

Spear stood behind the Mouth warriors with his arms folded over his bow and arrows. He watched everyone on the Honey side, Hairy especially. He knew that Hairy was no peace-lover. He'd kill as soon as he got excited.

Fruitman watched one Mouth warrior after another step forward to meet his relatives and friends from Honey. It was a new thing for him and Spear, siding with the old ways of our spirits at Mouth. But the fight didn't go well for Mouth. They shouldn't have laughed at the little clubs Honey had. Every Honey warrior, Won't-Grow, Bighead, Crossedeye, Toughfoot, and finally Trip, gave out the same quick whap-whap-whap-whap-whap to the Mouth warriors' head before he could get off a good swing with his big club. All their heads were bloody.

But our spirits were interested in more than just beating Honey. More than anything, we wanted to get Honey back to our old ways, to fighting, to drinking bones, to raids. So when Cloudy's son, Legbone, got mad and struck the fierce blow to

Slothtail's mother and laid her scalp open and Slothtail released the arrow, we all knew we were back to our old ways. Nothing would make our spirits dance more.

Slothtail's arrow was gone before anyone could stop it. He had never shot at a person before. But when this arrow left his bow, he knew exactly what it meant. He would kill that coward who hit his mother and throw his village into its first shooting war in his lifetime. And he knew the shot was perfect, headed squarely between the coward's shoulder blades. *We are back to our old ways now and nothing will stop it,* he thought. *A.H. and his friends will get their wish. It's war.*

"Not that! Not with arrows! No arrows! No arrows!" Shoefoot ran to the middle screaming before the arrow found its mark. Even though every shaman was irritated by Shoefoot's enemy spirit, we still knew that Shoefoot himself was our friend, everybody's friend. That's how he got the name No-Trouble in Toucan's village and Doesn't-Grab-Women in Shortman's village. And this day, though he had the weapons in hand to protect his family, he stood, arms stretched out, screaming for peace.

Fruitman knew that Slothtail's arrow meant he was in a shooting war with his closest friends. He wondered if he should have listened to A.H. and all the naba-talk.

But then the strangest thing happened that I have ever known. I know my spirits never would have caused it. Behind Legbone another Mouth warrior moved in and drew back his club as Slothtail's arrow flew. On its path, the club and the arrow met. The poisoned point hit the center of the club and splintered into pieces. It saved Legbone from certain death.

Suddenly every club disappeared and everyone had bows drawn.

At the center of the warriors, Shoefoot jumped and screamed. "Not that! No arrows!" he yelled over and over. His own hand held a bow and arrows, but they weren't in a shooting position. No one ever knew how he got them so fast.

Honey had many more warriors. A slaughter would be simple. And the Honey warriors wanted to do it. Only Shoefoot in the center stopped his people from filling the air with arrows.

"Go ahead! You cowards!" one of the young warriors from Mouth yelled. "Why don't you go ahead and kill us? Your women will burn some of you too. We'll make sure of that!"

He was right. But every warrior in Honey was willing to pay the price of a few dead to see Mouth completely wiped out.

With his screaming, Shoefoot was able to keep the Mouth warriors from shooting. Slowly the Mouth warriors backed toward the river with bows drawn. Their anger had been satisfied a little by the blow to Slothtail's mother. Maybe she would die. That would start a war for sure. The Honey anger had been satisfied a little when Slothtail showed them that Honey could kill too.

On the river they were loud and all talked at once.

"Wait till next time."

"They had spirit powder on their clubs."

"I wasn't afraid. Why didn't you hit them harder?"

"I would have done better, but the man who hit me had a powerful spirit."

Fruitman and Spear were quiet. They never meant for anyone to be killed. Fruitman wondered if he really wanted the old ways back. But the old ways were the only way he knew to get the women he wanted for his family.

"What shall we do now, Fruitman?" Someone woke him from his thoughts.

Fruitman shook his head. "I'll talk to the nabas again— A.H. and the other antros. They are the ones who have told us that the old ways are good. They must know how to keep Keleewa from getting in the middle and making trouble. Maybe they have more experience in these ways."

In Honey, Keleewa and his sisters took care of Slothtail's mother. All the women gathered around and began to wail.

"She's dying for sure."

"It was an awful blow."

"No one can survive that."

They wailed things that made her think she was dead even if she wasn't. Keleewa and his sisters could see that she wasn't going to die. They sewed her scalp back together.

A few days later the entire jungle talked about only one thing: the government plane was coming to Honey to take Keleewa to jail for murder. At first no one knew why. But then we learned that it was because of a story Fruitman had told them. A few seasons before, Keleewa had taken Fruitman's son to the doctors in the big naba villages. They were not able to help him and the boy had died. Now Fruitman was using this story to get revenge on Honey. Every Yanomamö was mad that they could do this to our Keleewa.

Even though my spirits had no comfort with Keleewa's spirit, I always knew that he was my friend. So we Indians asked ourselves, "Are the nabas crazy?" We knew that Keleewa had never killed anyone. Who would even say it?

But we also knew that the nabas were crazy. Hadn't we seen them for many seasons come into our land and just when we thought they were very smart and could teach us things, they started to copy us?

When government planes came into our land, they stopped at the Ocamo for fuel because there is a big field for landing the big planes. Tigerlip's village is right next to the big field.

When Tigerlip learned the news, he said to his people, "Keleewa has been a big help to us for all his life. We're not going to let them take him away. When the nabas land, we will ambush the airstrip, kill the guards, and take Keleewa. Then we'll take our village on wyumi and disappear with him into the jungle. They'll never find us."

Tigerlip and his warriors each found a hiding place at the edge of the jungle. They knew the spot where the plane would stop.

The whole village wailed when the guards came to Honey and took Keleewa away in their plane. The nabas said, "He'll come back, we think."

When the plane lifted from Honey, Tigerlip had his warriors ready at Ocamo. But this time the government plane turned the other way and didn't go to Ocamo. It took Keleewa straight to the big naba village. Tigerlip's village was sad that they were not able to rescue him.

Keleewa was in the naba's jail for many days and became very sick there. Because nabas can't talk Yanomamö, it took them a long time to learn from us that he was our friend and not a killer. When he finally came back to Honey, there was a great feast.

Hairy walked down to the bank of Blood River when he heard the motor. We call it Blood River because it is always so full of red dirt that it looks like the piranha are eating something. It was Keleewa, coming to see the new place that Hairy had chosen to move his village. They wanted to be closer to Honey. *This would be a good place,* Hairy thought. *The people from Honey can come all the way here by river. Now they will visit much more often.*

He stood on the bank thinking, knowing this would make things better. *It was wrong to kill that girl. I'm the one who has robbed my own sleep.* He shook his head. *She was a nice person; she just didn't like me. It wasn't her fault that she didn't like me.* He could still see the look on Yellowflower's face, her head pinned back against the ground as he squatted with one foot on each end of the stick that went across her neck. He had seen her face to face then, and he saw her now just as clearly, even though it had happened more than a generation ago.

Keleewa's canoe pulled up to the shore and they were excited to see each other. Trip came too. He never missed a chance to visit his home people. With Trip and Keleewa was a white naba they had named Doesn't-Miss after he shot a goose and some monkeys on the way to Hairy's village. They hung their hammocks in the lean-to shelter next to Hairy and the naba began to ask many strange questions.

Hairy had not seen many nabas, and almost none of them could talk. So every time the man talked, Keleewa would have to tell Hairy what the naba said. Then he would have to tell Doesn't-Miss what Hairy said back. So it took a long time to talk like that.

"The naba wants to know why you want to change the way you live out here in the jungle," Keleewa said to Hairy after Doesn't-Miss talked.

Hairy was surprised at the question. "Because we're miserable out here. We are miserable all the time. The people from Honey came here and made peace with us many seasons ago and their village keeps getting better. We want that for us. If it means throwing spirits away and taking new ones, we will do it. But we need someone to teach us these new ways."

Hairy didn't have spirits because he was not a shaman. But he followed everything the spirits told his shaman. I knew my spirits would be very irritated if Hairy quit following the spirits. No one who has killed as often and as long as Hairy could ever stop it.

"The naba says that many people think you don't really want someone to teach you new ways," Keleewa said. "You just want the trade goods that rich nabas bring."

"If you think that, then just send Indians to teach us," Hairy answered. "We don't want just *any* naba for his trade goods. Some nabas are no good at all. Tell him, Keleewa, what happened in my cousin's village up the Ocamo."

Keleewa told the story; everyone knows it. Hairy's cousin, Wabu, lives far up the Ocamo beyond Tigerlip's village. They wanted a naba to come to their village to teach them new ways. So they were excited when one came to visit.

"I'll come back to live with you and help you if you will build me a house to live in," the new naba told them. At last their dream of a naba would come true, someone to supply all the things they needed so bad. They built him a nice palm-leaf house just outside the shabono. And the naba spoke the truth; he did come back.

But when he got to the village his boat was almost empty. Everyone was disappointed. "What good is it to have him here if he has nothing we need?" one of the men asked Wabu.

"It might take him time to get his other things here," Wabu said. "Don't worry. They will come on another boat." But the other boat never came.

When the naba left to go downriver, Wabu told his people that this time he would certainly come back with his things. But the next time they saw him, he had nothing. "Next time he'll bring his things," Wabu said. "He has to have other things. And we'll be able to work for them."

Each time he came back, the village came to the river to see what he had brought. Each time they were disappointed. The women complained bitterly. "How will we ever get the medicine we need for our children if he never brings anything? All he ever brings is that stuff that nabas use to make marks on. What use is that?"

But what got the women real mad was that whenever their children got sick, the naba only watched the shaman work on the child. He never helped. He just stood there and watched, and made marks on his paper.

One child got worse and worse and still he never helped. Finally the child died. But he just stood around watching everyone wail with grief. And he made marks.

It wasn't long before everyone in the village was in agreement; he was useless. So the village leaders stopped protecting his house while he was away. Wabu and his friends got into the house and ate the naba's food.

When the white man came back, he went red with anger. He screamed at everyone in the village. But when he left, Wabu and his friends enjoyed his food again. They thought it would be the only thing they would ever get from this naba. Again he got red with rage and screamed at everyone in the village.

Wabu and his friends kept showing generosity to each other with the naba's food every time he was away. Finally the naba said that something terrible would happen to the people who kept stealing his food. Wabu was afraid and stayed away from the naba's house. But one of his friends refused.

"If this naba is going to live in our village and not help us, I am going to make it so hard for him that he will just leave," the boy told everyone. And he kept up his feeding habit until the naba found out who it was.

The naba got real mad. He screamed at Wabu's friend, who just lay in his hammock laughing. The laughter only made it worse.

"If you break into my house one more time you will die," the naba screamed, with veins showing on his neck. The threat worried the whole village. They decided that the best plan was to move the whole village away and leave the naba by himself. They warned the boy never to go near the naba's house again.

"If this naba is going to live in this village and never do us any good," the boy told them, "I will irritate him until he leaves. Why should *we* have to leave?"

"We have no idea how powerful his relatives might be," the village leader said. "How can you keep irritating him?"

One evening while the naba was away, the quiet was broken by screams outside the shabono. All the warriors grabbed their bows and arrows and ran out the opening, expecting to face a raiding party. There outside of the naba's house was Wabu's friend on the ground, wiggling and screaming, "He killed me! Mama, he killed me! The naba killed me! He used his magic to poison me!" He had broken into the naba's house again and eaten his food. This time, though, the naba had been ready for him.

There was nothing the shaman could do for him. He screamed for a little while and died. Wabu and his relatives burned the body, grieved, and waited for the naba to return. But he never did.

When Hairy saw that Keleewa was finished telling the story, he explained again. "We don't just want *any* naba. We need to be taught new ways. We want the kind of change that has happened at Honey."

Doesn't-Miss talked with Keleewa for a while. Keleewa paused and thought how to say what the naba said. Then he told Hairy, "He says there are many people in his land that don't think that he, or any of us, should be here helping you at all. They say that you're happy here and that we should leave you alone. He wants to know what an experienced killer like you would say to them."

Hairy grew even more serious. "I say to you, please don't listen to the people who say that. We need help so bad. We are so miserable here and our misery never stops. Night and day it goes on. Do those people think we don't suffer pain when the bugs bite us? If they think this is such a happy place out here in the jungle, why aren't they moving out here to enjoy this beautiful life with us?"

Doesn't-Miss was quiet. Then he got out of his hammock and walked down the trail to the canoe to get some of his things. When he was too far away to hear, Hairy said to Keleewa, "Is he stupid? Doesn't he have eyes? Can't he see these lean-tos we call houses? Can't he see us roam the jungle everyday, searching for food that isn't here, so we can starve slower? Can't he see that our village is almost gone, that this move we are making now is our last hope to stay alive?"

Keleewa was slow to answer. He knew Hairy wouldn't understand what he was about to say.

"Most nabas think just like him," Keleewa told Hairy, and shook his head because he knew he couldn't explain why.

"Nobody's that stupid," Hairy snapped. He was quiet for a while. "They must hate us. They think we're animals."

Keleewa didn't know what to say. They lay back on their hammocks in silence. So no one saw a tear come to Keleewa's eye. Maybe he should have kept the naba's words hidden from Hairy.

12

WHY DON'T YOU LEAVE?

Deemeoma's granddaughter is getting bigger and the children tease her about her black face. I trained Fredi to be a shaman and he lives in Forgetful Village. Hairy's village is settled at their new place. Fruitman and Spear have decided that they were tricked by A.H. and the other nabas. They broke with Mouth Village and went back to their relatives and friends in Honey. They were welcomed without even a fight.

One of my children died this season. It is a horrible time for me, as bad as when one of my wives died. She died a long time ago and I never told you because it always makes me so sad to say it. At that time we went to Honey to mourn with Shoefoot. Now we visit more often because there is so little left of my family.

I am very angry with my spirits over this. "Why have you not helped me more?" I often say to Jaguar while I lie in my hammock and watch the only wife I have left go about her work. "Just look around here. We have nothing. Our huge village is now so little that there's just me and my son and our wives. And what use is my son? He's got that worthless spirit from the deer. If anyone comes to the village, my son leaves for days. My heart feels nice for my son. I will mourn hard when he dies. But what will I lose? He is useless."

"We've done our best for you. Please don't throw us away, Father," Jaguar Spirit always answers me. That is all my spirits ever *do when I complain. They beg me not to throw them away. While they beg, I turn my attention to Charming. After all these seasons she is not even a little bit older. She is as young and beautiful as that first day she came to me. But I'm old now, and what good has this most beautiful woman done for me? "Don't throw them away," she begs. "I'll talk to them and find out why things have not gone right." She talks to them but nothing gets any better, and I'm still stuck with almost no family left and a son with a horrible spirit. I am upset almost all the time now.*

As the seasons go by, antros write more books about our people and now even more nabas come. Some of our people who have been to naba villages say that nabas sell pictures of our naked women. All our women who are rich enough wear clothes. But the nabas only buy the pictures of women without clothes.

Many moons later, Fruitman went up the Orinoco River to Mavaca. He was met there by Cesar, a Yanomamö Indian with much voice in the outside world.

"Why are you people over in Honey always so different from the rest of us?" Cesar asked.

"We want to be," Fruitman answered. "Why shouldn't we be different if we want to be?"

"Because you aren't Yanomamö any more, that's why," Cesar snapped back. "The old ways are good. We have learned so much from all the nabas that come through here and we still don't have to give up any of our old ways. Their ways go with our old ways very well."

"How?" Fruitman wondered.

"The drink in the cans," Cesar said. "It makes us happy just like the ebene used to. Some shamans even use it. And look at all the shotguns we have. It takes a great hunter to kill people with a bow and arrows, but with these naba weapons, any fool can kill. If your village joined us on a raid, we could wipe out anyone. Come on over here sometime with your relatives from Honey and we'll have a feast and drink bones and paint up and go steal some women. It will be a great time, and I just know that all of your relatives here will be so glad to see you back."

Fruitman looked at Cesar. This was the same talk he had heard from A.H. and the other nabas, the same talk he used to hear from his father, Spear, and the other great shamans before they threw their spirits away. *This man is really going to mess me up*, Fruitman thought. He would never forget the fight that had started over Falenci and Trip's girl and how close they came to war.

"Look around you at your village," Fruitman said to Cesar. "How do you like the way it looks?" Cesar looked at the jungle crowding in around the houses. And all the garbage that was mostly covered by creeping vines. Babies crawled in the dirt, rubbed it in their eyes and mouth. Then the dirt mixed with that stuff from their noses and the mixture covered their faces.

"How can you say that we live in misery because of what we have learned from the nabas?" Fruitman went on. "Use your eyes, Cesar. We aren't the ones who are in misery. You talk about all you have learned from the nabas, but what have you got to show for it? You're living out here just like animals. It's the same miserable life we used to live when we were out in the jungle on wyumi."

Fruitman traveled back down the Orinoco and turned up the Padamo toward Honey. The water was high and he stayed close to the side to stay away from the current. He couldn't stop thinking about the nabas who wanted him to keep the old ways. *They seem to like our ways as much as we do*, he thought, *maybe better. When they visit, we look at them and want to become like them. But after they spend a little time with us, they become just like us. Worse. I can understand wanting to chew our tobacco, but why would any smart person want to take his clothes off—to copy us?*

Halfway to home he rounded another bend and the sun danced on the water in front of the canoe. He remembered the time his mother, Noisy Privates, went to visit Tigerlip's village. She was met outside the village by the antros. "We are filming the Yanomamö with our cameras," they said, "and you have to take your clothes off so you will look like a real Indian." All around her people were dropping their pants and skirts because the nabas said to. She walked in with all her clothes on and they got mad.

Fruitman steered his dugout around a sharp bend. The overhanging jungle glided past. Thick foliage in front of him reminded him of the spirits he used to follow when he lived deep in the jungle. *Why*, he asked himself, *do the nabas, who can hardly talk and don't even know the spirits, say the same thing that the spirits say? Sometimes they even use the same words.*

Fruitman was thinking about Longbeard when his canoe came into the bank at Honey. Longbeard was a naba who lived in a far away village. He helped the people there and said he would teach them better ways and things about the great spirit. While he was there he decided to take a young girl for a wife. She didn't want him, but after he gave her parents gifts they forced her to go with him.

After a while she got used to him, like they all do. But every time he mistreated her, she ran home to her mother. Then he'd come and get her back and the whole problem would start all over again.

One time she struggled real hard and Longbeard was not able to overpower her. The village gathered around and laughed at him because he wasn't strong enough to control a girl. When she got away from him and began to run, he swung at her with his machete to stop her. But it hit her in the back of the neck and she fell down gushing blood. Longbeard moved to help her, but her relatives filled him full of arrows. He fell, but his body never touched the ground, held up by the arrows sticking out of him.

Fruitman looked around at Honey as he walked into the village. *Go back to the old way?* he thought. *I'll never make that mistake again.*

Each time I went with my wife to visit Shoefoot, we passed Forgetful Village where Fredi lived. One of my old friends named Hot lived there. He had helped capture Fredi and had defended him to keep him alive. He and his wife had a beautiful little girl. Even the nabas always noticed how pretty Yawalama was. When they visited Honey, she bounced on Keleewa's knee and he talked about her big, pretty eyes. When my friend promised to give her to Longfoot, her older brother, Raul, got angry.

"You can't!" Raul said to his parents. "He beats the wife he has. Do you want to see Yawalama abused the way he abuses his wife, Yoshicami?" Raul loved his beautiful little sister.

"He is a great hunter and provider. We must have the meat he can hunt in our old age," they told him.

"I'll hunt for you," he argued. "Yawalama will never want him when she grows up. No one wants him. He's so mean.

You have to wait until someone else comes along for her." The shabono was small. Everyone knew of the argument. The village didn't want to see Yawalama suffer.

Raul was sad when his parents began to take meat from Longfoot in exchange for the right to have her in marriage after she grew up. Raul became bitter. He did not plan to ever let his sister be taken by Longfoot.

Then Yoshicami became very sick. They called me, but even my spirits were not able to do anything to make her well. By this time I was old and not doing much healing any more. So they called Yawalama's father, Hot, who was a shaman. But his spirits were no help, either.

So Longfoot took Yoshicami to Honey. When they got there she was coughing blood. The nabas there told her that she might have a bad sickness that they called *teebee,* and they would have to take her on the long trip to the village of the nabas for treatment.

So Longfoot went with Yoshicami to the white people's village at Esmeralda and stayed there while their doctors worked on her. But she was slow to get well and Longfoot became impatient and told the doctors to let her go home. When they got back to Honey, the naba-doctor made the white people there explain to them that she must finish her medicine or the disease would kill her. Longfoot decided to stay in Honey with her until she finished taking all the medicine.

But it took a long time and Yoshicami didn't get better. She often coughed blood and looked as if she might die. Longfoot didn't think she would ever get well. One day in anger he said, "Why don't you just hurry up and die? Let's get this over with."

"Please don't say that," Yoshicami pleaded. "I need you more than ever now. And the two children. Look at this nice place that Shoefoot's brother has given us to stay in. Please don't talk like that." But she wasn't getting better. She looked awful. *I'll never get any more sex out of her,* Longfoot kept telling himself. Our relatives in Honey liked Yoshicami and encouraged Longfoot to stay, but he just got madder.

"Go on and die so I can get back to my village," he told her every day.

"Your wife is very sick," Shoefoot said to Longfoot. "She has been a good wife to you. It isn't right for you to leave her now when she needs you the most. You know what the right thing is. You have to feed your wife and children." The whole village agreed with Shoefoot, and every day the women came to look after Yoshicami and scold Longfoot.

Then word came from upriver in Forgetful Village that Yawalama had finished her woman rites. Longfoot looked at Yoshicami dying in her hammock. He knew he wouldn't get any more out of her. And now Yawalama was ripe and ready. He couldn't wait.

"I'm leaving," he said with all her relatives and friends listening. "I can't wait around here for you to die."

"What about our two children here?" she begged from her hammock, her fingers running through the hungry child's hair. "They need to eat too. You should be out catching some fish for us to eat instead of just standing around here telling me to die." He said nothing.

"How can you leave us here with nothing? The children are meat-hungry already. We'll starve." But he wouldn't answer.

"I know what you want. But I can't give it to you until I'm better, and I can't get better unless you help me."

Shoefoot and the rest of the village gathered around and encouraged Longfoot to have kindness on her and stay. But he wouldn't talk. He untied his hammock, gathered his things, and walked out the door.

All the villagers of Honey showed kindness to Yoshicami and her children in their hard time. She was Shoefoot's sister-cousin and related to many people in Honey. They shared their meat, and Shoefoot's sister-in-law cooked for her and the children. Yoshicami felt good that so many people cared for her. It helped to take away the pain of not having a husband who would meet her needs and protect her. Many times they thought she would die. But after a long time she got stronger and became healthy and pretty again.

One day a young man of the village, Redhair, came into the little house where she stayed. He had some fresh meat for the children. It was her favorite, wild turkey.

"Here. Take it," he said. "It's for the children. And for you." Yoshicami knew that this wasn't food that had been provided by her relatives. Their food was always brought by the women. Redhair turned and left before she could say anything. It felt strange to have someone really care enough to go on a good hunt and bring a fresh turkey. Just for me, she thought. As nice as it was to have the whole village taking care of her, knowing that there was one person who would do this made her feel even better. She had seen him before, but now he looked so wonderful. He was young, just starting out, but . . .

Her mind was full of kind thoughts as she put the turkey over the fire and blew smoke out of her eyes. They watered. Maybe from the smoke. But she thought maybe it was from her happiness. Her heart felt happier than it ever had as she watched the turkey cook. Maybe she would go to his hammock tonight. When the meat was cooked, she took a big bite and gave some to both of her little children. The three of them ate the whole turkey and it felt so good to be full.

She kept talking to herself. *But girls in Honey are so different. They don't just go to other men's hammocks unless they know he wants them for a wife. And even more surprising is that the men don't force them into their hammocks. When they do, they get in trouble from the other men. What a wonderful place this is. How can it be . . . ?*

The next day Redhair came with yucca from the garden and asked if she would like to go with him to help dig some more. She didn't answer; she didn't say anything. But when he left she followed him, and the children behind her. The four of them, one behind the other, walked through the village and across the airstrip to the garden. She saw that some of the villagers noticed her. If one person saw, everyone would know.

If only Longfoot could see this, he would know that I really am worth taking care of, Yoshicami thought. She wondered if Redhair would take her into the jungle. *He certainly deserves it,* she thought. *He brought me meat yesterday.* She watched his back as they walked across the field toward the garden. He was strong even though he was so young, and being with him made her feel safe.

On the way back from the garden Yoshicami was mixed up. Of course she didn't want him to take her into the jungle, but now she was disappointed that he hadn't. *Maybe he's not a complete man yet,* she wondered. *I'm a woman. Now that I'm not so weak with sickness, I could go to his hammock. Maybe tonight.*

By the time they returned to the village everyone knew that she had spent the afternoon working with Redhair. It had been many moons since they had seen her look so healthy. She grated the yucca, squeezed the poisonous juice out, and put it out to dry. Suddenly she was very tired and collapsed in her hammock.

Late that night she got up to stir the fire. Everyone was asleep. She slipped out the door and walked quietly over to Redhair's little leaf house. A dog stirred but didn't bark, and Redhair didn't even wake when she stepped through his door. When she got into his hammock, she knew what to do. She felt as if she had come alive again.

The next morning Redhair and Yoshicami were gone. They stayed out in the jungle for many days, long enough for Redhair to prove that she was really his. Yoshicami's parents and the people of Honey took care of her children while they were gone.

Soon word got to Longfoot in Forgetful Village that Yoshicami didn't die like he told her to. He heard she was so healthy that she had a man. So he came back in jealousy to take her back.

But she wouldn't go with him. And Redhair and his friends wouldn't let him take her by force. He went home in a rage.

Two days later, Longfoot came back with some warriors and threatened war on Honey if they didn't give Yoshicami back to him.

"She has a lot of medicine to finish," Shoefoot said. "After she is completely healthy, we will let her decide where she wants to live." When Forgetful Village heard that she needed more medicine, they went home. But Longfoot kept coming, trying to get her back. A few moons later, when her medicine was finished, he came with his warriors for a fight. On the grassy place between the houses, they were met by the Honey warriors.

"You are not going to have a fight here." Shoefoot stood in their path at the village center. He was joined by Fruitman and the other leaders of Honey. "We can call the government guards from Tama Tama to come up here and settle this matter. It's nothing to fight over."

Again Forgetful Village was satisfied, and the guards were called. Two days later, three guards in soldier's jungle clothes tied their boats at the Honey riverbank. Each one carried a big army rifle. With their guns in an open village, they had all the respect. But in the jungle, they would be no match for us.

Everyone gathered in the big building that they call church. Longfoot and the warriors from Forgetful Village were there. One of the guards told them that Yoshicami was a Venezuelan citizen and she could do what she wanted. He looked straight at her. "Tell us all now. Do you want to go back and live with your husband?"

"He's not my husband because I never wanted him," Yoshicami started quietly. "He's only my husband because my parents forced me to his hammock when I was a little girl. But I was willing to live with him even though he was so cruel. I had no choice. But then I got sick and almost died. And as soon as he heard that his next wife, Yawalama, was grown, he told me to go ahead and die and went away and left me with two small children to feed. No woman wants a husband like that.

"Then a long time later, when he heard I was healthy again, he came running back here to get me. I don't want him—none of him. I've found a good man here who wants me, and I'm his wife now."

The guards looked at Longfoot. "She has the right to do what she wants. We sure aren't going to force her to go back if she doesn't want to. That's Venezuelan law. She is free."

The guards took an angry crowd of Forgetful warriors back to their canoes. There was little they could say or do while the guards were there. But they would never let it stop with this humiliation.

Yoshicami was happy to stay in Honey and live with Red-hair.

Two days later, in the stillness before dawn, Yoshicami was wakened by a violent jerk on her arm that pulled her from her hammock into the dirt. She screamed. Ten men dragged her through the mud-wall doorway while Redhair fought with a few of them. Because he was sick with malaria, he couldn't give them much of a fight.

When the people of Honey heard the noise they were out of their houses, watching her struggle against Longfoot and his warriors. But no one wanted to get in the fight. Redhair didn't have a chance. Yoshicami's clothes were ripped off in the struggle and they dragged her down the airstrip toward the riverbank. Her brother ran along behind, trying to cover her nakedness with a pair of pants as she struggled to get loose. He failed.

Finally one of Redhair's friends jumped in to help him, but they still couldn't wrestle Yoshicami away. Then another joined, and another. Soon it was hard for the men to keep dragging her toward their canoe.

The rest of the village watched, still not willing to get in the fight. Redhair's friends couldn't get her loose, but they did stop them from moving closer to the river. The Forgetful Village warriors knew that she had been with Redhair long enough that she would be carrying a baby. So they knocked her to the ground in the middle of the mob and stamped on her stomach, trying to kill her baby. But they couldn't get her to the river.

"They're not going to give her up!" one of the enemy shouted. "Let's cut her." He began pushing the men away so he could get a good swing at her with his machete.

Until this time Pepe watched. He hated these fights. He wanted to stop them, but he couldn't without getting in the middle of the trouble. "No, no!" he shouted, jumping in and grabbing the man's arm. "Don't use a machete on her." Pepe never has hit a Yanomamö, but he will try to stop a killing. And he has grown very tired of fixing chopped knees.

The warrior pushed Pepe away. The push made Pepe slip on the wet morning grass and fall backward on his rear. When the people of Honey saw Pepe fall, their anger stormed. The whole village leaped at the warriors, like a jaguar all over a helpless turkey. Each of the enemy was grabbed and held by three or four warriors from Honey.

"No! No!" one Forgetful warrior yelled. "Don't all of you get in this!"

"It's too late for that now," Fruitman yelled back. "You knocked down our naba."

"We ought to bust your heads open right now!" Slothtail yelled.

But Shoefoot called out, "No, no! We've made our point." The whole village took Longfoot and his friends down to the riverbank and sent them home with empty hands. The women took Yoshicami, put the pants on her, and helped her to Pepe's house.

THE END

When Forgetful Village saw that Honey would not let them do anything they wanted with their women, they went over to the Orinoco to see Cesar. Because he was Yanomamö and had a little learning, the Venezuelan government had given him the work of keeping peace in Yanomamö jungles. Cesar decided to go to Honey and settle the matter.

News that Cesar was traveling to Honey to make peace passed to all the villages within a few-day walk. Everyone knew that Cesar's peacemaking would make a fight no one wanted to miss. Tigerlip's people came from the Ocamo. Mouth Village came. These bitter enemies from the past had now made peace with Honey.

Cesar's speedboat landed at Honey to the biggest gathering of Yanomamö he had ever seen. A naba-doctor we call Bearded-One came from Los Esmeralda. Even he expected trouble. He brought his camera.

The crowd was quiet, but very excited as they watched Cesar get out and tie his boat. Then an old woman called out to him, "Who are you to come here and solve our problems? We all know you're the biggest reason for fighting in our land."

"What about that girl you raped?" another yelled, before Cesar had even walked up the bank. "Did you ever punish yourself for that?"

"And when her father shot you in the chest, did he get in trouble for it?" another woman yelled.

"You're lucky he used a reloaded shell or you wouldn't be here, would you, Cesar?" *How could they possibly have known about that shell?* Cesar wondered.

"That's right. That whole war was the old father's fault, wasn't it? You sure helped bring peace to them, didn't you?"

When Yanomamö women get mad, they change. They suddenly know every story. They respect no one. And they forget nothing. You hear terrible things that you forgot long ago, and details you thought no one could ever know. And they have no need to exaggerate.

Cesar pretended not to notice, but he heard every word. He couldn't have known until this moment that his own people felt so hard about his behavior. *Why should they be so mad at me,* he thought. *I don't act any different from any other Yanomamö.*

The women kept on Cesar all the way across the village.

And the naba with him, Bearded-One—they would have loved to do some yelling at him. He had once given medicine to a Yanomamö woman and then asked her to pay for it with sex. She said no. So he wouldn't give her any more and she died. It was the perfect story for a time like this because only the women knew exactly how Bearded-One had tried to get sex from the woman; they might have even known something about his private part. But he was a naba . . .

So they kept yelling at Cesar. "What about that new wife you just raped a few days ago?" someone asked. Cesar smiled a little but didn't turn his head. *How did a story as unimportant as that get all the way over here so fast?* he wondered. He wouldn't forget her. She was young and very pretty—smart too, which really made her special. He had watched her leave his village with her new husband to go fishing. He had gotten three of his friends and followed. They had taken turns raping her while the others held her husband down.

"Don't look so surprised," a woman yelled. "We know all about it, and we know all about you."

"Yes. Why don't you call the guards? We'll tell them about you and your peacemaking! When it comes to crime, you are the best. This problem is nothing compared to what you do. Go on. Call the guards up here."

Tigerlip's wife had a lot to yell at Bearded-One, but she was afraid to. She remembered the time in her village when she had been shot by a poisoned arrow. When Bearded-One couldn't remove the point, the whole village wanted him to take her in the government plane to get it removed. After a long argument, Bearded-One had said, "That woman isn't worth the $200 it will cost to fly her out." He had said it using naba words, but everyone understood. If he weren't a naba, he would have been surprised at all he would have heard that morning.

By the time they reached the church, the biggest gathering of Yanomamö anyone could remember had heard a vicious telling of almost everything Cesar had done. He knew that it would be hard to send the girl back with all this anger. There were hundreds of Indians pressing around him and all agreeing with Honey.

The building was packed with angry people when Cesar finally got them all to listen. "The guards were here a few days ago. What did they say?" he asked.

"They said she can live wherever she wants," a few people answered together.

"Well, that's right," Cesar said and looked relieved that he could agree with the angry crowd. "I'm only here to tell you what the government says. I'm not here to start any trouble with you people here at Honey. The guards are right. She can live wherever she wants. As a Venezuelan, that is her right."

It was just what everyone wanted to hear. No one was happier than Yoshicami. She stood in the center of the building surrounded by protectors from her new village. They had given her life back to her when everyone expected her to die. So they thought of her as a part of them. Her brother-cousin, Shoefoot, and others stood close around her. All her beauty had come back to her full round face. Everyone could see the wonderful feeling in her big, brown eyes and it made them happy.

Cesar turned to Yoshicami. "Tell us where you want to live," he said. It was a wonderful chance for her to speak her own thoughts and tell everyone. For the first time in her life she felt the power to do whatever she chose. And so many warriors around her to help her. What a feeling, to be loved and wanted! She had never known a feeling like it. Cesar had no power to make her go, even if he wanted to. And she knew it.

"I will never go back to him," she called out, "no matter what anyone does or says. Even if you could force me to go back to Forgetful Village, I will never go back to Longfoot. Never."

Cesar turned to Yoshicami's father and the group from Forgetful Village. "This is not exactly what you told me she would say. Why did I come all the way over here? To go against the guards and make her live where she doesn't want and sleep with a man she doesn't want?" He turned to Yoshicami with a look of relief. "The guards are right. It is your right to live wherever you want and with whoever you want."

Bearded-One, the doctor from Esmeralda, had come out of curiosity like all the others. He waved Cesar to come outside for a talk. It was over, and because Forgetful Village was so small, they probably wouldn't start a fight now. But everyone watched and wondered as Cesar went outside with

Bearded-One. Shortman followed them because he is Cesar's brother-cousin.

"You can't interfere with these people like this," Bearded-One told Cesar when they were outside the building and away from the crowd. "She is a Yanomamö woman and doesn't have any rights. Her only right is to do what her husband tells her. You and your people are Yanomamö and you always will be. You have always settled your problems your own way, with clubs and arrows. And you have no right to change that with all this 'Venezuelan government' talk."

Cesar knew that Bearded-One had great influence with the government and over the people who gave Cesar his money. Bearded-One could see Cesar thinking. "Now you go back in there and tell that girl that she must do what any Yanomamö woman must do—go home with her husband. This is the chance you've been waiting for to make this village go back to your old ways. If they want to fight about it, that's the Yanomamö way. Let them fight."

Cesar turned to go back into the church. He knew this meant war. *At least my own village won't be a part of it,* he thought. *These people are getting too boastful about their new ways of peace, anyway. It might be a good lesson for them to get back into a war.*

The crowd roared with surprise and anger when Cesar told them that Yoshicami would have to return to Longfoot. He could see that all the visiting villages were going to side with Honey, and he couldn't make her go anywhere. This was going to be a short, one-sided fight and someone from Forgetful Village would be killed.

Fruitman stood there listening and watching Cesar. He remembered telling Cesar that Honey didn't want to go back to fighting. *Now Cesar is taking his chance to show us who's in control,* Fruitman thought. *If only I had an arrow, I'd shoot it at Cesar and say, "Here's the first arrow for the old ways—right in your chest."*

But Fruitman didn't have an arrow. Now he began thinking about going after his bow and arrows.

Shortman had heard everything Bearded-One said to Cesar. He wanted to show Bearded-One what Yanomamö ways were all about with a club over the top of his head. So before Bearded-One could follow Cesar back into the church,

Shortman asked him, "What are you doing here? Why don't you just leave?" Bearded-One's mouth dropped open. No Indian had ever spoken to him like that.

But Shortman was mad and not about to stop. "Who asked you to come here and interfere in our village? You want Cesar to leave us alone? Then why don't *you* leave us alone?"

Bearded-One stood with his mouth open and Shortman went right on talking. "You are a naba who knows nothing. I didn't see anyone here ask you to tell Cesar what to say. We know your kind. You are here with that camera of yours to take pictures of us when we start killing each other."

Bearded-One's face filled with anger at this talk from an Indian. "You don't know who I am, boy," he yelled back at Shortman. He did know who Bearded-One was. He knew about Tigerlip's wife and about the woman Bearded-One wanted sex from. She was a relative of his lifelong friend, Hairylip.

Inside the church Shoefoot stepped to the front. The crowd was silent, waiting to hear if this leader would talk against Cesar. "Yoshicami," he said to her slowly, "this naba, Bearded-One, has made everyone so mad that our people are ready to kill. If we start a fight here, someone is going to die. I'm your brother-cousin. Your father here is my father-uncle. You know I'm not going to let any harm come to you. Here's what I want you to do."

The Honey warriors had heard enough. They knew that Shoefoot would do anything to not have a fight. They walked very quietly out of the angry crowd and backed out of the church. Shoefoot saw them and knew where they were going. He didn't have much time.

"We will call the guards," he said faster, "and get them to come back and straighten this out. But until they come, I want you to go back with your parents to Forgetful Village. You don't need to go back to Longfoot. Just go for now with your parents. When the guards get here, we will come and get you back." Yoshicami knew he cared about her. He cared about everybody who came to his village.

On the grass outside the church, Bearded-One was still yelling at Shortman. "I'm a government official! If you don't shut your mouth, I'm going to call the guards to come out here and arrest you."

"Call them," Shortman answered as he watched all his friends run past on their way to the far end of the village. They were headed for weapons. They had a long way to run and were wondering why they hadn't brought their bows and shotguns with them.

Bearded-One was even more surprised. He pulled a little card from his pocket. "I'm on the special Indian Commission and the guards do what I tell them."

"Call them," Shortman said again.

"You are in trouble now!" Bearded-One yelled. "The guards will arrest you for sure."

Inside the church, Yoshicami hung her head. Shoefoot was right. She would be sick with sorrow if anyone was killed. By the time Shoefoot was finished talking, all the Honey warriors were gone. "Come on *now*," he said, "let's go fast. They've all gone for weapons. My people don't always do what I tell them."

He took Yoshicami, her parents, Longfoot, and the Forgetful Village warriors and rushed them out of the church toward the riverbank. "Hurry!" he yelled as he pushed them along. "They'll be back fast with weapons." Shoefoot's crowd rushed past Bearded-One, still threatening to call the guards up to arrest Shortman.

"Call them!" Shortman yelled back. "Why am I standing here saying the same thing over and over?"

"Go! Go! Faster!" Shoefoot yelled, and Bearded-One started following them toward the river.

"Call them, Mr. Indian Commissioner!" Shortman kept getting louder as he followed Bearded-One who followed Shoefoot who pushed Forgetful Village toward their canoes. "I can't wait to hear you tell them that a Yanomamö girl has no rights as a citizen of Venezuela. Come on." He waved and pointed Bearded-One toward a small building. "I'll take you over to the radio room right now and you can call them out here to arrest me. Let's go." Bearded-One pretended not to hear and kept following Shoefoot toward the river.

At the other end of the village Shortman saw Funnyman, Slothtail, Won't-Grow, Fruitman, Bighead and all the rest coming out of their houses with bows and arrows and shotguns. They hadn't even bothered to get clubs.

"Look, boy," Bearded-One yelled. "You don't know nothing! The guards are nothing but a bunch of criminals anyway. We put them there in Tama Tama as a punishment for their crimes." Shoefoot's crowd disappeared over the bank with Yoshicami.

Shortman's anger grew as he saw her disappear from sight. "Call them!" he shouted. "I can't wait to hear you tell them that. What are you afraid of? I'm going to call the guards whether you do or not." *I'm wasting my energy yelling at a fool,* he thought, *and there's no time left.* He ran toward the river with a hardwood club. No one ever found out how he got it that fast.

Shoefoot stood at the top of the bank yelling at Forgetful Village to hurry. Keleewa and his brother Miqie stood in an empty canoe and helped them load. Then Keleewa pushed their canoe out into the water. They started the motor and slowly moved into the current toward the other shore. The canoe was so packed with warriors that they had to hold very still to keep water from coming over the sides. Each warrior had bow and arrows ready. But they were an easy target for any fighter on shore.

Shortman got to the river before the others with his hardwood club, about as long as his arm. He ran past Shoefoot down the bank and threw it as hard as he could at the escaping canoe. It twisted through the air like a jungle vine and came within a finger of hitting Yoshicami's father in the head. It hit the far side of the canoe with a heavy clunk, bounced high into the air, fell straight into the water without a splash, and sank like a rock to the bottom of the river.

"No, no!" Shoefoot yelled as the rest of the warriors came with weapons. "We'll get the guards! We'll get the guards." The canoe moved away from the bank until it was out of range. Shoefoot breathed a sigh of relief.

And they did call the guards, even though Bearded-One decided not to help them make the call.

Shortman walked slow, one step at a time, back up the bank with his head down. His mind was full of confusion. *First they tell us that the government has no authority here and we must go back to our old ways,* he thought. *So when we try to use our old ways, which are to keep her by force, then they say that they are in authority and we must let her go.* He knew that he was right and Bearded-One was wrong.

From the top of the bank Shortman watched Bearded-One walk down toward his boat. He wasn't sure he could hold the anger he felt coming up inside his chest. He wanted to run down the bank and give Bearded-One a swift whack over the top of his head with a hardwood club. That would give him a feeling of the old ways.

And that is what really mixed Shortman's head. If he did what he really wanted to do—club Bearded-One over the head—that would be a complete return to the old ways. *This is what Bearded-One wants,* he thought. *And I'm mad because I don't want the old ways, but I would love to club Bearded-One.* He stood and thought and watched Bearded-One's boat leave the shore.

Because he's from the Siapa, Shortman has had much to do with the whites. As Bearded-One's engine roared, Shortman remembered the time he had gone in his canoe over to the Orinoco and been met by the antro there with the words, "Boy, don't you just think you're someone special all dressed in clothes and wearing a watch! Who do you think you are, anyway?" Shortman had answered him politely in Spanish.

"Don't you ever speak to me in Spanish!" the antro snapped back. "You are a Yanomamö and will always be a Yanomamö. You have no business throwing away your true ways and trying to copy nabas with their clothes, watches, motors, and now even changing to Spanish! Don't ever speak to me in Spanish again! You want to talk to me? Use Yanomamö!"

Shortman had pointed at the big bulge in the white man's lower lip. "What's that in your lower lip, there?" Shortman asked, speaking our Yanomamö talk.

"That's my wad of tobacco," the antro answered.

"Where did you learn to chew tobacco that way?" asked Shortman.

"I learned it from your people."

"You saw us chew tobacco that way and you tried it and you liked it. So you copied us, didn't you?"

"That's right," the antro said, with some pride in his Indian ways.

Shortman shrugged. "If you can copy us," he paused with a puzzled look, "then we can copy you." The naba said nothing.

Another time an antro had scolded him for traveling in a

speedboat. "Didn't Simon Bolivar, your white father, come here on a horse?" Shortman had asked the naba. When the naba didn't answer, Shortman said, "Where's *your* horse?" The antro had a funny look on his face and Shortman wasn't sure if he understood. "Well? Where's your horse?"

As he watched Bearded-One steer his boat out into the Padamo River, Shortman remembered many talks with the nabas.

Yoshicami was gone. *Will these nabas ever leave us alone?* he wondered.

13

VENGEANCE IS MINE

N ow Honey Village has the same split in their minds that we Yanomamö have had since that first season we visited the nabas. At first we want to be like them. Then after we watch them for a while, we don't. We now know that a naba took Shetary's head; we even know who did it. No Yanomamö would ever want to be like that.

But one thing we know; nabas can make things. We all want the things they have. But they make such a split in the head too. Some tell us not to fight. Some tell us to fight. Some tell us to throw our spirits away. Some tell us to keep our spirits. They might be able to make things—but they don't think very good.

A feeling of despair fell on the village of Honey, as thick as the morning clouds that sometimes came over, despair that they had not known in a long time. I wondered if this could be the result of all the curses I had spoken against them. But I hadn't made any curses for many seasons. I remembered very well the time I warned them that the armadillo would destroy their homes and the jaguar would hunt on their trails. It was a waste of my spiritual energy, just like all my other curses against them. If it is true that the spirits caused the trouble that Honey had, it was not the result of my power.

Redhair lay in his hammock for two days because of the

beating he got in the fight with Forgetful Village. Finally he fell asleep from all the pain and his family thought he was almost dead. They ran to get the nabas to come and help. Everyone came into the house while they worked on Redhair. They knew he was near death, and they began wailing and mourning.

"This young man is one of our own," one of the men said. "He was born here. He grew up here. If he dies, we'll have to go teach Forgetful Village a good lesson and take Yoshicami back." They all knew he was right. Something would have to be done about this killing.

Then suddenly Redhair sat up perfectly well. Quiet fell over everyone. He smiled. For the first time since the fight, all his family could see he had no pain. Everyone was excited.

"I feel just fine," he said. "Please listen to what I have to tell you. You have all known me all my life. Like so many of you, I'm a child of Yai Pada, the great spirit. Now, as you can see all around you," he said pointing around the house, "his people have come here to take me home. So I'm going with them now, and I just want to say before I go that I don't want any of you to even think about taking revenge against Forgetful Village."

When Redhair talked about the people sent by Yai Pada, their excitement turned to concern. "There's no one here to take you," they said, looking around. "You're well. You're going to be fine."

Redhair was shocked. "Can't you see these people?" he said. "They're standing all around here, waiting for me to finish talking to you." Everyone stared at him and shook their heads. "I can't believe you can't see them! *Look,* right there," he said, pointing to places around the house. No one saw anything.

"Open your eyes!" Redhair kept pointing all around. "Can't you see them?" But they all just stared at him with sad faces and shook their heads.

"Well, they're here for me and I'm going with them to Yai Pada. We won't need revenge where I'm going, so please don't take any on Forgetful Village."

For the first time a crowd of Yanomamö had nothing to say. They watched quietly as Redhair lay back down on his hammock, curled up and died.

Now Honey didn't know what to do; one of their own had died at the evil hands of others. Redhair was a Yanomamö. His relatives would have to take revenge, no matter what he had said before he died. Surely now the village that had wandered away for so long would have to return to the old ways of vengeance.

Then word came about what they were saying in Forgetful Village. "He got just what he deserved," they said. "And your leader, Shoefoot, is not a Yanomamö any more. He's too much of a coward to get revenge for Redhair's death."

Their talk would force Honey to act. Even though I had been an enemy for so long against Honey, if they had a war I would be on their side. It would be good to be back together again in a war.

Honey met that night at the church to decide what to do. Everyone was mad. But Shoefoot and Spear were still against taking revenge. "We cannot go back to our old ways!" Shoefoot kept saying. He would say it like each word was a separate idea all its own. "It's easy to start a war. It might even be easy to win the first battles. But try to stop a war after it gets started. It would be easier to get a swarm of bees to go back in their hive."

"We cannot allow killing to go unpunished in this village," Fruitman answered in anger. Everyone disagreed with Shoefoot and Spear. "We will go fight without you," they said.

Redhair's closest brother was Bighead. He hadn't said anything. Everyone knew he was in heavy sorrow. Finally he got up to speak. Everyone listened.

"You all remember what my brother said when he died," Bighead began slowly. "We thought he was well and over his pain. But he was only staying alive to leave us a message that we should not take revenge." Bighead then told the whole story, saying again every word Redhair had said.

"This spirit that we now follow," Bighead went on, "the one we call Yai Pada, this spirit of peace—we now know that we will see him some day. The people we are about to take revenge on will not. They follow other spirits that tell them to kill. That's why they are going to the fire pit. You all know that I love my brother. I would love to get revenge for his death. But I'm not going to take revenge for the death of my brother, who has already gone to Yai Pada's happy land, by killing people that I know will go to the fire pit. Let anybody talk if he thinks I am wrong." Bighead sat down.

Everyone was quiet. Bighead's talk wasn't the Yanomamö way. Redhair's relatives deserved *some* revenge. But his talk was so full of love and kindness toward all of our relatives in Forgetful Village that no one wanted to speak anything against it. They all left, quiet and thinking.

The next day a story came from upriver that Yoshicami had been tied up to keep her from running away. Shoefoot told the village again that she would not have to keep suffering much longer because the guards would come soon. Two days later another visitor said that every night she was tied into her hammock and sometimes during the day she was tied to a pole.

The next day a report came from the guards. They had been traveling toward Honey when they stopped at Las Esmeralda. That is where the Indian commissioner Bearded-One works. When they got to Las Esmeralda they were told that the trouble in Honey had been settled. So they turned back and wouldn't be coming.

Shortman was standing in the radio room when the report came. He had already taken far more than he ever thought he could. Yoshicami was a close relative of his wife.

"What do we do now?" he asked Keleewa. "What do we do now? I'm a Yanomamö. I know we have given up the old ways. But a Yanomamö never turns his back on his own relative! Never!"

Keleewa shook his head. Shortman was about to cry. "She is my wife's relative. Tell me, Keleewa. What do we do now?" The sun was high. The day was hot. It was a perfect Yanomamö day for making war. Keleewa couldn't think of any way to answer Shortman. Within minutes everyone was armed and ready to leave. They met in the middle of the village. Shoefoot and Spear begged them not to go.

"We'll call the guards again!" they pleaded. "It will only be a few more days."

"Everyone knows that Bearded-One stopped the guards and he'll do it again," Shortman answered.

"It doesn't matter," Won't-Grow said, stepping to the front and speaking for everyone. "It's what they are saying about you, Shoefoot, that we will not stand any longer. They are calling you a coward. They say you are not Yanomamö any-more." Slothtail, Fruitman, Bighead, Funnyman, Shortman, and all the warriors were behind Won't-Grow, agreeing with him. The bright sun reflected off their brown faces. Shoefoot saw deep lines in every face. "They say that you are a coward and have led us all to being cowards." All the men showed great sorrow at what Won't-Grow said.

"We can't let them talk like that about you," Slothtail added.

Shoefoot thought about it. Why am I doing this? he asked himself. *Why not let them go slaughter Forgetful Village? It will show them I'm no coward and I'll be the most powerful leader in our whole territory. Why not? It would be nice to be a man with power again.*

When Spear heard Won't-Grow's talk, he changed his mind and joined all the others. Shoefoot was now completely alone. Shortman stepped up. "Shoefoot, we love you and we have always respected you and followed you. But this is one time that all of us disagree with you. We all know we have to go up there and knock some heads. If we do that, and give Yoshicami a chance to come back to this village, then other people will finally leave us alone."

Keleewa and his brother Miqie refused to take sides. Later we learned that they didn't know which side to take. The sun burned harder.

Shoefoot really wanted to join them. *If they think Redhair got what he deserved, if they think we are cowards, why not go teach them a lesson?* And it felt good to think that he had the power to do it, too. He felt that same flood of power that he used to have when his spirits excited him to go on raids. The same feeling we all got when we fought. A feeling that says, "I am the fiercest and I'll prove it." *Why not?* Shoefoot wondered. *We'll show them who really has the power.*

Shoefoot caught himself for a moment. *No*, he thought. *These thoughts are the first step back to war.*

"I have the same thoughts you have right now," he said to his friends. "I know exactly how you all feel. You feel a crav-ing to beat another person and show him he's wrong. I know we're right. And we have the right. We have the power too. But that feeling, that craving to beat another person and teach him who's right—that is what is wrong."

It was the most passionate talk of his life. "I hurt for Yoshi-cami too," Shoefoot said. "She's my sister cousin. But there is one thing that many of you don't know. The old ways. You young men don't know the old ways. You don't know what war is like. Even you old men have forgotten. Spear, have you forgotten how we all suffered after every victory? We suffered so much that a victory wasn't a victory."

Spear did remember. Shoefoot knew how well Spear remembered. His son Fruitman knew too. Spear could still see the face of the young warrior screaming, "Don't kill me, older brother, don't kill me!"

Shoefoot kept talking. "When we got up in the morning we were so afraid we couldn't walk outside the shabono. We were so afraid all day that we couldn't go out to find food for our families. That's why so many of them died. Then we were so afraid at night that we couldn't sleep. We lived our whole lives like that. If you had any idea how horrible those old ways were, you would never go on this raid."

Everyone shook his head. "It is what they are saying about you," they all said to Shoefoot. "That's why we have to do this."

Everyone listened to all that Shoefoot had to say. He was right. They *didn't* know. But they all knew what they had to do. They listened. But they left. Armed with bows, arrows, clubs, and shotguns, they all loaded into their canoes. Even the women went with them. The sun sparkled over the water.

Shoefoot stood with Keleewa and Miqie and watched two long dug-outs, overloaded with warriors and women and children, move slowly up the Padamo River until they disappeared behind the foliage around the first bend. He fought back tears. He was old now, but he could still cry. Keleewa and Miqie could see he was about to cry for what he knew was going to happen. But they couldn't think of anything to say. He turned and walked slowly toward the church.

It was late afternoon. The village was empty. Only a few old women were left to watch the little ones. And Shoefoot's wife and children stayed. Shoefoot looked back at the empty village and turned and went in the church.

He sat on a bench in the back and remembered how the guards had told Yoshicami that she could do what she wanted. Then he remembered the next meeting with the troublemaker, Cesar. Even that would have been all right if Bearded-One hadn't come. He remembered how he had kept the fight from starting. Now he felt so helpless.

He had done all he could do. But he failed. All he could do now was talk to Yai Pada. His eyes filled with tears at the thought that his village was going to war, and against their own relatives. *Those people in Forgetful Village are my relatives too, and they don't have a chance against us,* he said, pleading with Yai Pada. *Who will celebrate when we win?*

Two bends downriver from Forgetful Village is a tiny village that has broken away from them. The Honey warriors stopped there for the night. "It's too late to fight today. We will fight them in the good light of the morning," Fierce-One said. Fierce-One never said much; he was so fierce he didn't have to. But now that the village was going to fight, Fierce-One was suddenly the leader. He had never given up the old ways.

Shoefoot walked home. He tried to help his wife a little. But he could see that he wasn't any help, so he went back to the church. The mud walls and palm roof made it cool inside. But so empty. *Am I really the only one who wants peace?* Shoefoot wondered. He was so alone. He walked past the spot where Yoshicami stood a few days before, and where Cesar stood, and Bearded-One.

How long must we suffer with these white nabas who have evil spirits? Shoefoot asked Yai Pada. They have evil spirits and they don't even know it. He sat in the chair he always used and remembered them; there was a boy from a visiting village who the children called One-Who-Strokes-A.H.'s-Penis, after they found out how he had earned his beautiful watch. How he got that name was too dirty for Shoefoot to even think about. The adults in Honey made the children stop using the name.

And Howashi Spirit wasn't the worst spirit the smart white man had. *Yai Pada help us!* was all Shoefoot could think when he remembered the horror of what the naba had done. *You are our only hope against people like him.*

The story he was remembering was the story of Shetary's missing head. It took many seasons of quiet talking before we all knew what had happened that terrible day. A small bunch of young warriors had left Shetary's village after they saw that the people were sick and dying. They were led by the white naba, A.H. He stopped when they came to the heeheeka that held Shetary's son. "Climb up there and cut that thing down," he said to one of the boys. They were too surprised to move. They couldn't believe what they had heard. "I want that head!" A.H. had said with a hard face. Every Indian clicked his tongue and shook his head in fear when they realized what he was saying.

It's true. A.H. had spirits that no shaman would ever want. Shoefoot sat in the church remembering every detail of the horror story that every Yanomamö knew. We knew the story as well as if we'd been there. Only the nabas didn't know. *Nabas will never understand things that are so clear to us,* Shoefoot thought. *Why would anyone be wicked enough to steal a dead man's head?*

"Never," the young warrior had answered A.H., even though he was afraid of him.

"Come on!" A.H. shouted back with excitement. "I want that head. I really want it bad. It's worth a lot of money. I just have to have it." He was almost jumping up and down. Everyone was horrified at the thought of cutting the head off of the boy. A.H. ordered a different warrior to climb up and cut it down.

"We wouldn't do that to the body of our worst enemy!" the man answered. "If you want that, you'll have to get it yourself."

"I have to have it!" A.H. repeated. "It's worth a lot of money." The Indians clicked their tongues again at the horror of the thought. *How could anyone even think of anything so evil?* they all thought. A.H. asked each Indian, but of course he couldn't get anyone to help him with his wicked idea.

So he leaned a pole up against the cross-pole at the larger end of the heeheeka. The Indians backed away in terror as they watched him climb the pole and cut the vines. The heeheeka crashed to the jungle floor. Then A.H. took some things out of his bag that they had never seen. They were real thin, almost white, stretched tight over his hands, and reached all the way up to his elbows. Then he took out a thing that was thin and white and shaped like a gourd cut in half. It fit exactly over his nose and mouth and was tied there with little strings that went around his head.

The Indians were so surprised to see a smart white person shame a dead body by cutting open the heeheeka. They were horrified to see that the hair and lips were already gone and the chest was full of maggots. *What will his father do to us,* they wondered, *when he comes back and finds this? He has done nothing to any of us to deserve something so wicked.* They shook their heads and clicked their tongues as they watched A.H. cut the head off and put it in a bag. Then everyone ran in fear down the trail and didn't stop until they reached the boat.

Downriver, the village did not understand why the Indians and A.H. went by so fast and didn't even stop. And they didn't stop anywhere along the river, or even talk until they got far away from that place. When they did stop, A.H. put the head inside a metal thing he had with him, filled it with some kind of special water, put a top over it real tight, and put it away. No one ever saw it again.

The Indians agreed among themselves that they would never tell anyone what had happened. How could they live with the shame of what they had let an evil naba do? We did many bad things, but none of us had ever thought of anything this wicked.

But a story like this cannot possibly stay untold. Everybody will trust somebody not to tell anybody. Soon everybody knows even though they never tell. Even to this day the warriors who were with A.H. will say that they weren't because they are so ashamed that they let it happen. But everybody knows exactly what happened, and Shoefoot sat there in the church and remembered each detail. *Why haven't you delivered us from these nabas?* he asked Yai Pada.

Early the next morning Shoefoot walked again across his empty village to the church building. It was too quiet with everyone gone.

Two bends downriver from Forgetful Village, Catalina untied her hammock, then Slothtail's and the children's. The other wives did the same. The men gathered pots from dying fires. Won't-Grow and Shortman passed each other on the trail as they loaded the canoes. No one could remember when they had all traveled together as warriors like this. "Warrior" is not the right word for these men—they are hunters, not raiders. The feeling of the old days was in the air and Shortman felt it, old days he really didn't want to go back to.

When they rounded the first bend in the river that morning, they saw ahead the second bend. Around it lay Forgetful Village. The sun was halfway up and shone off the water. "We'll sound a warning shot when we round that bend!" Won't-Grow yelled, and everyone got his shotgun loaded.

Around the second bend, with only open water between them and the village, Won't-Grow signaled and every man shot his shotgun at the same time. The sound was so loud it hurt their ears. They left their guns and bows and arrows with the women and children and walked to the village only with clubs. Fights almost always start small. They didn't want to kill, only crack a few heads. But they certainly had the right to kill. If anyone died, they would go back fast for the killing weapons.

Forgetful Village still lived in a shabono because they didn't know how to build houses. But the entrance was so overgrown with jungle that the Honey warriors had to spend half the morning working with their machetes to clear away the brush for the fight.

"We hear you out there!" a warrior called from inside. "It's so nice of you to clear our jungle for us."

"Yes!" another one called, "especially when all you'll get for it is a bunch of cracked heads."

"Hurry up! We can't wait for you to get in here and teach us a lesson."

Their long time of being different was over. Honey was now ready to do just what my spirits and I had always wanted, ready to join with us again in our ways. Now they would go back to being real Yanomamö. We would be a united tribe again. Our long time of separation was about to be over and my spirits celebrated with me. They were wild with delight. *Now I can go back to Honey,* I told myself, *and we will all celebrate together as we used to, drink the bones of our relatives, and go on raids together again.* The thought was wonderful. *Maybe I'll even teach Shoefoot again to be a shaman. He was so good. I know he could be as good as I am. My wife will be so happy to see her brother's village back with us.*

Yai Pada, Shoefoot begged. But he'd already said everything he knew to say. He had said it so many times he just knew that Yai Pada must be tired of hearing it. *Please . . .* he pleaded. Pleading was all that was left for him.

He remembered so many seasons back, back to the time when I was still teaching him to be a shaman, how Pepe had asked Yai Pada that his soul would be spared from judgment. He called it "praying." After Pepe finished, Shoefoot had prayed. But he wasn't really sure what he said or what it meant, something about following the new ways of the great spirit. Then he had left Pepe's leaf house and walked out into the jungle to be alone. He remembered it like yesterday.

A long way from the village Shoefoot had left the trail so he couldn't be followed. He sat on a cushion of jungle leaves, leaned back against the huge trunk of a hardwood, and looked up at the roof of foliage over his head. "This is a wonderful place," he had said, "but so mysterious."

He had talked to this new spirit, saying things he could never say with Pepe listening. Pepe couldn't understand what we shamans knew. "I can't throw these spirits of mine away," Shoefoot had said to Yai Wana Naba Laywa. "They will kill me before they will ever leave. I'll let you take them away if you can. But I don't know why you would. You are the unfriendly spirit, the enemy spirit. If you have noticed me or care about me, then you know I've always needed another spirit. My own spirits have told me that. If you are the spirit I need, then you'll have to get rid of the others. But I can't throw them away."

Shoefoot never again took ebene after that and never spoke to his spirits. He waited for them to try to kill him just like they tried to do when I was first training him.

A few days later it happened, but it was not what he had expected.

He had been lying in his hammock almost asleep when Omawa himself, the leader of all our spirits, had come to him from deep in the jungle. As he came he swooped his hand down into the jungle and gathered from it all the sweetest smells in the world. His beauty, his power, and his sweet smell were so wonderful that Shoefoot knew right away that he could never resist him. Shoefoot's body was filled with excitement. He was important enough to be visited by Omawa himself!

Omawa had scooped Shoefoot up from his hammock and they began to dance across the jungle. This was better than ebene or women or anything Shoefoot could imagine, even though he knew that Omawa would soon take him back to his spirits. Still, this was a moment that couldn't be resisted.

Just as they had been about to dance forever out into the jungle, they were suddenly hit with a white light as bright as many suns, more dazzling than anything Shoefoot had ever seen. It was like the sharpest flame of lightning but it didn't stop. The bright light stayed there, and the warmth from it filled Shoefoot with a new feeling he had never felt, a feeling of safety. It felt so good.

Just when the light appeared a huge voice had said, "You can't have him. He's mine." And Omawa ran in terror! Across the top of the jungle he ran until he was out of sight. *It's him,* Shoefoot thought, when he heard the voice. *It's Yai Pada, the great spirit—and he's not the enemy! He heard me when I asked him to chase my spirits away! He must be friendly to me after all!*

The light, the warmth, the safety, the care of the most powerful spirit—it was all too good for Shoefoot to hold in one moment.

Now Shoefoot sat in his chair at the front of the church at Honey Village and remembered. He had been young then and now he was old. But he could still remember that day and the brightness of Omawa's beauty. How charming he was! But Shoefoot knew that all his spirits from Omawa were the reason for so much of his misery. That day had been the beginning of his new life with Yai Wana Naba Laywa, the enemy spirit who turned out to be a friend. After that day, Shoefoot had never seen or heard from Omawa or any of the other spirits again.

I've failed, Yai Pada, he cried now. *I've done all I can and I failed,* he kept saying. *These people are just too stubborn to understand. Even the nabas don't understand, even Keleewa. They are all against me. You are all I have left. You brought me and my people from starving misery. Why would you do all this and then let us go back to war? But even if you did fail me, I wouldn't go back to my spirits now—not after the life I've had with you. Your spirit has made me free from the fear I had all the time of so many wars. You took so much pain when you became one of us to make us free from these wars. Please don't let us go back to it.*

Shoefoot stayed all morning in the little building saying these things.

Outside the shabono entrance at Forgetful Village the Honey warriors had finally finished clearing away the jungle. Now they gathered to make one attack all together. There was Shortman, Won't-Grow, Fruitman, Funnyman, Slothtail, Big-head and the rest of the men, all looking to Fierce-One to lead the attack. Except for a few fights with Mouth Village, they had never fought another village. As they attacked the shabono opening, the Honey warriors were met by the three bravest warriors from Forgetful Village, the ones who bragged that they would never get inside. Just like the fight with Mouth, it was Honey's little clubs that worked so well. Whap-whap-whap-whap-whap the club sounded on the head of the leader. He was on the ground before he was able to make one hit. The other two brave warriors took the same fast hits to the head and Honey warriors streamed over the top of them into the shabono.

Women and children screamed and scattered in all directions. Most of the warriors ran when they saw how easily and quickly their best fighters were clubbed down. But brave warriors never run. That's why they don't live to be old men. All the brave warriors of Forgetful Village were clubbed until they staggered and fell to the ground.

It was all over so fast. Those who ran came slowly back into the shabono when they realized no one was chasing them and their leaders were being clubbed, but not to death. The women also came back into the shabono. It was the first Yanomamö victory where the women weren't raped.

"Where's Yoshicami?" Shortman yelled at her father, who sat holding his bloody head, muttering something to himself about why he hadn't let her stay at Honey. "She finally got away."

"If she'd gotten away, she would have run to Honey," Shortman said. "Where is she?"

"When she heard that Redhair died, she got so upset that she ran off into the jungle, and we can't find her. She is carrying his child."

"Let's burn this place to the ground," Funnyman said, and ran back to the canoe. He came back with a can of gas.

"Wait, wait!" Won't-Grow and Slothtail shouted. "Put that gas away. We didn't come here to give the children pain. Look around, Funnyman. Where is a man without a bashed head?" Funnyman looked at the gas can in his hand. He thought about the children. Then a lot of shame came into him.

Everyone on both sides looked around. No one from Honey had even been hit. The enemy all looked like Yoshicami's father, blood running down faces, dripping onto chests and into the dirt. "We've done what we came for."

Shortman shook his finger at the bloody warriors. "If we still had our old ways we would kill every one of you. Don't you ever forget that." They didn't have the strength to look up at him. But they heard. "And we'd take Yoshicami and all the rest of your women. And you know what we'd do with them too. We're going to leave now, but don't let us ever hear again that you are tying that girl up. If we hear that, we'll come right back."

Yoshicami's father was very old, but he had a good memory. He remembered that big raid on Potato Village. He remembered all the people they slaughtered that morning and all the women they raped.

The old man sat with a mixed-up head. All the blood running off his head didn't help him think very clear. He looked up at Shortman with questions in his eyes. These people, he told himself, *who I thought weren't brave enough to be Yanomamö, have just shown their bravery by protecting my daughter. And now they show me they are not Yanomamö by letting us live and not stealing or raping our women.*

Two days later was the first day of the week, and the village of Honey gathered at the church for their weekly meeting. Shoefoot got up to speak.

"I want to talk to you about one little thing today," he started. "Those of you who can read have seen in Yai Pada's book where it says, 'If it is possible, as much as you can, live at peace with all men. And never take vengeance into your own hands, but leave room for Yai Pada's anger.' Yai Pada says, 'Vengeance is mine, I will pay back.' "

Shoefoot was quiet for just a little, while he let everyone think about what he was going to say.

"Because you are all my family and my best friends in the

world, I want you to know that I think Yai Pada wrote those words just for us Yanomamö. You all know that our whole life all we ever wanted was vengeance. You old women know how you saved the bones of your relatives, waiting for your boys to grow up so they could drink those bones and go kill. You know that our old spirits always told us to kill for vengeance. Now we follow a spirit that tells us to do completely different.

"I tell you that Yai Pada wrote this for the Yanomamö because no one knows more about war than we do. We all know that no fight ever ends. We always make sure that it goes on and on.

"If we let Yai Pada take care of vengeance, then our fights will always get smaller. If *he* wants to kill them, let him. But we won't be blamed for it when it happens, and the fight will never get bigger."

Shoefoot watched his people wiggle on their benches as he talked. "I'm not going to say I'm glad about what you did. You were wrong to try to take vengeance yourselves. When you take the fight to them, it always gets worse. It is just what Bearded-One wanted. The new spirit we now follow is making this very clear to us, and I want you who have learned reading to read it for yourselves and read it to your parents.

"This new spirit wants us to give up our old life of vengeance. If someone in Forgetful Village had been killed, we would be in a war. You all know that many of these well-taught nabas like Bearded-One want us here at Honey to go back to our old ways. They know that all the Yanomamö are looking to us here at Honey and hoping that they can become like us. The nabas know that if we fail in this new way, all the other Yanomamö will stay in their old ways. So the nabas would love for us to go back to the old ways."

Everyone was quiet. They could hear so much feeling in his voice as he ended with the words, *"But we never will!"*

Shoefoot sat down. Fruitman got up to speak. He always thought he should have been the leader of this village, so he often challenged Shoefoot. That's why Fruitman had been so anxious for revenge. But he didn't want the old ways back. Now he could see that Shoefoot was right.

"We aren't proud of what we did," he said to everyone. "We're not sorry that we did it, but we're not going to do it again. Some of you younger men have been bragging about how bad we beat them. Stop doing that. We thought we had to do it, and we did it. But it is nothing to brag about. Using your mouth like that is what stirs up more trouble."

After a short time, Yoshicami became so unhappy in Forgetful Village that she ran to another village where she had relatives. She never went back to Forgetful Village. Longfoot was left with only one wife, the beautiful little Yawalama.

I told you before about Yawalama—how her brother Raul tried to stop their parents from giving her to Longfoot. He knew that Longfoot would be just as cruel to his little sister as he had been to Yoshicami.

Yawalama had no desire to live in the same misery as Yoshicami. Every night Longfoot had to drag her kicking and screaming to his hammock. Then she would disturb the whole village all night with her loud crying. It was a big mess, but it is the Yanomamö way, and her family knew that in time she would get used to him and learn to accept her life with him. At least she would soon learn that all the fussing was a waste of energy.

Two moons later, the village was real tired of the noise every night. Finally, Longfoot learned that she really wanted one of the young men her own age.

"You mess around with another man and I'll kill you," he said to Yawalama so everyone could hear.

"She is my sister," Raul told him, "and I won't just stand around and watch you kill her. If you treat her good, better than you did Yoshicami, she will learn to like you after awhile. Talking about killing is not going to make her like you." But Longfoot's treatment didn't get better, and every night he did the same thing—dragged her screaming to his hammock. The village got irritated. She was taking far too long getting used to her husband. The griping and whining should have stopped long ago.

One day all the men went hunting. It was a perfect day for a hunt, so Raul thought it was strange when his brother-in-law dropped out of the hunting party without saying anything. Longfoot went back to the shabono, untied his hammock, and picked up all his things. Then he went into the jungle and hid his things in the brush. When he went back to the shabono, he spent a long time sharpening his machete.

"Where are you traveling to?" one of the women asked him.

"I'm going to visit my family," he said. His family lived far up in the headwaters of the Padamo River. The women didn't believe him, so two of them went looking for the men.

Yawalama was out in the garden digging yucca. She dug out another yucca root and added it to the stack that she and her friend were piling up to peel and grate. "We've got a lot of yucca this season," she said. When she looked up, there was her husband walking toward her through the yucca plants. His machete flashed in the sunlight, and in his eyes she saw a man determined to end his problem. She screamed and turned to run.

The women found the hunting party. "Come quick," they said to Raul. "We think he's going to do something to Yawalama!"

Yawalama was out of the garden and onto the jungle trail when Longfoot caught her and threw her to the ground. She jumped to her feet and he chopped one leg out from underneath her. With her back on the ground she used her arms to protect herself from his machete. He chopped her like a mad animal and left her to die.

Raul heard the wailing of the women before he reached the shabono. *It's too late,* he thought, *she's already dead.* His mother met him on the trail. "It's too late," she wept. "She's by the garden."

She must be alive, Raul hoped. He ran toward the garden and saw some brush where all the leaves were covered with blood, even up over his head. He pulled the brush apart. There on the ground in a pool of blood was the sister he had tried so hard to protect. She looked like a butchered animal. Some of her bones were completely cut and only hanging by the meat. White bones and tendons stuck out everywhere.

Raul sent his uncle paddling downriver to their enemy village, Honey, to call for help. "How bad is she?" Keleewa asked the breathless man.

"She might not be alive when we get back," the uncle said. The people of Honey knew Yawalama well. With her beautiful big brown eyes and wavy black hair, she had won everyone's heart.

Funnyman took two men with him and jumped into the

dugout canoe. It was almost dark when he pulled the cord and started the engine. The front of the canoe raised out of the water, the engine threw a wave that crashed onto the bank, and the boat moved out into the current and turned upriver. *Just two moons ago I tried to burn this village,* Funnyman thought. *Now we're out to help them.*

It was the middle of the night when Funnyman pulled the canoe onto the bank at Honey. I'm wasting my time, he thought, looking at the girl all chopped up. Raul was with him. They were met by half the village holding flashlights. Their faces turned to horror when the people of Honey saw Yawalama. It took five people to carry her because so many extra hands were needed to hold the parts that were nearly cut off. Deemeoma did whatever she could to help.

"She's ruined!" the women whispered together.

"She's dead!" others moaned, and a mourning wail began. Even the men joined.

In the light of the hut they use for medicine, Keleewa and his wife and sisters looked at her. "What have you done to this girl!" Keleewa shouted in shock at everyone. He remembered her so clearly eight seasons before—how she had jumped and giggled and played, her big eyes twinkling at everybody. He remembered bouncing her on his lap. Now he held her hand and forearm with two bones sticking out, completely separated from the upper arm except by a little muscle. In his right hand he held her wrist with two more bones sticking out.

Tears came to his eyes. *Why did God get me into this place?* he asked himself. "God" was the naba name for Yai Pada.

"You should all be taken out and shot!" he yelled. "This girl was so pretty. She's only thirteen seasons old and you've butchered her like an animal!" He wiped dirt and leaves off the muscle and pressed the arm back together. "This is what you get for giving these girls to people they don't want. When will you ever learn? If I had my way, I'd take you people out and beat every one of you. Better than that, I'd shoot you! This beautiful little girl doesn't have a chance to live. She's going to close her eyes any second, and we'll never see her again. The devil owns you people! What am I doing down here in this god-forsaken place?"

Keleewa was trying to cover Yawalama's leg muscle with some loose skin when he looked up and saw Raul's eyes.

There he saw the same despair he felt. He had been yelling at the prey.

Keleewa stepped over to Raul and put his bloody arms around him. "We'll do everything we can." He turned back to Yawalama, shaking his head, and muttered to himself, "It won't be much. Nobody's ever going to survive this." He turned and looked at her face to see if she was still with him. She knew Keleewa. Everybody knew Keleewa, the best friend the Yanomamö people ever had. Now it was her turn to get his kindness. Her big eyes stared at him, and she smiled a little. *That smile won't be there long,* he thought. *She'll leave here in a minute, we'll burn her body, and then I'm leaving and not coming back.*

But she didn't die. And Keleewa and his wife and sisters spent the rest of the night cleaning her wounds and putting muscles back on arms and legs. They tied the parts onto sticks of wood to hold them together and jammed pads and white cloths against them as tight as possible. The knee cap was cut off and tendons stuck out. They stuck it back and taped it together. Every few minutes Keleewa looked to see if she was still alive. She was so close to death that she felt no pain. It looked as if she had lost most of her blood. Raul stood watching and weeping. Women wailed.

All night they worked on her. They couldn't talk on the radio for help, because the plane couldn't fly at night.

When the sun finally came, Yawalama was still alive. Keleewa's wife used the radio to call for the plane. Three hours later they placed her carefully on a long stiff hammock and put her into the back of the plane. Raul watched it carry his sister down the long grass strip and then up into the air.

He shook his head and cried. Would he ever see her again? Would his people always live like this? Could they somehow, some time, be able to live the way they do in Honey?

The plane lifted and flew across the river and over the trees. Raul stood watching while the rest of the villagers left. *Is there any hope?* he wondered. *Even if she lives, what will she come back to? Women don't have a chance out here in this jungle.* He remembered that horrible smell the day a man got mad at his wife. He had knocked her to the ground and stood on one of her ankles. Then he picked up her other ankle with his hands and with her legs apart he held a stick from the fire up between them. "If you don't want to have me, you won't have anyone for a while," Raul remembered the man shouting. He held it there until it made the whole place stink from the burning flesh.

Raul watched until the plane was out of sight. *Maybe I'll stay in this village for a time,* he thought. *The men here are so strange. They are not even afraid to be seen helping their women. Maybe I can learn what makes them different.*

14

KILLERS LIKE ME

*he people in Honey are very rich. And they get richer every season.
But mostly they are happy. Shoefoot's children are healthy and
beautiful. And his wife and his friends, they are happy.*

*And what about me? Why haven't I been able to be rich? And
why am I so unhappy? My village is nothing. All my children have
died except my only son. And he's got Deer Spirit. Well, he says he has
Deer Spirit. But he doesn't; Deer Spirit has him. He's useless to me! I
would move our whole village to Honey, but Deer Spirit will never let
my son come. And I want my son with me too much to leave him. It's
all Deer Spirit's fault.*

*What do I have? What good thing is mine after all my life with
these spirits?*

I left Honey one day in a canoe to go back upriver. My
wife was happy for the time she had spent with Shoefoot and
his wife and children. They were so happy in Honey, and she
was always happy every time we visited. Funnyman steered
the little engine and moved the canoe around the sandbars.
This is such a nicer way to travel than the old paddling, I started to
think while I watched the overhanging jungle pass slowly by. I
began to think about my misery.

We passed Forgetful Village and I remembered Longfoot

and the pain he had caused Yoshicami and Yawalama. It reminded me of the pain I had caused Deemeoma.

"Don't throw us away, Father," Jaguar Spirit begged me again, and he was joined by the others. They crowded in around me like terrified bats.

"Why do you want me any more?" I asked. "I'm old now. I'm no more use to you." But they kept upsetting me again. Now I was having these bad thoughts about my spirits each time after we visited Honey. But my spirits were always so troubled by my thoughts that I never finished thinking them.

I'll finish these thoughts today, I told myself. And I did. They were thoughts that I have always known. But my spirits had always kept me from thinking them. Not today though.

I've got nothing! I've been a fool! All my life I've been a fool, and now I don't even have a family. The only love and care I get comes from these relatives who have thrown away all our spirits and all our ways.

"It's not our fault," Charming begged. "You need the spirit of Families-Together to help you. We'll help you find the spirit and your family will be better, even as good as the families in Honey." I didn't answer her. I've heard all these excuses all my life: "Don't blame us," "We're not the spirit for that problem," "You need another spirit," and on and on they have always gone.

But I already had more spirits than anybody. What I didn't have was enough time left in my life for anything to get any better.

My spirits hated my thoughts that day as Funnyman took us around each bend in the river. But I thought them anyway.

Not long after, I was walking down the trail one morning, coming back from fishing. I hadn't caught anything. It was a bright sunny day, but the jungle trail was dark and cool. I was alone with my thoughts when I saw my spirits come up behind me with machetes. Many of my spirits had already left and gone to younger shamans. It's normal—I'm old.

They took one mighty swing and hit me in the back of the neck. I looked to see if my head was chopped off and rolling down the trail. Then I fell and everything went dark. But I knew what was happening. My time was over. I had taught all my shamans this. We all know that when your usefulness is over, they will come and take you away—kill you, is what I mean.

But I never thought they would come for me. I think we all felt that way. We would never say it out loud, but I think we had the feeling, "Spirits come and kill old shamans, but somehow *my* time won't come." I especially had the right to feel that way because I had always had such a special relationship with all my spirits.

Surprised as I was, there was nothing I could do. They were trying to kill me.

Back at the shabono, my son and the other shaman could feel what was happening. They looked at each other and my son yelled, "The spirits are killing father! They've already chopped him in the back of the neck!"

My wife screamed, "Get down there and help him!" The whole village jumped up and ran out of the shabono entrance and down the trail. But I was a long way.

When I woke up I was lying on the ground. My spirits pounded on my chest. I jumped up and ran through the jungle like I have never run. I came to a clearing and tripped and fell to the jungle floor. Again they began to pound on my chest. My breath left me, but I felt no pain. I lay in the long grass and watched one fist after another hit my chest with great force. But I couldn't feel anything. Even though I knew I should expect it, I couldn't believe that my closest friends in all the world were doing this to me. Even Charming was with them.

Just before they killed me, a bright light came. It was so bright that I couldn't see anything. And there was something very warm like I have never felt. A creature stood over me, more dazzling than anyone could ever think. As soon as I felt him, I knew who he was. He was the one we have always called Yai Wana Naba Laywa—the unfriendly spirit, the enemy spirit. He was the same one who has eaten the spirits of our children, the one we and all our spirits have hated, the one I've always been so afraid of at Honey. He was the same spirit that my follower, Shoefoot, had taken when he threw away the spirits I found for him. All those times he had angered me with stories about a great spirit who became a man and made a trail to his land—I knew it was that spirit. I have never seen such beautiful light.

I lay on the ground in the cloud of brightness and I saw my whole life, and I saw how completely tricked I had been. I remembered all the things my spirits had told me. Now suddenly in this bright light, I saw that they were all lies. Everything they ever said was a lie. And such clever lies too! All our revenge, every habit, our chest-pounding, all of it was to make us unhappy. I had been used by my spirits for their pleasure.

I saw Shecoima dancing to save the baby eagle. What a lie! I saw myself chasing souls of children. They weren't being eaten—they were going to be with Yai Wana Naba Laywa in his beautiful land of the clear river. I saw the dead people I had hung out in the jungle and the dirty job it was to clean the meat off their bones so we could grind them. How tricked I was!

I've run from this creature of beauty all my life, I thought. *No wonder I have nothing.*

All of it happened in the snap of a bowstring. Yai Wana Naba Laywa reached out and grabbed me. I felt so safe. *That's why it doesn't hurt,* I thought. He stood over me, pulled me away from my spirits, and said to me, "Don't worry. You'll be all right. I'm here to protect you." Then with a big voice the spirit said to my spirits, "Leave him alone. He's mine." They scampered in every direction, like a herd of terrified hogs. And he was right; I was his.

At that moment I felt safer than ever in my life. I watched my spirits running so far away from me. When I saw their terror, all the fear of my whole life just ran away with them. Just when I needed another spirit most, Shoefoot's spirit suddenly decided to free me from my spirits.

Right then my village came. They found me in the clearing, sitting in the grass along the side of the trail. I was dizzy over what I had just seen. We always thought that Yai Wana Naba Laywa was hot, like in a fire. But he wasn't hot at all, just warm. So very warm.

"You're dying!" my son yelled as they ran to me.

"No, I feel good," I said. But I couldn't say how good it felt.

"No, you're dying," the others said. "The spirits have come to kill you. We know you are dying."

"No, I'm good," I said while they helped me to stand up. "It's true, they did come to kill me. But while I was dying from their blows, Yai Wana Naba Laywa came and saved me."

"We'll go to Honey to get help for you."

"No. I don't need it. I feel good," I said. They could tell that there was something wrong with me. So they sent someone to Honey to tell them I was dying. There was nothing I could say to stop them.

That night I lay in my hammock and for the first time in my life there were no spirits coming to me, wanting to chant and dance and talk. I had always thought I could never live without them. But I lay in my hammock and felt so happy to hear the sound of quiet. And not only happy, but so peaceful and so secure. There was no more noisy crowding or darkness in my shabono. I wondered if it could be all this happiness, peace and quiet that my spirits had been so afraid of when they always begged me not to throw them away. "Yai Wana Naba Laywa," I said, "do you have ears like the others?" I could tell that he heard me. So I asked him to keep me out of the fire pit, the place all us shamans feared.

When the people from Honey came, I told them that I wasn't sick and that they came for nothing. But I knew I had to go back with them to learn more about my amazing new spirit.

On the trip down to Honey I was still thinking about all the things I had understood about my spirits in that moment on the trail. In Honey I began to learn from Keleewa about the spirit of forgiveness instead of revenge, the spirit of kindness instead of fierceness. Keleewa said all these ideas came from my new spirit. We shamans have always called him Yai Wana Naba Laywa, but now that I know he isn't our enemy, I call him Yai Pada, the great spirit. Now as they told me about how he became a man and cut a trail for us to follow him to his beautiful land, I could see how true it all was.

"I know," I said. "You told me before about how the great spirit had become a man, but I was kept from seeing it. But I know that he is the one who rescued me from my spirits on the trail."

I shook my head and clicked my tongue again. How had I missed it for so long? Everything was now so clear, and so different.

One day a visitor from Hairy's village came to Honey with horrible news for Keleewa. Someone had blown alowali on Hairy's brother and he was dying. He begged Keleewa to go back to the village with him.

After two days on the river and through the jungle, they found Hairy's brother almost dead with malaria. After they gave him medicine he got better. Keleewa warned the village strongly that it was not alowali that made him sick, and they should not be asking spirits for someone to blame.

It was easy to see now. Alowali was another big lie the spirits had told us.

"We won't," Hairy promised. "We will learn the new ways and follow a new spirit. What do we have to do to get someone to come and teach us about your Yai Pada? We would like to clear a place here in the jungle so that the plane can land right here where we are." Keleewa wondered if Hairy knew what he was saying.

"If you clear it, we will come," Keleewa told him. Hairy knew that he meant it.

Hairy pushed the canoe carrying Keleewa, Trip, and the others out into the water and watched them turn downstream toward Honey. He remembered the wife he had killed. *I don't want to treat women like that any more*, he thought. *I don't want my children to be killers like me. I want them to follow the spirit of this man of peace. I want all of us to be free of our past. I want to sleep again.*

That day Hairy and all his people began clearing the jungle. Friends and enemies from other villages came to laugh. There were huge trees to cut and stumps to dig out. Then trouble struck again. Hairy's brother became very sick again.

This time Keleewa's brother Miqie went from Honey with Funnyman and a few others. They got there just before dark. Hairy's brother was just about to die. In the middle of the night he woke up and told them that he wasn't coming back. At dawn he was dead. The killer malaria would take many that season.

The fire for burning his body was set. Miqie, Funnyman, and the others could smell the smoke as they hurried down the trail to bring the news back to Honey.

Almost everyone in Honey went to Hairy's village. They stayed for a long time and mourned with Hairy and his people. They strongly warned them not to turn back to their spirits to get revenge. Now it was easy for me to see that revenge was the worst trick. What a lie! How it ruled us. And we had always thought that *we* ruled the spirits!

"We will never do that," Hairy said with many tears of sorrow for his brother. His brother had also been a great warrior and killer. Now all the leadership would be left to Hairy. "If we finish clearing the jungle for the airplane to land, will you send someone here to help us?" Hairy asked.

"If you clear it, someone will come," Miqie said to them all.

Each time something like this happened, I saw how we had been tricked by our spirits in so many ways. But the new spirit didn't just do everything that anyone wanted. One day Won't-Grow came to Pepe with a question. "This new spirit that we follow," Won't-Grow asked him, "is he able to take that big black mark off Yaiyomee's face?" Won't-Grow knew how much his girl was bothered by it. She was learning to hold her head so people couldn't see her face.

"Certainly he can," Pepe answered—maybe a little too fast, he thought. But why not? After he had seen a village of killers turned into such active peace-lovers that they forgave their enemies, what was a little birthmark? "You come to my house tomorrow and we'll talk to Yai Pada." *It really wasn't very little,* Pepe thought.

Won't-Grow came and they prayed. Nothing happened. He came the next day and they prayed. And the next day and the next. This went on for moons, placing Pepe in a clumsy spot.

"Yai Pada doesn't always do just what we want him to," Pepe told Won't-Grow one day. "But we can keep on asking anyway." So Won't-Grow continued to go to Pepe's house. But nothing ever happened. It reminded him of the time I called on the spirits to send armadillos to dig under the walls of Pepe's house and to make the jaguars lie in wait on the trails. But the spirits couldn't do it. Now Won't-Grow decided that Yai Pada couldn't do everything either. But Won't-Grow kept going to Pepe's house.

I never had asked my old spirits to do magical things like Won't-Grow was asking from Yai Pada. I only wanted them to take away some of our misery and help us live better. And now I saw all the ways my old spirits had stopped us from living better.

About this time word came to Honey that Toucan was very sick with malaria. His people helped him make the trip to the nabas, but he knew he wouldn't get there in time. When he thought he was about to go to sleep, he made all his relatives promise that they would not drink his bones or take revenge for his death. Soon after they came to the nabas' houses, Toucan died.

When word came to Honey, there was great mourning in the village. Many thought that there would have to be a raid and a killing to get vengeance for him. The death of a great man like Toucan cannot happen without vengeance. But to this day no one has ever drank his bones, and no vengeance has been taken for his death.

Toucan was one of the big memories from my past. What a great fight I and my spirits had against him and his people. Even though he had been our enemy, he is now our friend. And all of Honey cried for him. We were comforted by knowing that he wasn't killed by his spirits.

I know that my time is coming soon and it is good to know that I won't be killed by my spirits.

Toucan's death was special because I knew very well where he went. He was the first of a new generation of us shamans to throw away our spirits and follow Yai Pada's trail to his beautiful land. Our spirits had always told us that if we tried to throw them away, they would kill us—maybe the biggest lie of all.

EPILOGUE:

BE GOOD TO HER

Fredi was never happy in Forgetful Village. Even though I helped him find so many spirits, he never had the right one. When he thought he couldn't get any sadder, the limb of a tree fell on his daughter and killed her. In sorrow, he went back to Honey, threw away all the spirits that I had given him, and hung his desires on the spirit-man, Yai Pada. My relatives in Honey are very good to him. Now that he is old, he feels comfort that the great sadness of his life is passed.

Yawalama has recovered almost completely. Today she can walk and use both of her hands. She never did go back to Longfoot and has been taken as a wife by a young man in another village.

Yoshicami had so much sorrow over Redhair's death that she ran away from Forgetful Village and never went back. She suffered much from the time they fought for her and stamped on her stomach. Not long after, before her stomach got big, she got her birth pains and lost Redhair's baby.

She found a man in another village to care for her and her children. When she was very big with his baby, she became sick and burned with malaria. They brought her back to

Honey. She was only half awake and the baby was ready to come. But she was too weak, and both she and the baby died. The people of Honey burned her body and mourned for her. They still hold Bearded-One responsible for her death.

After Yoshicami died, an Indian named Carl came from another village to live and work in Honey. But Carl got all the men in Honey mad at him when he gave his daughter to a man who was the same age as his own grandfather. Then he decided to give his next daughter to Longfoot, the same man who left Yoshicami and chopped Yawalama. The men of Honey told Carl that they wouldn't let him do it.

Carl went back to his old village to ask his father what to do. "Of course you can give her to Longfoot," his father said. "We're Yanomamö; we can give any girl to anyone we want. That's our way. But why do such a terrible thing to your own daughter? You know our ways are horrible for little girls. So if you're going to follow that strange new spirit in Honey, then you can't give her to Longfoot; you have to be good to her."

But Carl gave her to Longfoot anyway. When Shoefoot heard this, he told Carl that no one in Honey would ever say that she belonged to Longfoot and that Carl would have to leave Honey and not come back.

The naba they call Doesn't-Miss was visiting Honey when this happened. He asked Shoefoot why he forced his own people to change their ways.

Shoefoot explained. "Even before we knew better, we knew that our ways were bad. But it was all we knew. Now that we know a better way to live, we can't let someone come here and enjoy all the good that we have in our village and then treat his daughter in those terrible old ways. If we did, it would be the start of us going back to the old ways ourselves. And we'll never do that."

But Doesn't-Miss said that Shoefoot only gave up his old ways because he listened to nabas like Pepe and Keleewa and that if he would listen to nabas like Irritating-Bee, he would keep the old ways like so many other Indians did.

Shoefoot said he could listen to whoever he wanted.

So Doesn't-Miss told Shoefoot what most nabas say—that the people of Honey have been tricked by nabas who give them trade goods so that they will throw their spirits away and come to church. The people of Honey are poor, so they do it.

"Nabas who say things like that are good at writing books and making money selling pictures of our naked women," Shoefoot said to Doesn't-Miss. "They mock my people. I've lived my whole life here in this jungle. If they think they know the best way to live here, let them come and show us. And tell them not to bring any guns with them. And no clothes. We'll even show them how to grow yucca before we send them off to their wonderful life in the jungle."

He pointed across the river to the green that went on forever. "People who talk like that do not know of the pain of my people who still live in misery every day. Am I a dog, that I should have my wife and children live in pain all the time because of what your people in your land say?"

Doesn't-Miss didn't ask any more questions.

One of the nabas who came into Yanomamö land and did many things to help our people was a man they called Doctor Anduce. When he was young he worked hard to try to heal people and always treated Indians with kindness. Later he became one of the leaders of the country.

One time he made the guards get A.H. and take him away from the territory. They took A.H. out of the jungle in big metal bracelets and chains. But after many moons he came back.

Dr. Anduce tried to get the bones of the boy who died after stealing the naba's food, saying that he was poisoned by the naba. The doctor told the people he could tell by looking at the bones if the boy had been poisoned. The people trusted Anduce, but they could not give up any of the bones of their dead.

Over many seasons he kept trying to get the bones, to get A.H. taken from our land, and to protect our people from gold miners and other nabas. He wanted to make sure we were able to live here as we wanted. But before he got any of these things done, Dr. Anduce died.

Hairy and his people finished clearing the jungle for the plane to land. The whole village gathered when they heard the sound of a motor over the treetops, a sound they had never heard over their village. Children jumped. Young men danced. Old women laughed. Hairy stood like he always did—

arms folded over his bow and arrows, one hand over his mouth. It was a new day for his people. The plane floated down and glided toward him. Tears came. And he didn't know why he should be crying. He was happier than he could ever remember. He had never had this kind of tears before.

Keleewa's sister moved with her husband and children to Hairy's village. They still live there.

One day a naba visited Honey. He saw the big, black mark on Yaiyomee's face. It was the biggest, ugliest mark he had ever seen. He asked Pepe about it. The children still teased her, so she always kept her head down.

Finally he said, "In my country I'm a doctor. If her parents want, I'll take that off." He paused. "No cost."

Pepe smiled. He had never doubted that Yai Pada *could* answer Won't-Grow's prayer, but he had often wondered if he would. "I'll ask them," he said.

Today Yaiyomee is beautiful. All the young men quarreled with each other over who would get her for a wife. After she married, she moved with her husband to Forgetful Village to help them. She now has many children. Her grandmother, Deemeoma, is very happy.

The territory where the head was stolen was called unsafe for any naba to travel into. Finally government people talked Keleewa into making a trip into the territory to tell Shetary that they hadn't stolen his son's head, and to ask him to let them travel safely there. Keleewa did and Shetary said that he wouldn't kill anyone but A.H. No one has ever seen A.H. in that part of the jungle again.

Longbeard, who killed his Indian wife and was killed by her relatives, became known as a great person in the world of the nabas. The nabas have a special word for a great person who is willing to be killed while trying to do something very important. Nabas can be so slow in the head when they want to be. Like so many things here in Yanomamö land, it's a split-truth. He was trying to do something very important—important to him. But the dead girl's relatives know what the "important" thing really was, and the nabas probably never even found out that there was a dead girl.

Padre Gonzales died. He was a wonderful man and a great person to our people. The nabas should have forgotten about Longbeard and used their special word on Padre Gonzales.

To this day the people in Tigerlip's village still mourn for Padre Coco and are sorry that they did not listen to him.

Many seasons after Irritating-Bee left, Kaobawa became angry with his spirits because of all the misery that kept coming to his people. All his brothers died, and his children. His spirits kept telling him to kill. Finally he threw them away in disgust. He thought they might kill him, but he didn't care.

Many seasons later he traveled to Honey to learn about Yai Pada. After learning about a good spirit, Kaobawa said, "I'm really mad now, because Irritating-Bee lied to me about the naba spirit and left me here suffering with my awful spirits. My village is miserable. Why did he lie to me?"

My people all over the jungle still fight and kill. Honey is the only place where they don't. Men from Honey often travel to other villages to try to get them to stop their wars. Shortman traveled to his home village at Sahael and to Sahael's enemy village to try to get them to give up their killing ways and try peace. But they didn't listen to him.

Shortman thought many sad thoughts as he traveled back up the Padamo River toward Honey. *Now my relatives face a double nightmare,* he thought. *They have their need for revenge and have added the weapons of the nabas. It's the nabas who really know about evil. Maybe the shamans are right about Omawa,* he wondered. *Maybe he did go to the world of the nabas to teach them the things he taught us. And he's taught them better. They have sex habits that have brought us even worse diseases, and they have much better killing tools than we do.*

Shortman whispered to Yai Pada for help. He shook his head at the thought of his relatives. *Is there any hope that it will ever end?* he wondered.

Now, about me: I still live upriver from Honey with Shoe-foot's sister. And we are so happy here, happier than I've ever been. I haven't seen any of my spirits since that day Yai Pada scared them away. Now I lie in my hammock and talk to him at night just like I used to do with my old spirits. And now even I have stopped many of the old ways. We don't kill any more or drink bones or rape or take ebene.

The only sad thing is my son. He still has that disgusting spirit of the deer. Whenever friends come to visit, he disappears into the jungle and doesn't come back for days. But not even the peace and beauty of the jungle can hide the war of fear that runs wild in him.

The white naba, the one they named Doesn't-Miss, the one who asked Shoefoot and Hairy about change, thought a lot about their answers. He decided to help us make our lives better and spent many days listening to me and all my new friends. He put all of these words of mine on paper so that you could see them.

I wish I had known the truth about Yai Wana Naba Laywa when I was a young man—it would have saved me so much pain and misery. But how could I? My spirits lied so much to me and tricked me. They were so beautiful, so wonderful, so hard not to want. They were the best at telling me split-truth. Now I'm at the end of this life, and I'm ready to begin my real life with Yai Pada.

16

AUTHOR'S ADDENDUM: SO MANY OF THEM ARE DEAD

On April 14, 1994, Jungleman died. Looking back, I think I hardly knew him after all, a great misfortune. By this I mean that the whole time I knew him, all we ever did together was tell and retell stories. I knew him well in that respect, but never as a friend. We never went hunting together, never ran the river, never lay in hammocks with fish line in the water. By the time I met him, he was too old to do all those things.

I shouldn't have been so surprised at Jungleman's death. He was old and close to death that first day when we sat to talk. But his stories were so lively and his enthusiasm so great that I didn't notice the generational gap between us. Within minutes of our meeting he was recounting one story after another in graphic detail, so graphic I kept wondering how much detail was surviving the translation. Dignity prohibits a complete description of Jungleman's talent. Keleewa, a person of considerable humility and piety, struggled in vain to translate Jungleman into palatable English while I asked myself, "How am I going to write this? No matter how much I tone this man down, I can still hear the critics: 'Too much sex—too much violence—too degrading of women.'" Still, I admit my surprise when major publishing houses turned this book down, citing its violence as a reason.

But now he is gone and his story is on the record. If it is (as one professor labeled it) "crap," we would expect it to be exposed in the future by additional evidence and stories. But if Jungleman has represented his people fairly and accurately, a new view of the Yanomamö will have emerged.

Since the first release of this book, Shoefoot, Keleewa, and I have made four tours to promote it. Anthropologist Neil L.

Whitehead, respected tribal warfare authority at the University of Wisconsin, called these tours "eloquent testimony to the resentment felt by some at the iconic representation of the Yanomamö." Whatever else it may be, touring the U.S. with a Yanomamö Indian is pure adventure. And the height of adventure would be a chance for Shoefoot to meet again Irritating-Bee, the anthropologist who had made his people so famous. By now Dr. Napoleon Chagnon's book on the Yanomamö had become the bestselling anthropological book of all time.

That's why there was a pent-up feeling of anticipation as we entered a luxurious room on the twelfth floor of the downtown San Francisco Hilton. It was the annual convention of the American Anthropological Association, and Chagnon had agreed to meet us at his booth that afternoon. Shoefoot hadn't been invited to the convention, so I was nervous about how we would be received.

Shoefoot didn't seem to share my anxiety. He surveyed the opulent room and said, "Now, this is how I deserve to be treated." It was Yanomamö humor; we'd been staying at Motel 6 up to that point.

But I knew that when it came to Chagnon, Shoefoot's humor was in short supply. The Yanomamö are naturally very confrontational. Shoefoot had long ago given up physical confrontation—but verbal? If a Yanomamö has a grievance against a person, he doesn't start with small talk. The first words out of his mouth will go straight to the heart of the problem. It doesn't matter how old the grievance, he will address it, and in the fewest possible words. This can be intimidating when in public, even if in another language. Although I didn't know what Shoefoot would say, it promised to be an interesting afternoon.

While Shoefoot and Keleewa rested in the room, I registered us. Outside the huge room displaying all the products of the anthropological world I nearly bumped into Professor Neil Whitehead. He apparently recognized me by my badge or the copy of *Spirit of the Rainforest* in my hand. "You're Mark Ritchie. You're gonna get sued," he said, in as friendly a way as is possible to a perfect stranger. When he invited me to sit for a chat, I hoped he couldn't read intimidation written across my face.

Within an hour of meeting Whitehead, I introduced him to Shoefoot and we went to our appointed meeting at Chagnon's booth. By this time no one could have missed the intimidation I felt. We had inadvertently placed Shoefoot's "everything is a lie" charge too close to Chagnon's name on the back cover of the first edition of this book. And we had made too big a deal of his "bums, beggars, and prostitutes" comment. Moreover, Chagnon's reputation for dramatic confrontations is well known. But my anxiety was mounting for nothing. He didn't show up. Later I reached Dr. Chagnon by phone and we agreed on another time for him to meet Shoefoot at his booth.

Escorting a Yanomamö Indian through the Hilton's lobbies filled with the world's leading anthropologists is an experience in itself. Shoefoot is so short he can't possibly stand out in a crowd. There are thousands of scholars and hundreds of papers to be presented. Escalators took us from one magnificent floor to another, past chandeliers with lights and glass that went on forever. Shoefoot struggled to get onto the escalator. I wondered if I could possibly tell him that if we had just one of those chandeliers we could sell it and build a medical clinic in Honey Village.

Next day, waiting at Chagnon's booth, we began to watch the newly released CD-ROM showing Yanomamö Indians engaged in a small axe fight. The selling point: it was interactive. The student could manipulate the CD in order to actually interact in some way with the Indians. I had already seen the CD and warned Keleewa that it might be painful for Shoefoot, who possibly had deceased relatives in it. But he wanted to see it.

On the high-resolution computer screen, surrounded by the world's leading scholars, Shoefoot was taken on a visual trip to a past he had long ago put behind him, a life of warfare, disease, pain, and ultimately the dread of extinction. He watched his people humiliate themselves with fighting words that led to violence. One doesn't need a translator to read pain in a man's face, or grief in his eyes. Shoefoot shook his head and quietly said, "So many of them are dead," and Professor Whitehead was there.

We waited for about an hour at the booth, but once again Shoefoot was disappointed that Chagnon wasn't able to make it.

"He's afraid of me," Shoefoot said. It was hard for me to

imagine at the time. I didn't say anything, but I had the feeling that he might not fully understand the situation.

Then I read Whitehead's review of *Spirit of the Rainforest*. He wrote of the uncomfortable irony "that those who are studied might offer their own self-understanding in place of our ethnographies, and write ethnographies of our fieldwork practice, instead of our fieldwork producing their ethnography." This sentence is profound, not merely because he has stated it so much better than I, but because he appears to be the first scholar to make such an observation, even labeling it an irony. Whitehead actually applied the word "conceit" to the CD-ROM project. While scholars have been listening to and studying the Yanomamö for decades, Whitehead may have been the first to hear and see a Yanomamö respond to Yanomamology. Their response to the very word "Yanomamology" would be enlightening enough. (See p. 256 for quotes from Whitehead's review, and my response.)

Introducing Shoefoot to the AAA at the Hilton was a bit like showing him the house that anthropology built. It reminded me of the time he told an audience, "We Yanomamö are tired of people coming to our lands in order to make money studying us." The comment created such an offense with a few of the scholars present that Shoefoot was obliged to explain. He told of a picture postcard he had found for sale in Caracas, of a beautiful Yanomamö woman. He had asked Keleewa how much it would cost so that he could buy and destroy it. (What he didn't tell the audience was that the woman was a deceased relative.)

"The more you buy, the more they make," Keleewa had explained to his old friend. Thus had begun Shoefoot's education into the ways of the nabas.

"So I have guessed," Shoefoot concluded to his audience that day, "that someone makes money studying my people."

But Shoefoot could never have guessed that they made enough money to convene by the thousands at the San Francisco Hilton. I didn't have the heart to tell him that if we had the money spent on this week-long meeting, we could build a school in every Yanomamö village. I knew what Shoefoot would say: anthropologists wouldn't want a school in *any* Yanomamö village.

Shoefoot's understanding of anthropology was about to get

a course correction. After leaving the AAA we went to Stanford, where we visited a medical anthropology class. Dr. Clifford Barnett, the professor, had just stepped off the plane from Asia and cordially invited us to speak to his students.

Afterward students gathered around Shoefoot with questions and reactions while I spoke to Barnett, who made a comment I'd been waiting to hear: "Whenever an anthropologist is finished studying a culture, he's obligated to give something back to it to help the people improve their lives." I immediately called Shoefoot and Keleewa over, insisted that Barnett repeat himself, and watched for Shoefoot's reaction.

"He's an anthropologist?" Shoefoot asked, pointing at Barnett with a look of disbelief. It was a special moment. *Even Yanomamö have stereotypes,* I thought, keeping my laughter to myself. "I'm learning a lot on this trip," Shoefoot would later confide.

"If you don't like people to come and study you, what kind of people *do* you want to come into your land?" a student asked.

"I'm not an animal to be studied," was his response. "We want people who will help us improve our way of life, not just write books about us." That was his short answer to the question. On this particular day he elaborated.

"We want people who will really care about us, like the man who came into my village and put his arm around me when I was covered with dirt, sweat, saliva, and mucous. This man shared in our suffering. He cared about our children. He showed us something we knew nothing about—love." Shoefoot's audience was on the verge of tears.

Naturally, not all missionaries are like the man Shoefoot described that day. Chagnon writes of a missionary who yelled and screamed at the Indians, calling their habits the demonic work of filthy spirits, intimidating them with waving arms and pictures of hell. Chagnon makes a strong point. I myself write of a missionary who "spanked" an Indian woman with a stick, another who had an inappropriate relationship with an underage girl, and others who were overtly racist against Indians. One semimissionary actually killed his Indian wife. These stories have garnered both Chagnon and me plenty of wrath from mission circles.

Shoefoot's point was simple: *We want people to help us, not study us like animals.* Then he sees his deceased relatives exposed and humiliated on a CD-ROM and is told that it is the latest advance in ethnography.

Having spent years with the Yanomamö, Chagnon isn't one to fall victim to the delusion that manipulation of a CD-ROM provides ethnographic exposure to the Yanomamö. The irony is that the CD didn't work. But even if it had worked, such ethnography doesn't work. Could it be possible to become so focused on ethnography that one doesn't hear the people speak?

There is a curious footnote to this particular story. The kind missionary of whom Shoefoot speaks and the harsh missionary Chagnon describes? They're the same person: Joe Dawson. This demonstrates the general lack of reliability built into data coming from isolated cultures in distant lands. Verifiability is nearly always quite impractical. Whitehead's criticism that the CD-ROM places the Yanomamö "out of time" is an unverifiable guess—unless a Yanomamö shows up to give it some support. In this exceedingly rare instance, one did. How enlightening it might have been had Chagnon been able to engage this dialogue.

After the AAA we traveled to Colorado, where we found ourselves in a radio studio sitting across the table from a young and very sweet African-American talk show host— an Oprah in the making. I'm used to the talk-show circuit by now, but I was ill prepared for the turn this discussion abruptly took. A caller engaged us in a debate over our general credibility and the destruction of both the rainforest and the Yanomamö culture. The man, obviously educated and well spoken, became frustrated that Shoefoot couldn't be dissuaded and referred to him as a "token nigger."

It was one of those moments when your mind fills with thoughts, memories, pictures, more than you could ever express. I recalled a myriad of racial and class inequities I'd experienced: the extreme poor I'd played with in the streets of Afghanistan as a boy; the almost outcast poor I'd gone to school with; using the word "Jew" as a verb; how much the Yanomamö have to teach us; how much they taught Chagnon "about being human"; how the death of a shaman is like "a library being burned down."

And now Shoefoot, this man with the wisdom of the ages,

having disputed the opinion of a few educated callers, found himself labeled a token nigger. Nevertheless, he answered the man gracefully, even humbly. He suggested that even though the man sounded like he knew a lot about the Yanomamö people, Shoefoot guessed that he had probably never been there or met a Yanomamö. He suggested that the caller was mocking his people.

We walked out of the studio that morning into a typically gorgeous Colorado day. And once again I had the same thought that has recurred since the release of this book: *This is an intellectual discussion about a group of people my audience has never seen, met, or even cared about. What is the source of all this venom?* Some theories came to mind as we made our way to Washington, D.C. and a visit to PBS.

On Derek McGinty's show he ignored Shoefoot for a moment, turned directly to me and said, "This is a question of your credibility." I don't mind McGinty or anyone else challenging my credibility. In his case it was refreshing. He's African-American; I could be assured my friend wasn't going to be called any racist names. But one can't ignore Shoefoot in this debate. Indeed, the attempt to ignore Shoefoot is what this story is about. One doesn't need to listen very long to him before his credibility is quite established. One man came to Shoefoot after hearing him and apologized, saying, "I wasn't talking about *your* jungle when I said not to develop it. I wasn't talking about *your* people when I said to leave them alone."

At a gathering of university activity directors we were displaying the book at a booth and encountered a student who recognized it as a text she had been assigned for one of her courses. She told me how controversial the story had been and how heated the class discussions. I asked, "How many of the class thought I concocted the whole story?" She gave me that how-did-you-know look. What she didn't know was that Shoefoot was sitting only a few feet away from us. I introduced them, saying, "Tell him exactly what students are saying about his book." She did—and he told her that every story in the book represents precisely what Jungleman and his people have said.

A certain contemporary book about the Aborigines is classified as fiction, but the author strongly hints in her opening material that it actually happened. There is no hinting in *Spirit of the Rainforest.* What you've read is not fiction. Every significant detail is written just as the Indians told it to me and every attempt has been made to avoid meddling with it myself. Every detail that was difficult to believe was double-checked with a variety of sources.

Some have asked what an *insignificant* detail might be. Page 12 is a good example of it; I am the source of the writing. On page 21, since Jungleman never did speak his name and I had the decency not to ask him, I placed the word "Jungleman" in his mouth and created the setting in which it was used. This is reasonable author liberty. However, as he begins in the next paragraph to tell of his childhood in the jungle, every detail is his alone.

Details, whether specific or general, make a story believable. All details in this story came from and belong to the Indians. I have no idea of the color of babies' brains. Nor do I know at what age a child's head is hard enough that it could not be broken on a shabono pole. It could be argued that I could have done a little medical research and discovered these details. I didn't. And I have no idea whether it is possible for a body to be supported in the sitting position by arrows protruding from it. I have no idea of the color of the gloves A.H. used to steal the head. (From the Indians' own description, it sounds as though they may have been surgical gloves and a surgical mask.) Anyone could speculate that I made up the description. The truth is that I got every detailed description from the Indians.

The best example I can give of this story belonging to the Yanomamö in every detail is the matter of the missing head. One senior anthropologist of national repute told me, "No one will ever believe that story. It will serve only to destroy the credibility of the book." His opinion has been echoed by others.

So I returned to my Indian sources. As we motored downstream on the Padamo toward the Orinoco, Won't-Grow asked what brought me to the jungle again. I mentioned wanting to make sure that all the stories about A.H. were true, and to see what Won't-Grow and his friends would say about removing the story of the stolen head.

"My people say they will never believe that story," I told him.

Won't-Grow and Shortman started to talk. Miqie was with

us and translated. Two people can talk fairly well in a dugout canoe, but hardly four. I suggested we pull into the soft backside of a sandbar. Within minutes I had the camera set and, sitting high on top of a huge log, they began giving details. While Miqie translated into one channel of the stereo camera, I monitored on an earpiece.

Over the years I had come to know both Won't-Grow and Shortman quite well. They both visited me in the U.S. when Won't-Grow came to get Yaiyomee after her face surgery. I had introduced them to *Chicago Sun Times* reporter Neil Steinberg, who took us to the top of the Sears Tower during an interview. Shortman made the *Sun Times* "Quote of the Day" when he said, "Nothing about killing someone gives you pleasure."

Now they sat together, wild green jungle for a backdrop, and began to talk about Bosinawalewa (A.H.). But they struggled with embarrassment over the sexual stories. It is a mystery how modest the Yanomamö people can be; they quickly forget that they grew up naked. Embarrassment soon turned to shy snickering. Wanting all the facts as straight as I could get them, I tried to keep the material serious. But as long as they were talking, I let them go.

Finally Shortman said, "This really isn't all that funny. I suppose we shouldn't be laughing." A hush fell over us. I had the feeling that Shortman had made another quote for the day. A shaman's apprentice, a killer, a man with a horrible past, observed that the behavior of the white naba was too shameful for levity.

Their message was clear: "We don't care what your nabas believe. A.H. *did* all those things, including stealing the head."

It was a gorgeous day. Back in the canoe, the motor droned around never-ending turns of overhanging foliage and I contemplated my dilemma. I had given them my word that I would tell *their* story, not mine, and now I had been considering deleting a story in order to preserve my credibility in my own culture. As much as I told myself, "Take out the part about the stolen head. Save it for a later edition. Earn credibility first," I could not censor their story because of my audience. The story stayed.

As it turns out, the story of the stolen head has actually enhanced credibility in the eyes of the very few who are in the know. As one anthropologist put it, "No one would be foolish enough to make up a story that outrageous!"

One critic claimed that *Spirit of the Rainforest* was written by a secret Chagnon supporter in order to make Chagnon look good by comparison to A.H. I make mention of this more for comic relief than anything else. This notion is simply erroneous. I've never met Chagnon. Neither have I ever met the person who wants to look good by comparison with A.H.

It has been suggested that I failed to mention a number of scandalous charges that could have made certain characters look much worse. This is true. However, it is quite irrelevant to this book. My commitment has been to tell the *Indians'* story, not grind an axe against any individual.

Scandalous and false charges have been made about me, too. I view them with gratitude. They've helped me appreciate how easy it is to pass on false charges unwittingly. Each repetition adds to the appearance of credibility, and usually distorts the charge as well.

But all the charges made in this book come to the reader from the Yanomamö Indians themselves. Because I'm committed to the accuracy of every story here, the more outlandish the story, the more witnesses and details I've demanded to substantiate it. And no one has yet identified so much as one line of this book that is anything short of accurate.

Over the last seventeen years since meeting Shoefoot and his people, I myself have viewed with skepticism much of what was told me. To date, however, that skepticism has proven unfounded. The fact that Shoefoot speaks no English and I don't write Ph.D. after my name does nothing to diminish the longevity of the truth we speak. In fact, one cannot imagine the confidence we have in it.

In concluding the matter of credibility, I have one overriding theme: Let the people themselves speak. Those who have heard Shoefoot have been given abundant data for consideration. A professor who declined to invite him, saying, "He would countermand all I have taught about the Yanomamö," simply missed out. The professor who said, "*Spirit of the Rainforest* is a bunch of crap," has surely never heard Shoefoot.

Shoefoot is personally acquainted with many of the scholars who have studied his people and published their studies. He watched with intrigue a number of authorities speak about his people on a nationally televised documentary released by ABC's "Prime Time Live." At its conclusion he commented, "Everything they say on your TV about my people is a lie."

Now we have arrived at a most unsettling point: The object of study has said to those who studied him, "Why did you describe me thus?" In his review, Neil Whitehead used phrases like "uncomfortable irony for us all" and "unsettling professional complacency" to capture the impact of an Indian speaking back.

Lest anyone think that Shoefoot has stooped to the level of returning insults, let me clarify. It is not any of the degrading statements made about his people that he calls a lie. Shoefoot was referring to the overarching conclusion drawn about the Yanomamö people which sees them as *living in Eden*. This view of the Yanomamö is best summarized by the subtitle to the popular version of Chagnon's book: *The Last Days of Eden*. The phrase is thoroughly inaccurate.

I have traveled the world over. If I could find James Hilton's Shangri La, I would move there. Alas, Hilton was a writer of fiction. I know not one single person subscribing to the Eden theory who has relocated to Eden with the goal of enjoying it—not one.

Surprising though it may be, Chagnon appears to agree with me on this point. How often do you see an author disavow his own title in the preface to his book? Yet that is precisely what Chagnon does. Without naming Eden as the specifically objectionable word, he argues forcefully that the Yanomamö are violent and against the broad majority opinion that isolated peoples live in peaceful tranquility. (Nothing is more important to a Yanomamö male than to be fierce.) Chagnon may have his critics, but on the subject of violence he is to be commended.

And he openly admits that his own anthropological community is the source of the error. "There is a definite bias in cultural anthropology," he writes and quotes a colleague who said of violence, "Even if they are that way, we do not want others to know about it—it will give them the wrong impression." So Eden is the "right" impression. Chagnon compares this mental state to the close-minded attitude of the anti-evolutionist, a refreshingly candid admission. (*Yanomamö: The Last Days of Eden*, 1992, Harcourt Brace and Company,

p. xv. The reader will find Chagnon's preface well worth reading in its entirety.)

Nothing has changed since Jungleman's death. The raiding, killing, and raping are still an integral part of Yanomamö life. A.H.'s village got into a war. He moved them to Mouth village for mutual defense and armed them with guns and ammo. Girls were raped and stolen for wives. A.H.'s village actually fought with their own Mouth allies and the people of Mouth killed some of them with the ammo A.H. had given for their defense. If there is any change it is only because they now have better killing weapons. Premature deaths are still the rule. Jungleman's death was a rare exception. Fredi is dead. Runner is dead. Dedeheiwa, to whom Chagnon dedicated his book, is dead.

"All my arrows are gone," Kaobawa said, meaning all his sons. Shoefoot summarized it plainly: "So many of them are dead."

A group of anthropology students took a trip to visit a different country and experience that culture in all its various aspects. Well, maybe not all. While there some of the students were raped and one of the girls murdered, a tragedy of the highest order. Let no one ever suggest that what I am about to write next is meant in any way to detract from the horror of this experience.

In a village close to Honey there was a dispute over a girl at the time she came to puberty. Being a good Yanomamö girl, she would have consented to live with and serve whatever man she was forced to go with. But before she could perform her duties as a wife, the dispute over her ownership would have to be settled. In a culture where possession is ten-tenths of the law, she became the object of a tug of war. She was too young and too small and soon died.

The story of this girl's death, a part of everyday life among the Yanomamö, is a tragedy equal to the death of the anthropology student. To say that one girl's life ended in tragedy and that the other girl lives in "Eden" is to make a mockery of the Yanomamö people.

Why do the Yanomamö stir such controversy and emotion? My theory now, looking back with better hindsight, is that we have come to see in the Yanomamö a mirror image of ourselves a few centuries removed. We don't want them to be violent because we don't want to think of ourselves as violent. We don't want them to be rapists because we don't want to think of ourselves as rapists. We need to believe that an Eden is possible. Above all, we want to believe in our own fundamental goodness.

But now let Shoefoot and his mentor, Jungleman, enter the scene, both of them shamans extraordinaire. They live in "Eden" and possess the wisdom of the rainforest, their brains virtual libraries. Both of them convert to Christianity and recommend that the rest of their tribe do the same. One student summarized a common question when she asked, "But can't you change for the better without becoming so religious?"

It is absolutely impossible for Shoefoot to answer that question in any way consistent with the tolerance expected in our culture. He genuinely believes that following the spirits of the shamans is detrimental to his culture and people. So he has no way to soften his answer to make it even appear palatable. Again and again he has repeated, "The spirits are evil. The only hope for my people is to stop following those spirits."

He has even identified the signs and symbols of many of the spirits right here in our "civilized" culture. He has no problem understanding the Columbine High School massacre (Colorado, 1999), or any other killing spree. The spirits of anger and hatred that own and drive a person are spirits he has known personally. He knows what it means to kill under the influence of something or someone. So when a student asks a natural follow-up question, "Why can't you get rid of your spirits without converting to Christianity?" his answer is simple: "I don't know any other way to get rid of the spirits that are destroying us. And no other shaman does either."

Shoefoot sees the world through spiritual eyes. He knows that apart from a small miracle, his tribe will either become extinct or will live out Chagnon's (and my) worst fear by becoming bums, beggars, and prostitutes. Herein lies the ultimate difference between Shoefoot and us. We study ethnography and don't believe in miracles. But Shoefoot himself is a small miracle of sorts. He once would have valued the skillful murdering work of the two assassins of Columbine High School. Now he is a brilliant leader of his people and a paragon of virtue.

I have a theory about the vitriolic reactions we've encountered. Remember the extreme spiritual and emotional tension often felt by shamans when in the presence of a person with the spirit of Yai Pada? I have a feeling that some people experience that same dramatic inner turmoil when confronted by Shoefoot and his message. I'll leave you, the reader, to be the final judge on this point. You tell me: When you think of Yai Pada, a spirit of love and forgiveness, do you have the same feelings of bitter inner conflict that Hot, Toucan, and other shamans had? When you think of Shoefoot converting to Christianity, do you have the same animosity over it that others have had? I am most curious to hear what you say on this point (write me in care of the publisher).

These highly charged emotional responses to Shoefoot, sometimes accompanied by fighting words, make me wonder if it might not be an inner conflict that merely reveals itself in ugly insults? This is only a guess on my part, but Shoefoot thinks so.

Jungleman is dead. But he spoke so respectfully of Yai Pada and his beautiful land, and his expectation of enjoying immortality there. Though I knew him only briefly, if he is right, we will meet again.

APPENDIX

Review posted on the internet by Thomas Headland, anthropologist at the University of Texas at Arlington, January 24, 1998.

Yanomamö: Noble Savages or Hobbesian Brutes?

The 16,000 Yanomamö people are depicted as the most primitive, most violent, and most famous tribal society in the Amazon. Popularized by the most widely read book in the history of anthropology (*Yanomamö: The Fierce People*, by Napoleon Chagnon), these people are today suffering excruciating problems from gold miners and newly introduced diseases. Major debates have raged among anthropologists, and between anthropologists and missionaries, for 20 years over the "truth" of the Yanomamö culture. Do they live a wonderful life in a beautiful rainforest Eden, as Chagnon implies in his 1992 book, *The Last Days of Eden*, or do they live in fear and misery as some missionaries say?

Perhaps we should ask that question [of] the Yanomamö themselves, rather than [of] the anthropologists or the missionaries. Who does speak for the Yanomamö, anyway? Here, for the first time, author Mark Ritchie allows the

Yanomamö to speak for themselves to us. This is truly "a Yanomamö shaman's story," as the book's subtitle says. It is the autobiography of a Yanomamö shaman-chief named Jungleman. He, at least, is weary of his violent society, and fed up with the anthropologists, too.

Anyone who thinks the Yanomamö culture is idyllic must be a male: The women live in chronic danger of gang-rapes, savage beatings by their husbands, and kidnapping. And men suffer one of the highest homicide rates in the world from the frequent raiding between villages. If you think it's a romantic way of life, why don't you try it?

Non-specialists in Amazonian anthropology may be skeptical of Jungleman's descriptions of the sexual customs of a European anthropologist who the Yanomamö call "Ass Handler." A.H. has lived with the Yanomamö for many years and, says Jungleman, makes a regular practice of forcibly sodomizing Yanomamö boys. Disbelievers may want to ask the opinion of any anthropologist specializing on the Amazon.

This is a gripping book to read: hard to put down, violent (some would say pornographic), and gut-wrenching. Students who have read the other ethnographies on the Yanomamö will recognize that this book has, above all, a ring of truth. New Age seekers will be fascinated by Jungleman's descriptions of the spirit world that shamans have found. Anthropology students will be shocked by Jungleman's insider view of the political internecine intrigues among anthropologists and between anthropologists and missionaries.

Review posted on the internet by George Tucker, October 31, 1998.

Missionaries-1, Anthropologists-0

Read this book if:

You believe anthropologists are arrogant, foolish people.
You think shamans worship Satan.
You think Christian missionaries can save animists and pagans from their own violent natures
You suspect that many aboriginal peoples are jumping at the chance to follow Christ.

You support the intrusions of whitefolks into the economies, politics, and cultures of aboriginal peoples.

You've murdered lots of people and want forgiveness.

You think the establishment of a church in a village will turn it into a utopia.

You firmly believe non-Christians are savages.

You are a televangelist and want material for a sermon.

This book is not poorly written, but I think the author takes extreme liberties with the material — all the information is second hand at best.

Author's Response

Michener wrote that he never read anything his critics said about him and strongly advised other writers to exercise the same restraint. This must be a luxury reserved for fiction writers. While glowing reviews are great, nothing focuses one's attention like a strong dose of criticism. This one summarizes much of the critique we've heard. It demonstrates the passion Jungleman stirs. Allow me to address each of these crisply stated observations.

No single group of people has ever staked an exclusive claim to the title "foolish and arrogant" and neither I nor Jungleman ever imply this about anthropologists. Anthropology is a most worthy field of study.

You decide if the beings the shamans follow are anything like your concept of Satan.

Christian missionaries never saved anybody from anything (discounting immunizations). Only individuals making very traumatic inner choices turn from violent lifestyles.

The thesis that aboriginal people might like to improve their lives is worthy of consideration.

When I represented this commonly held majority opinion to Hairy, he responded with four lines I have never forgotten. He said, "Please don't listen to them. Nobody's that stupid. They must hate us. They think we're animals."

Forgiveness has made an amazing comeback these days, right up to the highest levels of the land. Everybody wants it. This might be a bit of an august thought: even murderers may occasionally want forgiveness.

I don't know enough about Utopia to comment here.

It is possible for human beings to be savage.

I've never met a televangelist, had any desire to do so, or any reason to think he might find any material here. (One Christian organization marketed *Spirit of the Rainforest* until severe criticism forced them to refuse to deliver purchased copies to their people—too much spirit activity and violence against women. Not much sermon material here, I'm afraid.)

No liberties have been taken with any of the significant material. (See p. 246 for a discussion of significant material.) With the exception of the shy females, I stared every source into the eyes as I listened to his story.

Excerpts from "Yanomamology, Missiology, and Anthropology," by Neil L. Whitehead, University of Wisconsin-Madison, in *American Anthropologist*, June 1998, pp. 507-19. The more I have read and studied this review, the greater respect I have gained for it. The reader is encouraged to consult the *American Anthropologist* for the complete text of Whitehead's review not only of *Spirit of the Rainforest*, but also of Salomone's book, *The Yanomamö and Their Interpreters: Fierce People or Fierce Interpreters?* and Chagnon's *Yanomamö Interactive: The Ax Fight.*

[The three works here reviewed] are far more likely to inform one as to anthropology's intellectual practice than as to the situation of native peoples in the Amazon....in San Francisco in 1996,...I stood beside the Yanomamö man, Shoefoot, with the author of *Spirit of the Rainforest*, Mark Ritchie, while watching the interactive CD-ROM *The Ax Fight*....it is the "context" to these texts [the works reviewed] that reveals their meaning, not simply those texts themselves.

It is something of an irony then that *Spirit of the Rainforest*, despite being a thinly veiled Salesian product . . . a most interesting document in its own right, both for the way in which it mimics the ethnographic form of "life-history" and for the vivid window it opens on aspects of Yanomamö shamanism. But the deep complicity between Mark Ritchie, Jungleman, and his interlocutor Mark Dawson in the very controversies that it claims to clarify also makes this a deeply problematical text....

But one cannot help but feel that there is an uncomfortable irony here for us all; that those who are studied might offer their own self-understanding in place of our ethnographies, and write ethnographies of our fieldwork practice, instead of our fieldwork producing their ethnography. Although *Spirit of the Rainforest* is a work of missionary propaganda, it is a good piece of propaganda, for it does its job of unsettling professional complacency and demonstrating that no one can claim to speak exclusively for others or authoritatively of others.

The deeper conceit that underlies the CD-ROM is clearly expressed...the suggestion is made that the disk will allow students to "do ethnography" by manipulating ethnographic and demographic data to explore alternative meanings of "raw data" (p. ix). But obviously only certain kinds of "alternative meaning" are accessible through this data set, which is not "raw" at all but the product of many earlier manipulations. In these ways the CD-ROM has serious technical and intellectual problems, but its novelty cannot be denied.

. . . one could do worse than conclude this review with the comment that Shoefoot made to me on seeing the CD-ROM... "so many of them are dead...so many." It is interaction with that kind of "raw data" that allows us to find alternative meanings, not the mirror of ethnographic representation and fierce interpretation.

Author's Response

Professor Neil L. Whitehead's review is groundbreaking on two fronts: Of all who have criticized *Spirit of the Rainforest,* Whitehead is the first to actually cite an example of an inaccuracy. And, he makes the invaluable distinction between raw data and high-tech data manipulation.

First, let us consider his criticism. Whitehead labels the book propaganda, but then calls it "good" propaganda. Could this be a concession that the book makes a good point no matter how one-sided or unfair it may be to the facts? He bases this "missionary propaganda" assertion on a number of observations that cause him to conclude that my work is a "deeply problematical text." For example, he observes that there exists a complicity between myself, Jungleman, and Mark Dawson who is the son of Salesian missionaries. Thus it is not a stretch for him to conclude that *Spirit of the Rainforest* is a "thinly veiled Salesian product."

All propaganda and problematic-text labels aside, I thank Whitehead for finally placing some facts on the table over which there can be some meaningful discussion. He is, however, somewhat misled. There is no Mark Dawson. I can only assume he means Gary Dawson. Neither Gary nor myself are sons of or related in any way to any Salesian missionary. I'm led to believe that Salesians take a vow of celibacy. His statement that this book is a "thinly veiled Salesian product" is a guess on his part. But it's also in error. To my knowledge, I've never met a Salesian.

What he's driving at is that Gary Dawson is the son of the missionary who had the confrontation with Chagnon some three decades ago. He does not explain, but leaves us to assume that the son of one of the parties to a confrontation might give a biased impression of what happened, thus making for what he calls a "deeply problematical text."

The story to which he refers is the highly dramatic confrontation between the colorful, spirit-chanting anthropologist and the missionary. It is just the sort of high drama that no writer can resist. But the story was first told by the anthropologist, himself one of the parties to the conflict.[1] Does that make his text "deeply problematical"? Whenever there is another side to a story, it is almost always told by someone on the other side. The problems in a story arise not because someone takes a side in the story, but because the facts he uses to support his position are less than accurate. In this case there is virtually no dispute over the facts, leaving no problem either for my text or Chagnon's.

Whitehead calls *Spirit of the Rainforest* a "work of missionary propaganda." From two of Gary Dawson's closest associates, both lifelong missionaries, I have angry letters that demonstrate this book to be anything but missionary propaganda. I write of a missionary who "spanked" an Indian woman with a stick, another who had an inappropriate relationship with an underage girl, others who were overtly racist against Indians, one who even killed his Indian wife. I can assure you that no missionary has yet thanked me for this propaganda.

In the overall scheme of Whitehead's review, however, these corrections are so minor as to be hardly worthy of mention. I do so merely to set the record straight.

Therefore let me turn to the second area in which Whitehead breaks new ground. In actual fact, the thrust of his comments are nothing short of brilliant. All criticism of Whitehead pales by comparison to the insight of his concluding paragraph. I first met Dr. Whitehead at the 1996 AAA in San Francisco. Within sixty seconds of our meeting, we were in an argument. About thirty seconds after that I discovered that I was in over my head.

So why do I label "brilliant" the review of a man who does not agree with me? Because Whitehead met Shoefoot. He stood next to him and watched him respond to Chagnon's high-tech, CD-ROM-supported spin on the Yanomamö. The CD-ROM shows the Yanomamö in their most uncomplimentary light.

In that experience Whitehead received a brief moment of what he calls "raw data," and which he quite rightly distinguishes from the data of the CD-ROM. And he did what too few have done: he listened. He heard the heart of a man who cares about the survival of his people. Not only did Whitehead get it exactly right, he got it in perspective. There is even a touch of emotion in his scholarly conclusion.

Whitehead could not be more insightful than when he applies the word "conceit" to the CD-ROM project. With our wonderful technology we don't have to meet the real people any more; now we can manipulate their raw data with a computer. Whitehead correctly observes that the data we manipulate has already been manipulated. Then we call all such manipulation ethnography. Whitehead didn't just get close with this one. He got the perfect word: conceit.

One could call it symbolic irony that the CD-ROM didn't work. But that's no problem. A computer whiz can fix that. But who can fix the conceit of a high-tech culture that overlooks tears in the eyes of a man as he says, "So many of them are dead?"

---

[1]*Yanomamö: The Fierce People*, 2nd Edition, p.158, also 3rd Edition, p. 210. This fascinating story appears only in these two editions.

GLOSSARY

ă·lä´nă: wall built across the shabono entrance to protect from raiders. In times of serious war, it would extend all the way around the outside of the shabono. This would force a raider to circle the shabono completely to arrive at the entrance.

ä·lō·wä´lï: magical powder blown on an enemy, resulting in an evil curse

ån´trōs: name given by the Indians to the people who come to study them

cåp·y·bä´ră: world's largest rodent, stands two feet tall, more than four feet long; looks like a giant guinea pig with partially webbed feet

e·be´nē: hallucinogenic drug growing on the ebene tree, used by shamans to assist in contacting their spirits

hee´hee´kă: casement formed by wrapping the walemashi around a corpse

hor´·dï·mō·shï´·ẘa: one given to play-acting, contemptible fool, stooge, dunce

hŏ·wä´shï: small monkey known for its mischievous behavior

nä´bă: non-Yanomamö

GLOSSARY

Ō·mä´wă: head of all spirits in the spirit world

shä´bŏ·nō: high wall extending in a huge circle; wall leans inward at about a 45-degree angle, constructed of poles and covered with palm leaves for protection from rain. Each family has a section of the leaning wall under which they hang their hammocks, build fires for cooking, and take care of other domestic needs.

shä´măn: person whose life is given to finding and communing with beings of the spirit world; usually becomes more interested in the spirit world than the real world and often cannot distinguish between the two

Tk!: loud click made when the tongue is released under pressure from the roof of the mouth; an expression of amazement, as in "Wow!" However, it is usually more serious in tone, as in "unbelievable" or "what a shame!"

ū´nō·kai: a rite of cleansing, approximately seven days in duration, through which a warrior must go after killing. Anything his hands touch during that time will be cursed.

wä´lē·mä·shï: poles woven together with vines, forming a mat into which a body is placed for hanging out in the jungle while it decays

wy·ū´mï: nomadic activity for the purpose of gathering any food to be found in the jungle

Yai Pä´dă: the greatest of the spirits, creator of everything, including the spirits, often referred to as the great spirit. See Yai Wana Naba Laywa

Yai Wä´nă Nä´bă Lāy´wă: same being as Yai Pada. This name, however, also labels him the unfriendly, unknowable, or foreign spirit (notice the term "naba"), and the enemy spirit. The use of "naba" in this name does not label this spirit as the spirit of the foreigners. It describes, rather, the nature of this spirit's relationship to the Yanomamö people.

Family Relations

Father-uncle: Your father's brothers are all called father because they might be sleeping with your mother (brothers often share their wives).

Mother-aunt: Your mother's sisters are all called mother because they might be sleeping with your father (sisters often share their husband).

Brother-cousin: Boy born to your father's brother, called a brother because it is assumed that your father and his brothers shared their wives with each other. Therefore any child born to your father's brother would be called a sibling, even though it would probably be a cousin. If you are a girl, marriage to this brother-cousin is incest—strictly taboo.

Sister-cousin: Girl born to your father's brother, called a sister because it is assumed that your father and his brothers shared their wives with each other. Like brother-cousin, any child born to your father's brother would be called a sibling, even though it would probably be a cousin. If you are a boy, marriage to this sister-cousin is incest—strictly taboo.

Mother-in-law-aunt: Most commonly your father's sister, but also your mother's brother's wife. This woman is called a mother-in-law whether or not you are married to any of her children, because she is a potential mother-in-law. Your potential marriage to her child lasts a lifetime; hence, she will never lose her mother-in-law title. Her children are potential spouses because they couldn't possibly be half siblings; no man would ever have sex with his sister. Therefore, one of your father's sister's children will make the perfect spouse. Also your mother's brother's children will make perfect spouses because they couldn't be your half-sibling (your mother's brother would never share his wife with your father). The birth defect of Anita's daughter (p. 156) was possibly due to this kind of cousin marriage. Won't Grow's mother was the sister of Anita's father. Won't Grow and Anita were considered the ideal match because they could not have been half-siblings.

Father-in-law-uncle: Most commonly your father's sister's husband, but also your mother's brother. Their children will be called your cousins. They are thought to make for you the ideal spouse or sibling-in-law.

Mother-in-law: Any woman who couldn't possibly be your mother, because you could marry her children without committing incest. If you are a male and you marry the daughter of a mother-in-law (a woman you have always "called" mother-in-law), you will from that time on never call her anything. In fact, you will never speak to her or even be seen with her in public or private. To do so would create the worst sort of scandal; just the thought that your wife's mother might bear your children is so repulsive that if you met this woman walking across the village, you (and she) would turn around and head the other way. Getting across the village (or anywhere) is never as important as avoiding your mother-in-law. In any public gathering, you would *always* position yourself on the opposite side of the group from your mother-in-law. It has been speculated that this trait has attracted so many anthropologists to the Yanomamö tribe.

LEGEND OF CHARACTERS AND LOCATIONS

A.H.: well-known anthropologist. Due to the serious nature of the allegations made against him, his identity has been withheld. Any regulatory agency interested in protecting the Indians from him could get ample testimony on these and other stories about him from the Indians, including, of course, his identity.

Anduce, Dr. Pablo: anthropologist and medical doctor who worked inside the Amazonas territory for many years and later held high office in the Venezuelan government. A long-time champion of Indian's rights

Bighead: Honey warrior, brother of Redhair (Spanish name, Julio)

Cesar: Indian appointed by the government to keep peace among the Yanomamö people

Crossedeye: Honey warrior (Spanish name, Augusto)

Deemeoma: young girl who was stolen in the slaughter of Potato Village. The story follows her to Honey Village where she grows to be an unusually compassionate woman.

Doesn't-Grab-Women: so named because of his inexplicable restraint. A man of such mystery that he changed the entire history of a village with one visit

Doesn't-Miss: foreigner who had brief encounters with Hairy and Shoefoot

Dye: Paul Dye, career missionary with New Tribes Mission

Fastman: best hunter in Honey

Forgetful Village: located upriver from Honey, commonly called Seducedawiteli

Fredi: childhood peer of Deemeoma

Fruitman: son of Spear and Noisy Privates, strongly influenced by foreigners (Spanish name, Octavio)

Funnyman: Honey warrior (Spanish name, Ramon)

Granny Troxel: elderly white woman, first-known white to take up residence in a Yanomamö village

Hairy: feared warrior, but not a shaman; strong leader

Hairy's Village: located on the Iyewei (Blood) River, commonly called Hallelusiteli

Honey Village: located on the Padamo River at 3°3' N, 65°11' W; commonly called Cosheloweteli

Irritating-Bee: Napoleon Chagnon, world-renowned anthropologist whose book, *Yanomamö, The Fierce People,* has now sold well over a million copies

Jungleman: narrator of the story. A shaman of extraordinary talent, articulate, likable, outgoing, leader, lover of the jungle, great hunter and fisherman, fierce warrior and killer of children

Kaobawa: longtime friend of Runner, leader of a village at Mavaca, important informant to Chagnon. Chagnon dedicated his book to Kaobawa as well as Runner and another Indian, saying that they taught him much about being human.

Keleewa: Gary Dawson, lifelong friend of many of the characters of this story

Legbone: fierce warrior from Mouth Village

Longbeard: missionary who took an Indian wife. His identity is withheld because it is impossible for me to review his side of the story. Almost any Yanomamö will know his identity.

Mavaca: name given to a Salesian mission and a group of Yanomamö villages located at the mouth of the Mavaca River

No-Trouble: strange visitor to Turkey's village

Noisy Privates: wife of Spear. Her name alone intimates the treatment of women.

Noweda: rubber merchant

Padre Coco: Catholic missionary, Tigerlip's mentor

Padre Gonzales: rugged outdoorsman, volunteer at a mission

Pepe: missionary Joe Dawson, one of the first white men ever to sustain long contact with the Yanomamö Indians

Redhair: young man in Honey who took Yoshicami for a wife; brother of Bighead (Spanish name, Ricardo)

Runner: traveled on the river with A.H., became one of the primary informants to whom Napoleon Chagnon dedicated his book (Yanomamö name, Rerebawa)

Shetary: Indian who would still like to kill the one responsible for the desecration of his son's body

Shoefoot: shaman-in-training; became leader of Honey (Spanish name, Baptista)

Shortman: child victim from the Siapa (Spanish name, Pablo Majias)

Slothtail: Honey warrior (Spanish name, Pavlino)

Smallmouth: warrior from Mouth Village

Spear: lifelong friend of Jungleman and Shoefoot, fierce shaman and killer, haunted by the memory of his victims and the death of his father; still lives in Honey (Spanish name, Luis)

Tigerlip: fierce shaman (Spanish name, Husto); settled on the Ocamo, became friend of Padre Coco

Tigerlip's Village: located at the mouth of the Ocamo River, commonly called Ocamo (2°47' N, 65°11' W)

Toucan: fierce shaman possessing special powers (Spanish name, Samuel)

Toughfoot: Honey warrior

Trip: nephew of Hairy, moved from Hairy's village to take a wife from Honey (Spanish name, Pedro)

Turkey: Relative of Shoefoot and leader of a village at Mavaca

Turkey's Village: located at the mouth of the Mavaca River. Turkey's and other villages located there as well as the nearby Catholic Salesian Mission are commonly known as Mavaca and are so designated on Venezuelan maps. Bisaasiteli is the Yanomamö name and the designation used by the anthropological community.

Won't-Grow: Honey warrior (Spanish name, Jaimie)

Wyteli: Deemeoma's father, famous for being hard to kill

Yaiyomee: child born with massive birthmark across face, considered to be a birth defect

Yawalama: second wife of Longfoot

Yoshicami: first wife of Longfoot, object of a struggle between Honey and Forgetful Village.

DOCUMENTATION

In the interest of preserving the flow of Jungleman's story, I have elected not to use footnotes. However, each significant event is listed below with its source and pertinent details. Witnesses to the events of Jungleman's life were initially recorded on tape by Gary Dawson on his many trips to villages in the headwaters of the Orinoco. Dawson recorded the tapes in the Yanomamö language, then transcribed them into English. In September 1990 I recorded the same stories in detail with Jungleman and all the other characters willing to speak. (Most were recorded in stereo with the person speaking Yanomamö on one channel and a simultaneous English translation on the other channel.)

The Indians most familiar with all these stories live in Honey Village (commonly known as Cosheloweteli), located on the Padamo River at 3°3' N, 65°11' W. All of the September 1990 recordings were made at this location. In January 1995 further documentation was made using video recordings, again with the Yanomamö on one channel and English on the other. Half of these were made at Cosheloweteli, the remaining being made at various locations on the Padamo and Orinoco Rivers.

Chapter 9

Page 141: Sodomizing of young boys

This anthropologist's identity is well known in Amazonas and these stories are common among the Yanomamö people. The stories were told in a number of settings and recorded in September 1990 at Honey Village on the Padamo River. Fruit-man (Octavio) and a group of other Indians reported these stories. None of those reporting the stories actually engaged in sex acts with the anthropologist. They merely reported the words of those to whom they had spoken who had done so. Translator Gary Dawson had an unrecorded conversation with a boy hired by A.H. to do sex acts. On January 21, 1995, Shortman (Pablo Majias), Won't-Grow (Jaimie) and Timoteo, all Indians living in Cosheloweteli on the Padamo, also report-ed these stories, all of which were recorded on video tape.

Page 146: Beating of Youngbird

The incident occurred in 1969 at Mavaca on the Orinoco River and was witnessed by translator Gary Dawson and many Indians in the village.

Page 148: Fight in which A.H. broke his arm

The fight occurred in 1972 or 1973 in a village on the Manaviche River, a tributary of the Orinoco located between Mavaca and Platanal. The incident was witnessed by a number of Indians and recorded in September 1990.

Page 151: Irritating-Bee taking drugs and doing shamanism

This fascinating story was first reported by Napoleon Chagnon in his bestselling book, *Yanomamö, The Fierce People*. I have now interviewed five witnesses to this intriguing event: the missionary whom Chagnon calls Pete (real name, Joe Dawson), Keleewa (Gary Dawson, Joe's son), Kaobawa, Runner (Rerebawa), and Shoefoot. All of their stories bear phenomenal resemblance to Chagnon's, with some additions which provide the most intriguing twists. Indeed, Kaobawa was so impressed with the accuracy of Chagnon's description of the spirit world that he said to me, "He must have written it himself." I was puzzled by this response. What could an illiterate Indian know about the art of writing that would make him reach the insightful conclusion that the words he had just heard could only have been written by Chagnon himself? His response can only be characterized as brilliant.

I was so amazed that I inquired of Kaobawa what he knew about the communication process that he would draw such a conclusion. He said simply that he knew that the description given from Chagnon's book could only have been written by someone who had really been there and had experienced the spirits himself.

Kaobawa actually demonstrated for me the dance and chant that Chagnon used to call Buzzard Spirit with the end result, according to Kaobawa, that Buzzard Spirit killed the spirit of a child in another village. Kaobawa claimed that the child died as a result of Chagnon's and Buzzard Spirit's work.

Much of what happens in the spirit world is commonly confused in the Yanomamö mind as to whether it actually happened in the physical world. This confusion presents no problem to Yanomamö reasoning. Their assumption is that if it happened in either world, it happened in the other as well. Therefore, it should be abundantly clear that neither Kaobawa nor any other witness has ever said that Chagnon killed the boy in the physical world. He said that Chagnon and Buzzard Spirit killed the boy (we would say by casting a spell) in the spirit world. When the boy died, the Indians would have credited his death to the shamanism of Chagnon.

It is possible that as a result of his drug-induced state Chagnon had no recollection of this sorcery-based killing. In that case, there can be no doubt that Kaobawa would have made him well aware of it. Such killings are the substance of considerable pride. This event, the spiritual killing of a child in another village, was arguably one of Chagnon's crowning achievements in the Yanomamö culture. When one considers the amount of space given by Chagnon to the study of Yanomamö cosmology and spiritism, one cannot help but wonder why he omitted the event from his writings.

But the most memorable aspect of this event to all of the witnesses was the exposure of the pink flesh at the bottom of the eye ball, referred to by the Yanomamö as pulling the eye down. Chagnon implies that pious men might curse in someone else's language and that this act could be thought of as cursing. But it would appear that this move, the pulling down of the eye, has no connection whatever to cursing. Chagnon also stated that it was equivalent to the use of the third finger (the actual word used in his case study, p. 158, was "the bird"). In all the interviews that I conducted, all responses were the same: the pulling of the eye has no sexual meaning whatever.

Pulling the eye down is the highest nonviolent insult that a Yanomamö person can give. It is a demonstration of total contempt. Every witness who told this story started with the eye-pulling encounter, repeated it a number of times throughout, and ended with the same climax—the pulling down of the eye.

It would appear to this author that the event was a significant moment in the memory of every party interviewed; all of the parties remembered, after 25 years, the very word the missionary used to describe his contempt for Chagnon. Even Kaobawa, although under the influence of drugs at the time, remembered that the actual word Joe Dawson used on Dr. Chagnon was "hordimoshiwa," meaning "contemptible hypocrite." According to Kaobawa and Shoefoot, the verbal and eye-pulling insult brought the spiritual encounter to an immediate, laughing halt.

The most significant aspect of this incident to Kaobawa was the deception to which he had been subjected by Chagnon. He insisted that the white foreigner had ruined his life and the lives of his people. I was intrigued at his repetition of this theme. "I'm really angry at how much I let him deceive me," he said time and again. "My life has been ruined by the deception of this foreigner." He claimed that if he had only given up his violent spirits when Joe Dawson had encouraged him to do so, his life would not have been so miserable and he would not have come to such a pathetic end. He spoke as candidly as a Yanomamö ever will about the suffering he had endured from the death of his many "arrows," meaning his sons.

I confess to being brought to tears when Kaobawa said, "I want you to ask Chagnon why he lied to me about the spirits." I told Kaobawa that Chagnon hadn't lied to him, but that he just didn't know about the spirits. Wasn't he, Kaobawa, the expert in matters of the spirit, and wasn't Chagnon the shaman's apprentice? "Yes, that is correct," Kaobawa answered. "I was the one who knew about the spirits. So I asked him why he would have listened to Chagnon. His reply: "Because he said that he knew about the foreigner spirits."

While much of Kaobawa's testimony is difficult to believe, some of it, such as the foregoing statement, is borne out by Chagnon's own words. He wrote that his experience with the spirits set the Indians' minds at ease: ". . . for was I not myself from Diosi-urihi-teri, and therefore knowledgeable about the machinations of Dios and the limitations on his power to destroy men with fire?" (*Yanomamö, The Fierce People*, second edition, p. 158. Diosi-urihi-teri means literally, "land of God.")

If Chagnon's claim to know about the foreigner spirits is hard to believe, Kaobawa's additional statements about Chagnon are even more erratic. He claimed that Chagnon told him that if he (Kaobawa) were to throw his spirits away and accept the spirit of Pepe, he would die. This is quite consistent with the teaching of the Yanomamö spirits and makes one wonder if Chagnon really did, as he claims, communicate with the spirits. Kaobawa further stated that Chagnon told him that if he continued to go to Pepe's meetings he would die.

I questioned Kaobawa at length on this claim. I told him that there was no way anyone in my country would believe that Chagnon would ever tell him anything like that. He could tell that I didn't believe him and I pushed him to the point of insulting him, maybe beyond. But he was adamant about it. "He can never deny that he said it. Because he said it."

Bizarre as Kaobawa's charge is, it appears credible for three reasons. First: The sincerity, conviction, and passion with which Kaobawa told his stories was quite compelling.

Second: Chagnon's own behavior demonstrated that he was interested in Kaobawa remaining a shaman and rejecting the missionary's message. Indeed, Chagnon exonerated the ways of shamanism as powerfully as he could.

Third: By his own admission, Chagnon was intellectually prejudiced in favor of Kaobawa's spiritual position. He wrote that Pepe's teaching made him "almost sick with anger and resentment" (p. 155). So predisposed was Chagnon against Pepe's encouragement of the Indians to give up their spirits that his opposition to the missionary gave him some improved moral feeling. He wrote, "I interfered in the 'work' of the missionary thereby, but I felt, somehow, morally better for having done so" (p. 155). It is therefore possible to believe that Chagnon may indeed have told Kaobawa that he would die if he converted to Christianity. The statement is quite consistent with Yanomamö demonology.

It is an interesting question whether a missionary is guilty of mind manipulation when he tells an ignorant Indian that an all-powerful being will destroy his world with fire. In the case I cite here, the missionary would probably respond that the Indian in question is far from ignorant. The shamans say that they had no need of missionaries to inform them of the concept of hell. It was with them long before any whites came (Shoefoot interview on video, January 26, 1995). So one could argue that a discussion between two men of spiritual interest—a missionary and a shaman—about God's future intent for His creation might provide a provocative interchange. While the missionary relies on holy writ for such conclusions, one wonders on what authority an anthropologist relies when he tells the Indian about the horrible fate that will befall him should he convert to Christianity.

Under the influence of Shoefoot and the people of Honey, Kaobawa has converted to Christianity, but he still expresses great regret that he was so badly misled.

Chapter 11

Page 182: Indian boy who died accusing a foreigner of poisoning him

The story is commonly told in the village of Wabutawiteli. At the time of the poisoning, the village was located at 3°5' N, 64°35' W. Dr. Pablo Anduce was never successful in getting the bones of this Indian to test for poison. The village has moved and is located today at 2°55.54' N, 64°45.32' W.

Chapter 12

Page 187: Filming of Indians

Foreigners of all varieties ask and pay Yanomamö Indians to take off their clothes for the camera in order to look more primitive. This happened almost yearly on the Ocamo and Orinoco Rivers during the decades of the '70s, '80s, and '90s.

The most common location is Tigerlip's village (commonly known as Ocamo, located on the Ocamo River at 2°47′ N, 65°11′ W). Perhaps as many as half the Indians one might meet there will tell a similar story.

Page 196: Woman harassed for sex

The story of the woman who died for lack of medical treatment because she refused the doctor's requests for sex was told by Shortman (Spanish name, Pablo) and was recorded September 27, 1990, on audiotape and January 23, 1995, on videotape. Pablo lives both at Cosheloweteli on the Padamo River and at Sahael on the Orinoco River. Most of the Indians at Sahael are familiar with the story.

Page 198: Confrontation between Cesar and Bearded-One at Honey

This event occurred in the spring of 1988 and was witnessed by hundreds of Yanomamö Indians. Recordings giving details of this event were made of Shoefoot, Octavio, Pablo, Pedro and others.

Chapter 13

Page 211: Stolen head

Of all the atrocities detailed in this book, none is as reprehensible in the minds of the Indians as the criminal desecration of Shetary's burial casket and the theft of his son's head. This story is still not admitted to by the eyewitnesses even though it is common knowledge. Though at one point I spoke to Runner, who was with A.H. when the head was taken, neither he nor any of the other Indians with him will ever admit to having allowed the foreigner to succeed in the commission of this crime.

Nevertheless, the story is known in intricate detail. It was relayed to me September 27, 1990 by Fruitman (Spanish name, Octavio) in Honey Village (Cosheloweteli, on the Padamo River). Octavio is the brother-cousin of the young man whose head was stolen. The details of his story were confirmed by Trip (Spanish name, Pedro) from Hairy's village (called Hallelusiteli), Shortman (Spanish name, Pablo), Timoteo, Spear (Luis) and Shoefoot.

Their stories and the words of others were recorded on audiotape. Their knowledge of details is uncanny. They knew that A.H. used gloves and a mask and that he was unable to get anyone else with him to give any assistance. They knew the color of the gloves and mask. They knew that the Indians had stood at a distance out of horror at what they were seeing. They knew that A.H. placed the head into a plastic bag. I asked and repeated so many detailed questions on this story that Fruitman finally said, "We can tell from your many questions that you don't believe us. But it is true. We can't prove it, and the people with him will never admit that they allowed it to happen, but every Yanomamö knows who took that head: the antro, A.H."

If you were to follow the Orinoco to the Ocamo and travel up the Ocamo to 3°15′ N, 64°35′ W, you would be at the location of this crime. If Runner were healthy enough and so inclined, it might be possible for him to return to the very scene.

The most difficult part of the story to confirm is the year. It occurred during peach-palm season, making it January or February, and the best guess on the year is 1973 or 1974. Mike Dawson visited this village in 1974 and was met on the trail by a group of warriors with bows drawn. They said they would have killed him but they recognized the Indian woman who walked the trail in front of him.

Shetary's village (also called Aloteteli) moved from their location in an attempt to escape the sorrow of this tragedy. They are now located at 3°10.62′ N, 64°44.6′ W. Indians in this village will confirm this story, but must be approached with care as they are still angry at and suspicious of whites. Trip (Pedro) and Phillipe confirmed the story again on video January 27, 1995.

Shetary's story and attitude is widely known. It is rumored that the Venezuelan government protested to a foreign government over the missing head.

INDEX

Afraid–of–Big–Water, 43
A.H.
  arrest of, 235
  arrival of, in Turkey's Village, 141
  beating of Youngbird by, 145–46
  breaking of arm in fight, 148
  dinner with Fruitman, 168–70
  fight with Padre Gonzales, 147–48
  fight with Runner, 143–44
  naming of, 142
  attitude toward young girls, 144
  sodomization of boys by, 142, 147
  sodomization of Lizzard by, 141
  and stealing of Shetary's son's head,
    211–13
  theft of belongings by children, 145
  whereabouts of, 236
  Yanomamö desire for revenge on,
    149–50, 236
Alana, 37
Alligator Spirit, 63
  assistance to Jungleman by, 65–66
  nature of, 64
Amazonas, 7, 8
Anduce, Pablo
  assistance to the Yanomamö by, 235
  author's consultation with, 7
  death of, 235
  as source of Yanomamö information, 7

Anita
  and acceptance of Yaiyomee's
    defect, 157
  and birth of Yaiyomee, 155–56
  as daughter of Deemeoma, 155
  as wife of Won't–Grow, 155
Antros, 168, 186, 188, 202–203
Armadillo Spirit, 117
Augusto. See Crossedeye
Baptista. See Shoefoot
Bearded–One
  and confrontation with Cesar, 198
  and confrontation with Shortman,
    199, 200–201
  harassment of woman for sex by, 199
  interference with peacekeeping by,
    208
  presence at Yoshicami dispute, 195
  and Tigerlip's wife, 196
  and Yoshicami's death, 234
Bighead (Julio)
  peacekeeping efforts of, after Red–
    hair's death, 207–208
  role of, in Honey–Mouth fight, 15,
    176
Bisaasiteli. See Turkey's Village
Blood (Iyewei) River, 179–80
Brazil, 61
Buto River, 158

Buzzard Spirit
  Irritating–Bee and, 151–52
  nature of, 151
Carl, 234
Casiquiare River, 45, 61, 132
Catalina
  and Falenci's forced mating, 165–66
  as sister of Fruitman, 169
  as wife of Slothtail, 165
Cesar
  Forgetful Village's request to, 195
  Fruitman's visit with, 186–87
  allegations of rapes by, 195, 196
  and trip to Honey over Yoshicami
    matter, 195–99
Chagnon, Napoleon. *See* Irritating–Bee
Charming Spirit
  Jungleman's encounters with, 25, 37
  teachings of, to Jungleman, 26
  protection of Jungleman by, 47
Cloudy. *See also* Smallmouth
  as father of Legbone, 176
  and Mouth's woman–stealing trip to
    Honey, 121–22
  visit with Spear by, 123–24
Cosheloweteli. *See* Honey Village
Creator Spirit, 81
Crossedeye (Augusto)
  father of, 64
  role of, in Honey–Mouth fight, 15,
    176
Dawson, Gary. *See* Keleewa
Dawson, Joe. *See* Pepe
Deemeoma
  as daughter of Wyteli, 26
  knowledge of tribe history and mem-
    bers by, 15, 18, 156–57
  life of, after Potato Village raid, 51
    chopping of, 95
    Honey's fight for, 94
    marriage of, 94–95
    midwife for grandchild's birth,
      155–56
    molestation of, 95
    move to Honey by, 77
    move from Jungleman's peo-
      ple by, 73
    presence at Honey–Mouth
      fight, 15, 176
    stolen by Forgetful Village, 93,
      94
  as mother-in-law of Won't Grow,
    176

slaughter of Potato Village and,
    26–32
  arrival of raiders, 29–32
  death of father, 30
  death of mother, 29
  death of uncle, 30
  killing of babies, 31
  life spared by enemy, 31
  sparing of healthy girls, 32
  father's role in protecting vil-
    lage, 27–28
  village's mourning, 28–29
Deer Spirit, 59
  and Jungleman's son, 225, 238
  nature of, 73
Doesn't–Grab–Women, 129
Doesn't–Miss
  naming of, 180
  and Jungleman, 238
  and Shoefoot, 234–35
  visit with Hairy, 180–83
Dye, Paul
  and Sahael people, 132
  visit with Fruitman, 136–37
Ebene
  at festival times, 71
  for hearing spirits, 22, 27–28, 41
  for talking with spirits after war vic-
    tories, 36
Esmeralda, 189, 195
Falenci
  as daughter of Slothtail, 165
  desire of, by Fruitman's relative, 165
  as granddaughter of Spear, 169
  rape of, 166–67
  rescue of, by Keleewa, 167
Fastman
  naming of, 117
  Pepe's challenge to, 117–18
  wife Sofia and, 118–19
  Yai Pada's protection of, 119
Fierce–One
  fame of, 171
  naming of, 171
  role of, in Honey–Mouth fight,
    171–72
  and Yoshicami incident, 211
Fish, 139
Forgetful Village (Seducedawiteli)
  attempts at stealing Yoshicami,
    192–93, 193–95
  and Cesar, 195
  Fredi's move to, 94

Honey's fight with, 214, 217–18
    reason for, 208–209, 218
    location of, 94
    reaction of, to Redhair's death, 207
    stealing of Deemeoma by, 93
    Yaiyomee's move to, 236
Fredi
    as child from Potato Village, 26–27
    conversion of, 233
    life of, after Potato Village raid
        death of daughter, 233
        marriage of, 94
        move to Forgetful Village, 94
        move to Honey, 77, 79
        move from Jungleman's peo-
            ple, 73
        return to Honey, 233
        shaman training of, 185
        taunting of , by children, 51
    life spared by enemy, 32, 34–35
    as property of Honey elder, 36
Fruitboy, 58. See also Fruitman
Fruitman (Octavio)
    and arrest of Keleewa, 178–79
    break with Mouth by, 185
    death of son and, 178–79
    and dinner with antros, 168–70
    and Falenci's forced mating, 165
    as husband of Juanita, 135
    naba's apology to, 136
    Paul Dye's visit with, 136–37
    return to Honey by, 185
    role of, in Honey–Mouth fight, 15,
        176, 178
    as son of Spear, 15
    and Spear's prevention of revenge,
        136
    spiritual warfare within, 169
    and visit with Cesar, 186–87
Funnyman (Ramon)
    assistance to Yawalama by, 222
    personality of, 16
    river travel skills of, 16
    role of, in Honey–Forgetful fight,
        217, 218
    role of, in Honey–Mouth fight, 15, 16
God. See Yai Pada
Granny Troxel, 79–80
Hairy
    brother of, 101
    as cousin of Wabu, 182
    death of brother and, 229–30
    death of Sara and, 98

fighting abilities of, 13
as husband of Sara, 98
and Keleewa, 230
killing of brother and, 106
and killing of Yellowflower, 101–102
and killing of Yellowflower's brother,
    106
and marriage to Yellowflower, 98–99
naming of, 98
nephew of, 107
new wives of, 106
nightmares of, 106–107
presence at Honey–Mouth fight,
    13–14, 15, 16, 17
and return of Yellowflower's bones,
    104
as uncle of Trip, 16
visit to, by Keleewa and
    Doesn't–Miss, 179–83
visit to, by Shoefoot and Pepe, 105
and wife from Honey, 105
Hairylip
    and Doesn't–Grab–Women's visit,
        130
    as teacher at naba school, 133
    trip to Honey by, 134
    visit to, by Shortman, 133–34
Hairy's Village (Hallelusiteli)
    and friendship with Honey, 16, 230
    and Honey–Mouth fight
        Hairy's presence at, 13–14, 15,
            16, 17
        Trip's role in, 15, 16, 17
    nabas' arrival in, 235–36
    and runaway girl, 107
    Shoefoot and Pepe's visit to, 105
    relocation of, 180
    revenge on Yellowflower's death and,
        105–106
    and truce with Honey, 105
    Yellowflower's escapes from, 99–100
Hawk people, 99
Hallelusiteli. See Hairy's Village
Healing Spirit, 47
Honey Village (Cosheloweteli)
    Carl's arrival in, 234
    conversion of, 117–18
        angelic guardians, 122
        assisting Yoshicami, 190
        church meetings, 218
        condolence visit to Hairy's Vil-
            lage, 230
        feeding children first, 119

no forcing of women, 191
peace with Mouth Village and
    Tigerlip's Village, 195
prayer in
    over food, 119
    for protection, 122
refusal to help Tigerlip with
    revenge, 121
Shoefoot on, 234
spells against them fail, 123,
    205
stops avenging attacks, 122,
    123, 125, 232
and fear of Jungleman's powers, 116
and fight with Forgetful Village, 214,
    217–18
    reason for, 208–209, 218
    Fierce-One's role in, 217
    Fruitman's reaction to, 219–20
    Funnyman's role in, 217, 218
    Shoefoot's reaction to, 218–19
    Shortman's role in, 208, 217,
        218
    Slothtail's role in, 218
    Won't-Grow's role in,
        208–209, 214, 218
and fight with Mouth Village, 13–18,
    170–72
    Bighead's role in, 15, 176
    Crossedeye's role in, 15, 176
    Deemeoma's presence at, 15,
        176
    Fierce-One's role in, 171–72
    Funnyman's role in, 15, 16
    Honey men's fighting strategy
        in, 16
    Jungleman's interpretation of,
        175, 176–77
    purpose of, 15, 16, 175–76
    Shoefoot's role in, 14, 172,
        177
    Slothtail's role in, 14, 18, 177
    Toughfoot's role in, 15, 176
    women's role in, 14–15
    Won't-Grow's role in, 15,
        175–76
Fruitman and
    return to, 185
    revenge on, 178–79
Jungleman and
    avoidance of, 120
    curse upon, 117
    visits to by, 87, 96–98, 116,
        159–60, 225–27

location of, 77
missionary's arrival at, 77
nabas and
    arrival at, 87
    departure from, 93
    spiritual confusion at, 87
naming of, 77
Mouth's woman-stealing attempt
    and, 121–22
Pepe's arrival at, 93
Shoefoot's people's move to, 77
and slaughter of Potato Village,
    26–32
    arrival of raiders, 29–32
        death of Deemeoma's
            father, 30
        death of Deemeoma's
            mother, 29
        death of Deemeoma's
            uncle, 30
        Deemeoma's life spared by
            enemy, 31
        hitting of captured women,
            34
        killing of babies, 31
        raping of women, 34
        sparing of healthy girls, 32
    cause of, 33
    led by Jungleman, 33
    and protection of Honey from
        retaliation, 37–38, 40
Spear's return to, 185
standing up to Jungleman's powers,
    116
and Toucan's death, 232
travels of, to naba land, 42–47, 61
    and Myc Indians, 43–44
    and naba spell, 47
    and Noweda, 43–46, 61
        goods given to Honey men
            by, 45, 46–47
        killing of Parrotbeak by, 46
        naming of Jungleman by,
            45
        treatment of Mycs by, 44,
            45, 46
        treatment of Yanomamö
            by, 44
        weapons of, 45
    and return home, 47
Trip's desire for girl from, 170
and truce with Hairy's Village, 105

Hot
  attempts by, to heal Yawalama, 189
  daughter Yawalama and, 188
  as friend of Jungleman, 188
  and promise of Yawalama to Long-
    foot, 188–89
  son Raul and, 188–89
Howashi Spirit, 129, 164
  nature of, 59, 72
Husto. *See* Tigerlip
Ice Spirit, 24
Irritating–Bee (Chagnon, Napoleon)
  arrival of, in Turkey's Village, 139–41
  and dinner with Fruitman, 168–70
  performance of shamanism by,
    151–52
  pulling–down of eye to, by Pepe, 152
Iyewei (Blood) River, 179–80
Jaguar Spirit
  advice of, 41–42, 48, 49
  and conversations with Jungleman,
    36, 83, 86
  nature of, 55, 64
Jaimie. *See* Won't–Grow
Juanita, 135
Julio. *See* Bighead
Jungleman. *See also* Shamans
  and acquisition of more killing spirits,
    64
  and Alligator Spirit, 63
  and attempted healing of Yawalama,
    189
  brother of, 44, 47
  brother–in–law of Shoefoot, 97
  and Charming Spirit
    help with sick son by, 66
    encounters with, 25, 37, 86
    introduction to Snakeman by,
      64
    teachings from, 26
  protection by, 47
  as Child–Eater, 65
  clairvoyance of, 8, 18
  control powers of, 46
  conversion of, 227–29, 237–38
  death of daughter and, 139
  death of sons and, 66, 113
  and Deer Spirit in son, 225, 238
  and Doesn't–Miss, 238
  early spirit experiences, 21–26
    mother's instruction regarding,
      22, 23
    talking animals, 22

talking leaves, 22
talking log, 21–22
visions during, 23–26
  Charming Spirit, 25, 26
  Ice Spirit, 24
  Omawa Spirit, 23–24
  Yai Wana Naba Laywa,
    24–25
and good spirits, 60
and Healing Spirit, 47
and Honey Village
  avoidance of, 120
  curse upon, 117, 119
  interpretation of
    Honey–Mouth fight, 175,
    176–77
  visits to, 87, 96–98, 116,
    159–60, 225–27
hunting methods of, 53–54
and killing of village child, 96
and jaguar encounters, 54
and Jaguar Spirit
  advice of, 41–42, 48, 49
  conversations with, 36, 83, 86
  nature of, 55
and Keleewa
  meeting of, 116
  spiritual instruction by, 229
as leader of raid on Potato Village, 33
marriage to Longhair, 63
naming of, 45
as narrator of Spirit of the Rainforest,
  8
niece of, 135
Ocamo relatives' revenge on, 70–71
and revenge on Ocamo relatives,
  83–86
and revenge on Shooting Village,
  66–67
second wife of, 79
and shaman training of Fredi, 185
and shaman training of Shoefoot, 14,
  73
    fasting of, 51–52
    first trip to spirit world by, 52
    joining Jungleman and Spear
      in spirit times, 52
    sequestering of, 51
    teaching about spirits, 55
Shoefoot's spiritual discussions with,
  159–60
and sister–in–law's childbirth, 134–35
and Snakeman

INDEX

assistance of, with son's illness,
86
introduction to, by Charming
Spirit, 64
spiritual discernment of, 60
spiritual warfare within, 97, 116,
119–20, 160–61, 185–86, 225–26
and splitting of village, 72–73
and Sucking–Out Spirit, 66, 96
and Toucan, 159
travels to naba land (Tama Tama),
42–47, 61
and Myc Indians, 43–44
and naba spell, 47
and Noweda, 43–46, 61
goods given to men by, 45,
46–47
killing of Parrotbeak by, 46
naming of Jungleman by,
45
treatment of Mycs by, 44,
45, 46
treatment of Yanomamö
by, 44
weapons of, 45
and return home, 47
Kaobawa
conversion of, 237
Pepe's spiritual conversation with,
151
shamanism with Irritating–Bee,
151–52
Keleewa (Dawson, Gary)
arrest of, 178–79
author's interviews with, 7, 8
and brother Miqie, 201, 209, 210,
230
defense of Youngbird, 145
departure from Honey Village, 135
and Hairy's Village, 229–30
and Jungleman
meeting, 116
spiritual discussions with, 229
and Littlecurl
friendship with, 82, 83
naming by, 82
reunion with, 161–63
presence at Honey–Mouth fight, 14
presence at Yoshicami dispute, 201
relationship of, with the Yanomamö,
8, 223
research work of, 8
residences of

A.H.'s village, 144–45
Honey, 93, 155
Tama Tama, 82
and Shecoima
healing baby, 111
mending wounds, 112
and Shetary, 236
and Shortman, 208
and Slothtail
argument over Falenci,
165–68
naba friend not trusted by,
163–65
friendship with, 14, 165
helping wounded mother of,
178
and Toucan, 158
translation work of, 7, 8
wife of
and Yaiyomee, 157
marriage to, 150
and Yawalama
as a little girl, 188
after chopping by Longfoot,
222–23
Laughing–Man. *See* Toucan
Leadeyes, 171–72
Legbone
and clubbing of Slothtail's mother, 17
humiliation of, by Trip, 17
as Mouth's best warrior, 16
role of, in Honey–Mouth fight, 14,
16, 17, 175–76
as son of Smallmouth, 16, 176
Littlecurl
and friendship with Keleewa, 82, 83
life of, among nabas, 83
as nephew of Tigerlip, 82
reunion of, with Keleewa, 161–63
return of, to Tigerlip's Village, 83
and son's accident, 162
Lizzard
and A.H.'s assaults on boys, 142
banishment of, 142
father of, 142
sodomization of, by A.H., 141
Longbeard, 188, 236
Longfoot
abandonment of Yoshicami by, 190
attempts of, at stealing Yoshicami,
192–93, 193–95
and Carl's daughter, 234
desire for Yawalama by, 188, 189, 190

and illness of Yoshicami, 189–90
Longhair
  death of son and, 66
  and marriage to Jungleman, 63
  and move toward the Padamo, 73
Luis. *See* Spear
Majias, Pablo. *See* Shortman
Malaria, 194, 230, 231
Mavaca
  A.H. at, 145
  beating of Youngbird at, 145–46
  Fruitman's trip to, 186–87
Mavaca River, 128
Metaconi River, 73, 77
Miqie, 201, 209, 210, 230
Monkeylip
  as brother of Fruitman, 170
  and fight for mate, 170–72
Mouth Village
  and fight with Honey, 13–18, 170–72
    Fruitman's role in, 15, 176,
      178
    Jungleman's interpretation of,
      175, 176–77
    Leadeyes's role in, 171–72
    Legbone's role in, 14, 16, 17,
      175–76
    purpose of, 15, 16, 175–76
    Smallmouth's presence at, 15,
      16
    Spear's role in, 15
  and forced mating of Falenci, 165
  formation of, 96
  Fruitman and Spear's break with,
    185
  grudge of, over Potato Village slaugh-
    ter, 170, 175–76
  location of, 96
  presence of, at Yoshicami dispute,
    195
  Tigerlip's alliance with, 121
  woman–stealing attempt of, on
    Honey, 121–22
Myc Indians, 43–44, 146, 163
Nabas. *See also* Tama Tama
  as cause of split thinking, 205
  exploitation of Yanomamö by, 133,
    186
  great spirit of, 75–76, 188
  houses of, 43, 45
  land of, 42
  Littlecurl's life among, 83
  orgies of, 61

  Shoefoot's friendship with, 14
  spell of, 47
  stinginess of, 88–89
  white people as, 13, 41
National Geographic, 7
Noisy Privates
  and encounter with antros, 187
  and marriage to Spear, 51
  as mother of Fruitman, 187
  naming of, 51
No–Trouble
  naming of, 115
  discussion of spirits with Toucan,
    113–15
Noweda, 43–46, 61
  goods given to men by, 45, 46–47
  killing of Parrotbeak by, 46
  naming of Jungleman, 45
  treatment of Myc by, 44, 45, 46
  treatment of Yanomamö by, 44
  weapons of, 45
Ocamo. *See* Tigerlip's Village
Ocamo River, 72, 158
Ocamo Village
  Jungleman's relatives of, 70
  Jungleman's revenge on, 83–86
  revenge of, 70–71
Octavio. *See* Fruitman
Omawa Spirit
  departure of, to naba world, 26
  as leader of all spirits, 23
  nature of, 23–24
  Shoefoot's experience with, 215–16
  teachings of, to the Yanomamö, 24,
    26, 44
  and tricking the Yanomamö, 159
Orinoco River, 127
Padamo River, 77, 94
Padre Coco, 80–81, 82, 237
Padre Gonzales, 147–48, 237
Parrotbeak, 45–46
Pavlino. *See* Slothtail
Pedro. *See* Trip
Pepe (Dawson, Joe)
  arrival of, at A.H.'s village, 144–45
  arrival of, at Honey, 93
  departure of from Honey Village, 135
  as father of Keleewa, 82
  and friendship with Tigerlip, 82
  healing of Deemeoma by, 95
  pulling–down of eye by, to Irritat-
    ing–Bee, 152

residences of
    A.H.'s village, 144–45
    Honey, 93
    Tama Tama, 82
spiritual teaching of
    to Kaobawa, 151
    to Runner, 151
    to Shoefoot, 215
    to Tigerlip and relatives, 82–83
    to Won't–Grow, 231
Potato Village
    as childhood home of Deemeoma, 26
    slaughter of, 26–32
        arrival of Honey Village
            raiders, 29–32
            death of Deemeoma's
                father, 30
            death of Deemeoma's
                mother, 29
            death of Deemeoma's
                uncle, 30
            Deemeoma's life spared by
                enemy, 31
            hitting of captured women,
                34
            killing of babies, 31
            raping of women, 34
            sparing of healthy girls, 32
        cause of, 33
        led by Jungleman, 33
    Wyteli's role in protecting village
        from enemies, 27–28
    village's mourning for the dead,
        28–29
Rainforest
    animals of
        bee, 23
        capybara, 143
        howashi monkey, 17, 40
        jaguar, 40, 54
        mosquito, 127
        ocelot, 22
        piranha, 144
        sloth, 102
        tapir, 71
        toucan, 17, 22
        turkey, 39, 53
    vegetation of
        ebene tree, 45
        hardwood palm tree, 41
        papaya, 45, 53
        yellow–flower tree, 74
        yucca, 39

Ramon. *See* Funnyman
Raul
    aid to Yawalama by, 221, 222, 223
    and decision to stay in Honey, 224
    defense of Yawalama by, 188–89, 220
Redhair
    beating of, 205–206
    death of, 206
    and Yoshicami, 191–92
Rerebawa. *See* Runner
Runner
    and A.H.
        defiance of, 143–44
        desire for revenge on, 149–50
        hunting with, 142–43
    and Pepe's spiritual discussion, 151
    and shamanism with Irritating–Bee,
        151–52
Samuel. *See* Toucan
Sahael
    exploitation of, by nabas, 133, 134
    location of, 132
    Paul Dye and, 133
    Shortman and
        trip to, 133
        witness to, 237
Sara
    death of, 98
    as sister of Yellowflower, 98
    as wife of Hairy, 98
Seducedawiteli. *See* Forgetful Village
Shabono, 26
Shamanism. *See* Yanomamö Indians,
    shamanism of
Shamans
    attracting more spirits by, 73–74
    blocking of trails by, 27
    calling of, 22
    as cause of diseases to enemies, 28
    clairvoyance of, 8, 18
    drinking relatives' bones by, 24
    and ebene–taking
        to hear spirits' advice, 22,
          27–28, 41
        to speak with spirits after war
          victories, 36
    healing by, 55, 63, 65, 107–109
    killing of, by spirits, 60
    and need for many spirits, 108
    Omawa's teachings to, 23, 24
    and pleasing the spirits, 69
    protective powers of, 43
    retrieving souls by, 24

and revelations from spirits, 18
role of, in village, 18
and sending spirits to kill enemy
    babies, 28
spell–casting by, 64–65
spiritual discernment of, 60
training of
    fasting, 51–52
    sequestering, 51
    and teachings on spirit world,
        55
Shecoima
    abandonment of, by husband,
        111–12
    arrival of, in Hairy's Village, 107
    childhood marriage of, 109–10
    and deaths of children, 109
    disfigurement of, 112
    healing of baby by Keleewa, 111
    and marriage to Hairy's nephew, 107
    naming of, 107
    rape of, in Wabu's Village, 110
Shetary
    hatred of nabas by, 139
    son of, 125–27
        death of, 126
        and desecration of body,
            127
        Keleewa's visit regarding,
            236
        outcome of missing–head
            mystery, 211–13
Shetaris, 99
Shoefoot (Baptista), 37
    as brother–cousin to Yoshicami, 197
    as brother–in–law of Jungleman, 97
    conversion of, 96–98, 216
        defense of Yaiyomee by, 156
        peaceful nature of, 14, 172,
            199–200, 201
        prayer to Yai Pada by, 211,
            216–17
        standing up to Jungleman by,
            116
        spiritual leadership of
            to Honey, 209–10, 218–19
            to Jungleman and Toucan,
                159–60
            to Turkey, 128–29
    on the conversion of Honey, 234
    and death of uncle, 38–39, 40
    desire of, for new spirit, 88
    as Doesn't–Grab–Women, 129

and Doesn't–Miss, 234–35
father of, 51, 64
    advice of, regarding troubles in
        village, 74
    conversations with, on great
        spirit, 76, 77
    and move to Honey, 77
and friendship with nabas, 14
as He's–Got–A–Mouth, 93–94
as Honey leader, 14, 172
learning about naba spirit, 87
mysterious nature of, 14
naming of, 94
as No–Trouble, 115
and people's move to Honey 77. See
    also Honey Village
and rift with brothers, 94
role of, in Honey–Mouth fight, 14,
    172, 177
as shaman–in–training under Jungle-
    man, 14, 64
    acquisition of more spirits, 70
    encounters with bad spirits,
        60, 61
    fasting of, 51–52
    first trip to spirit world, 52
    joining Jungleman and Spear
        in times with spirits, 52
    learning about spirits from
        Jungleman, 55
        Deer Spirit, 59, 73
        Howashi Spirit, 59
        Tiger Spirit, 73
    sequestering of, 51
and sister Sofia, 118
spiritual warfare within, 87–88,
    215–16
and splitting of Jungleman's village,
    72, 73
travel to naba world (Tama Tama) by,
    74–76
    father's advice regarding, 74
    and great spirit of the nabas,
        75–76, 77
    reason for, 74
    requests naba help for his peo-
        ple, 76, 77
uncle of, 59–60, 72
Shooting Village
    Jungleman's revenge on, 66–67
    naming of, 67
    and Toucan's wife, 67
    Toucan's meeting with nabas in,
        157–58

Shortman (Pablo Majias)
  confrontation of, with Bearded–One,
    199, 200–201
  and Doesn't–Grab–Women's visit,
    130
  and encounters with antros, 202–203
  and Keleewa, 208
  and move to Honey, 133
  role of, in Honey–Forgetful fight,
    208, 217, 218
  trip to Sahael by, 133
  village's name for Shoefoot, 177
  visit with Hairylip by, 133–34
  message to Sahael by, 237
Siapa River, 129
Siapa River people
  Doesn't–Grab–Women's visit to,
    129–30
  as enemies of Turkey, 128, 129
  moving of village by, 130–31, 132
  splitting of village by, 132. See also
    Sahael
Slothtail (Pavlino)
  clubbing of mother by Legbone, 17
  daughter of, 165
    desired by Fruitman's relative,
      165
    rape of, 166–67
    rescue of, by Keleewa, 167
  and Keleewa
    argument with, over Falenci,
      165–68
    distrusts naba friend of,
      163–65
    friendship with, 14, 165
  peaceful nature of, 14
  presence at Honey–Mouth fight, 14,
    16, 18, 177
  role of, in Honey–Forgetful fight,
    208–109, 214, 218
  shooting attempt of, on Legbone, 16,
    177
  wife of, 165
Smallmouth. See also Cloudy
  as father of Legbone, 16, 176
  presence at Honey–Mouth fight, 15,
    16
Snakeman
  assistance of, in illness, 86
  instructions of to Jungleman on
    revenge killing, 64
  introduction of to Jungleman by
    Charming Spirit, 64

Sofia, 118
Spear (Luis), 40
  abandonment of father by, 55–57
  and break with Mouth Village, 185
  conversion of, 113
    prevents Fruitman from strik-
      ing naba, 136
    reverts to old ways with Fruit-
      man, 170
    conversation about spirits with
      Cloudy, 123–24
  desire of, for new spirit, 88
  as father of Fruitman, 15
  as grandfather of Falenci, 169
  as Jungleman's fellow shaman, 36,
    37–38
  learning about God from nabas, 87
  and marriage to Noisy Privates, 51
  nightmares of, 58
  return of, to Honey, 185
  role of, in Honey–Mouth fight, 15, 18
  role of, in Potato Village slaughter, 35
  spiritual warfare within, 87
  and wyumi trip, 49, 53, 55
Sucking–Out Spirit, 66, 96, 107–108
Swampfish, 129
Tama Tama
  Dawson family in, 82
  Noweda's life in, 43–46, 61
    goods given to men by, 45,
      46–47
    killing of Parrotbeak by, 46
    naming of Jungleman by, 45
    treatment of Myc by, 44, 45,
      46
    treatment of Yanomamö by,
      44
    weapons of, 45
  Sahael's location near, 132
  Shoefoot's experiences with nabas at,
    75–76
Thunder Spirit, 76
Tiger–Ear, 84
Tigerlip (Husto)
  brother of, 82, 83
  Creator Spirit's blessing and, 81
  Granny Troxel and, 79–80
  and Honey's refusal to aid revenge,
    121
  naming of, 80
  Padre Coco and, 80–81, 82
  travel to Tama Tama by, 82–83

as village shaman, 80, 81, 82
spiritual teaching to
    by Padre Coco, 83
    by Pepe, 82–83
    and wounding of wife, 196
Tigerlip's Village (Ocamo)
    doctor's arrival at, 82
    forming of, 72–73
    Granny Troxel and, 79–80
    location of, 83
    naba disease in, 81
    nabas' trade with, 81
    Padre Coco and, 80–81, 82, 237
    presence of, at Yoshicami dispute,
        195
    Tyomi's move to, 73
Tiger Spirit, 73
Toucan (Samuel)
    conversion of, 120–21
        Keleewa's teachings to, 158
        and nabas in Shooting Village,
            157–58
        and reverting to old ways, 158
        trip to Honey by, 159
    death of, 231–32
    and death of Jungleman's son, 66
    fame of, 69
    first wife of, 67
    killing of second wife by, 67–70
    killings by, in Jungleman's village,
        65, 66
    as Laughing–Man, 120
    meeting of Jungleman, 159
    and Shooting Village, 67
    spiritual warfare within, 115, 120
    spiritual instruction from No–Trou-
        ble, 113–15
Toucan's Village
    illnesses in, 158
    name for Shoefoot by, 177
    shooting raid by, 158
Toughfoot, 15, 176
Trip (Pedro)
    desire of, for Honey girl, 16
    discovery of Yellowflower's body by,
        102–103
    as nephew of Hairy, 16
    role of, in Honey–Mouth fight, 15,
        16, 17, 176
    victory of, over Legbone, 17
Turkey
    as relative of Shoefoot, 128
    Shoefoot's message to, 128–29

Turkey's Village (Bisaasiteli)
    Fish's trade visits to, 139
    Irritating–Bee's arrival in, 139–41
    location of, 128
    Shoefoot's visit to, 127–29
Tyomi
    death of baby, 28–29
    Deemeoma's sister, 26
    marriage of, 63
    move to Tigerlip's Village (Ocamo),
        73
    rape of, 34
Unokai, 35–36, 37, 40, 41
Venezuela, 127
    home of the Yanomamö, 7
    rainforest of, 7
Wabu
    as cousin of Hairy, 181
    and naba's arrival at village, 181–83
Wabu's Village (Wabutawiteli)
    naba's arrival at, 181
    alleged poisoning of boy at, 182–83
    rape of Shecoima by, 110
White people. See Nabas
Won't–Grow (Jaimie)
    as father of Yaiyomee, 156
    as husband of Anita, 155
    and Pepe, 231
    reaction of, to Yoshicami incident ,
        208–209
    role of, in Honey–Mouth fight, 15,
        175–76
    sickly childhood of, 15
    as son–in–law of Deemeoma, 176
Wyteli
    death of, 30
    as father of Deemeoma, 26
    as Hard–to–Kill, 29, 30
    as shaman of Potato Village, 27–28
Wyumi
    hardships of, 55
    nature of, 49, 53
Yai Pada
    as creator of all, 83, 114
    death of
        foreknowledge of, 159
        as unokai, 159
    as "eater" of souls, 114
    following, 164
    incarnation of, 159
    love of, for people, 124
    as most powerful spirit, 89
    naba name for, 222

prayers to, 119, 122
protection of Fastman by, 119
return from the dead by, 160
Yai Wana Naba Laywa
  as great enemy spirit, 24
  nature of, 24–25, 76, 77
  and souls, 65, 76
Yaiyomee
  Anita's acceptance of, 157
  birth of, 155–56
  birthmark of, 156, 231, 236
  marriage of, 236
  move of, to Forgetful Village, 236
  Shoefoot's defense of, 156
  Won't–Grow's acceptance of, 156
Yanomamö Culture
  canoe–making of, 74
  customs of
    burning of the dead, 48, 71
    chewing tobacco, 13
    ebene–taking at festival times,
      71
    male's childhood name
      becomes an insult, 51, 65
    multiple names for people, 21
    penis–tying, 27, 34
    pulling–down of eye as worst
      insult, 152
    stealing and returning others'
      belongings, 145
    stealing from neighbors' gar-
      dens, 43–44
  diet of
    bananas, 24
    capybara, 143
    cashew fruit, 86
    honey, 38
    monkey, 42
    palm fruit, 61
    papaya, 53
    sloth, 102–103
    tapir, 71
    turkey, 53
    yucca as staple, 38
  dwellings of, 26
  food–gathering (wyumi), 49, 53, 55
  heeheekas of, 125
  hunting abilities of, 7
  location of, 6, 7
  mores of
    caring for a baby once it's been
      touched, 156
    feeding adults first, children

  last, 52, 53, 86–87
    fighting fair, 148, 172
    generosity even to enemies, 84
    leaving the elderly behind to
      die, 55–57
    protecting the weak, 18
    providing for elderly in–laws,
      165
  oral tradition of, 21
  religious practices of. See shamanism
    of
  rituals of
    chest–striking, 48
    ebene–taking. See Ebene
    killer's cleaning (unokai),
      35–36, 37, 40, 41
    wailing over the dead, 47–48,
      57
    woman rites, 190
  shabonos of, 26
  shamanism of. See also various
    names of spirits
    and calling as a people, 24
    dwelling–place of spirits, 86,
      97
    drinking of dead relatives'
      bones, 24
    and enemy spirits, 26
      blocking of trails against,
        27
      grabbing of souls by, 24
    and fire pit, 84–85
    and good spirits
      instruction by, of whom to
        kill, 33
      protection of, against naba
        disease, 48
    and Ice Spirit, 24
    and personal spirits, 108
    and Omawa Spirit, 23–24, 26
    and revenge for death of adult,
      24, 26, 40
    voices of spirits and, 22
    and Yai Pada, 83
    and Yai Wana Naba Laywa
      as great enemy spirit, 24
      nature of, 24–25, 76, 77
      and souls, 65, 76
  shamans of. See Shamans
  size of, 7
  strength of, 7
  taboos of
    asking for someone's name(s), 21

bragging about never having
killed, 14
desecration of a corpse, 127
eating of pets, 80
sex in public, 61
shooting at children, 30
showing fear, 42, 59
showing remorse for killing,
70
speaking a dead person's
name, 8, 128
speaking someone's name, 21,
64–65
taking revenge for death of
child, 26
and war with Myc Indians, 43–44
war practices of
ambush, 39, 44
axes as weapons, 84
bashing of enemy babies'
heads, 31
boasting of kills, 34, 35
clubbing, 13, 17
insulting, 14–15
killers' cleaning ritual
(unokai), 35–36, 37, 40, 41
poison arrows, 14, 41
protecting village from retaliation, 37–38, 41
raping of enemy women, 34
sparing lives of healthy enemy
girls, 32
women's role in, 14–15
women of
abuse of
beating, 34, 99
chopping, 63, 67–68, 95,
221
clubbing, 17
disfigurement, 112
forced mating, 165–67
killing, 67–70, 101–102
name-calling, 51
molesting, 95
raping, 34, 109–10
stealing of, 35, 93, 94
torture, 223–24
roles of
insulting enemy, 14–15,
195–96

keeping children from
speaking names, 65
preventing wars by fabri-
cating stories, 103
subservience, 102
wyumi of
hardships of, 55
nature of, 49, 53
Yawalama
chopping of, 221
as daughter of Hot, 188
Longfoot's abuse of, 220
Longfoot's desire for, 188, 189, 190
marriage of, 233
Raul's defense of, 188–89, 220
recovery of, 233
Yellowflower
beatings of, 99, 100
escapes from Hairy's Village, 99–100
killing of, 101–102
and marriage to Hairy, 98–99
as sister of Sara, 98
Yoblobeteli, 40
Yoshicami
abandonment of, by Longfoot, 190
death of, 233–34
departure of, from Forgetful Village,
220
dispute over
Cesar's attempt to settle,
195–99
Shoefoot's peacekeeping during, 199–200, 201
father of, 218
flight of, to Forgetful Village,
199–200
illness of, 189–90
Longfoot's attempts to steal, 192–93,
193–95
Pepe's attempt to rescue, 194
reaction of, to Redhair's death, 217,
233
Redhair and, 191–92
Shoefoot's defense of, 190, 193
testimony of, to government guards,
193